Park Synagogue

JANUARY 2000

Presented By:  DAVID APPLE

In Memory Of:  SHMUEL APPLE

A Portrait of the
American Jewish Community

A PORTRAIT OF THE AMERICAN JEWISH COMMUNITY

edited by

Norman Linzer, David J. Schnall,
and Jerome A. Chanes

with a Foreword by

Jack Wertheimer

PRAEGER

Westport, Connecticut
London

Library of Congress Cataloging-in-Publication Data

A portrait of the American Jewish community / edited by Norman Linzer,
   David J. Schnall, and Jerome A. Chanes ; foreword by Jack
   Wertheimer.
        p.   cm.
     Includes bibliographical references and index.
     ISBN 0-275-96022-6 (alk. paper)
        1. Jews—United States—Politics and government. 2. Jews—United
     States—Identity. 3. Judaism—United States. 4. Jews—United
     States—Social conditions. 5. United States—Ethnic relations.
     I. Linzer, Norman. II. Schnall, David J. III. Chanes, Jerome A.
     E184.J5P637   1998
     305.892´4073—DC21   97-38800

British Library Cataloguing in Publication Data is available.

Library of Congress Catalog Card Number: 97-38800
ISBN: 0-275-96022-6

First published in 1998

Praeger Publishers, 88 Post Road West, Westport, CT 06881
An imprint of Greenwood Publishing Group, Inc.

Printed in the United States of America

The paper used in this book complies with the
Permanent Paper Standard issued by the National
Information Standards Organization (Z39.48–1984).

10 9 8 7 6 5 4 3 2 1

Copyright Acknowledgments

The editors gratefully acknowledge the following publications for their permissions to
reprint previously published material: **Chapter 1:** "The Changing Nature of Jewish
Identity," reprinted with permission from *The Journal of Jewish Communal Service,* Vol.
72, No. 3, Spring 1996; **Chapter 4:** An earlier and abbreviated version of this chapter
was prepared for the 1997 supplement to the nineteenth edition of the *Encyclopedia of
Social Work,* published by the NASW Press. Copyright © 1997, National Association of
Social Workers, Inc., *Encyclopedia of Social Work Supplement 1997;* **Chapter 5:** An
earlier and abbreviated version of "The Jewish Federations: The First Hundred Years" is
reprinted with permission from *The Journal of Jewish Communal Service,* Vol. 72, Nos.
1/2, Fall/Winter 1995/1996; **Chapter 12:** "Reengineering the Jewish Community,"
reprinted with permission from *The Journal of Jewish Communal Service,* Vol. 73, No.
1, Fall 1996.

Contents

Foreword

The closing decade of the twentieth century has been punctuated by a series of spirited—at times, acrimonious—debates over the current direction and future prospects of the American Jewish community. This, in itself, represents a shift from the strong consensus that undergirded much of the policy of the organized Jewish community just a few decades ago and enabled that community to mount self-confident campaigns to aid needy Jews abroad during the decades after the Holocaust. Now that other Jewish communities in distress have been rescued and rebuilt, American Jews have begun to look inward and have found cause to worry. The new contentiousness arises from a growing preoccupation with the health of American Jewry and the vitality of its organizational life.

Some of these controversies center on matters of communal priorities. As American Jewry addresses threats to its own "continuity," how much funding should be spent on enriching the Jewish lives of young people at the possible expense of obligations to other populations in need—the aged, families in distress, new immigrants? Given the finite resources available to the community, which populations should receive special attention? And what proportion of communal philanthropy should go to aid Jews abroad, as opposed to funds allocated for domestic Jewish needs?

Barely hidden beneath these concrete allocation decisions are agonizing questions about the future direction of Jewish life in the United States. Does the porousness of American society pose a dire threat to the integrity of the Jewish community, or does it offer new opportunities? Should we regard the spiraling incidence of intermarriage as an opportunity to enlarge the community by bringing in "the unchurched," or does it portend a disastrous depletion of the Jewish population because most "interfaith" families opt out of Jewish communal life? And more generally, does the community need to define sharper boundaries in order to clarify the limits of its tolerance for diversity, or should American Jews learn to live with ambiguity?

Many of these concerns are relatively new in the American Jewish self-consciousness. After all, for much of the middle decades of the century American Jews labored to rescue and succor Jews in need around the globe. The endangered Jewish communities were far away, and American Jews magnanimously—and often quite heroically—offered political aid and financial support to their coreligionists abroad. It is therefore shocking to American Jews to consider that their own community is now in crisis and that financial allocations alone will not offer solutions to the challenges to their group existence. Rather, the community must address deeper questions about its Jewish values and worldview, and the ways these relate to the larger culture. It is hardly surprising that such discussions are polarizing American Jews, based as they are on profoundly differing conceptions of Judaism, Jewish identity, and Judaic cultural values.

A Portrait of the American Jewish Community provides a rich introduction to some of these pressing issues. Written primarily by engaged academics and leading communal servants, the essays in this volume offer insightful and provocative views of the most critical questions on the current agenda of the American Jewish polity.

JACK WERTHEIMER
Joseph and Martha Mendelson Professor of American Jewish History,
Jewish Theological Seminary of America

Acknowledgments

A number of the chapters in this book had originally been delivered in a lecture series to students of the Wurzweiler School of Social Work, Yeshiva University, under the auspices of the Atran Foundation. We acknowledge the generosity of the Atran Foundation, which has supported numerous lectures, conferences, and the *Jewish Social Work Forum*—the journal of the Wurzweiler Alumni Association—over the years.

Dr. Sheldon R. Gelman, the Dorothy and David I. Schachne Dean of the Wurzweiler School of Social Work, has given unstinting and unwavering support in bringing this project to fruition. He has provided the administrative staff, the facilities, and resources of the school.

Tessie Spivey, in particular, has invested a considerable amount of time in preparing the manuscript. Her meticulous attention to detail enhanced its quality. We owe her a debt of gratitude for her commitment to excellence.

Introduction

For those of us who are obliged to track the workings of the Jewish community, these are puzzling times. The contours of the communal agenda for the American Jewish community have changed dramatically in recent years. Priorities for communal action are shifting, religious and social views are becoming increasingly polarized, Jewish organizations are changing their focus and structure, and issues labeled as "survival" or "security" concerns are receding from the forefront of American Jewish consciousness. At bottom is the way in which American Jews view and envision the organized community, the Jewish polity.

One can have two contrasting views and visions of the American Jewish community in the closing years of the twentieth century. On the one hand, the Jewish community in America is the largest, wealthiest, best-educated, and most successful Diaspora community in history. It enjoys unprecedented levels of freedom, acceptance, and security. Its communal institutions are thriving. American Jews are accepted in virtually every arena of activity in the American polity, and enjoy leadership in many. America has indeed become the "*goldene medina*"—the "golden land"—envisioned by the immigrant generation.

At the same time, a darker view delimns the horizon. In this view American Jews are beset—indeed fatally stricken—with assimilation, Jewish illiteracy, shrinking population, and (if the reported statistics are accurate) intermarriage at an unprecedented rate. The benefits of pluralism, argue those who hold this dark view, have been more a burden than a blessing, and have in some instances been destructive to Jewish identity and to Jewish community. Moreover, in this vision anti-Semitism is still rampant, even in a democratic America.

More deeply, at the level of communal *angst*, a specter haunts the American Jewish community: that of a community whose organizations are shrinking for lack of support, whose communal agencies are weakened, whose funding is collapsing, whose agendas are irrelevant—all this precisely at a time when the creative continuity of the community is being called into question, and the community needs the resources and energy that will fuel activity and activism in this area.

This ongoing debate, played out in one way or another over the past forty-five years, is well known to Jewish social thinkers as the sparring between "assimilationists" and "transformationalists," earlier known as "integrationists" and "particularists" or "survivalists." The fundamental question in the discussion is whether the Jewish community is headed toward assimilation, irrelevance, and therefore ultimately disappearance; or whether it is merely "transforming" the ways in which the Jewish experience is taking place.

Transformationalists argue that matters are not worse for Jews in the United States, only different; they may even be better. They point to American Jewish successes and argue that American Jewish society is unique in time and place and therefore ought not be judged by the standards of other Jewish societies of different eras and places. Indeed, the American Jewish community is a highly successful response to the challenge of modernity.

Assimilationists, on the other hand, assert that intermarriage, low levels of philanthropic support, and, most of all, religious and cultural illiteracy threaten Jewish survival. That threat is informed precisely by Jewish integration into American society. Jews are in many ways victims of their success. To the assimilationists, American Jews have not merely *acculturated*—they have *assimilated.*

These discussions of the assimilationists *versus* the transformationalists need to be explored through the prism of the quintessentially American dynamic of democratic and cultural pluralism. Pluralism is the central dynamic that informs American associationalism, and is the engine that drives voluntarism. American Jews have found in the American-pluralist experiment a context in which the community can be integrated into the workings of the society, at little cost to group distinctiveness. But this model has been questioned in recent years, and the question of "at what cost?" has been raised, as communal dilemmas continue to mount.

This book addresses a range of issues that collectively illumine the landscape of American Jewry, and uses these issues as vehicles for the exploration of pluralism and conflicting visions in the construct of American Jewry.

We begin with an exploration of Jewish identity, set a historical context, and examine demographic data. We then look at how a range of substantive issues are addressed by the American Jewish polity, and examine some of the instrumentalities that are designated to act on behalf of Jews. We close with a provocative prescriptive essay.

In Chapter 1, Norman Linzer observes that "Jewish identity is an issue that has never been resolved," and concludes that solutions are not likely to be at hand. Identity is an exceedingly complex dynamic, informed by heritage, ancestry, religion, culture, nationality, and a host of other factors. One important point to be noted with respect to the author's concentrated discussion of "Jewish identity by choice" is that there are many recent data that demonstrate that Americans are increasingly exercising ethnic choices, or asserting "options." Americans are saying that they no longer feel obliged by birth or by ancestry to articulate a discrete identity, but that they can and will choose amongst ethnicities.

Setting a historical context for the volume is Jeffrey Gurock's chapter, "America's Challenge to Jewish Identity" (Chapter 2). Gurock offers a historical perspective for a profile of American Jewry, in which he traces the acculturation and "Americanization" of successive waves of Jewish immigrants and of discrete Jewish groups, and explores how these patterns affected Jewish identity. Associationalism and voluntarism—quintessentially and uniquely American phenomena—informed the patterns of assimilation and raised for American Jews the questions: America, good or bad?

Rounding out historian Gurock's context is demographer Jeffrey Scheckner's analysis in Chapter 3 of the 1990 National Jewish Population Survey (NJPS), the latest, most comprehensive—and certainly most provocative—of recent studies of the American Jewish community. The NJPS tells us that there is good news and bad news: good news in that (for example) some Jewish holidays are widely observed and that Jewish education for children is at higher levels than in previous decades, both indicating serious attachment to Jewish identity. The bad news are the burgeoning rate of intermarriage, the weakening of attachment to Jewish organizations, the patterns of conversion—these and other findings point toward increased assimilation.

The NJPS is a valuable document in assaying the American Jewish present. But there yet needs to be serious evaluation of the survey's disparate data. For example, when American Jews who identified themselves as "Jews" were asked to specify whether they were "national," "religious," "ethnic," or "cultural," the overwhelming majority identified "cultural" as salient for them. But there was limited follow-up to this important finding: does "cultural" mean eating bagels?, or does it signify a deeper form of expression, perhaps an indigenously American expression?

Further, the by now well-known, dramatic statistic of a 52 percent rate of intermarriage—a finding that has become crucial to the "Jewish-continuity" agenda of the Jewish community—requires serious analysis and, in the view of a number of observers, reevaluation. Demographers have suggested a number of flaws in the intermarriage numbers. For example, the techniques used in the NJPS unfairly weigh poor and rural Jews who, contrary to other ethnic populations, respond at the same rate as do urban, middle-class, and affluent Jews. Yet rural and small-city Jews are *more* likely to intermarry. Their responses, therefore, carry more weight than those of urban Jews, who are somewhat *less* likely to intermarry. The percentage ought to be reduced "off the top."

Additionally, the survey lumps all ages in intermarriage, including intermarriage among elderly folk, those Jews who intermarry for a second or third marriage and who may have no intention of having children. Social scientists suggest that to be a valid indicator of Jewish continuity the intermarriage numbers ought to be restricted to Jews in those age groups (say 18 to 50) that are likely to raise families.

The national survey, and the issues it addresses, point to the need and role of Jewish communal agencies in strengthening Jewish identity and Jewish community. An elaborate and, contrary to conventional wisdom, well-coordinated network of Jewish communal agencies has been developed as part of the federal consensus to look after Jewish interests in the varied spheres of activity: social services, public affairs and community relations, Israel and international affairs,[1] religion, education, and culture,

In their chapter (Chapter 4) on the arena of Jewish communal service, David J. Schnall and Sheldon R. Gelman begin with a summary of the Jewish religious imperative to engage in *tzedakah*—charitable justice—which informs the responsibility of individuals and the community to provide social services. The chapter surveys the range of services, and some of the organizational structures that are instrumentalities for service delivery. Emphasis is placed on services for the aged, health care, community centers, immigration and immigrant services, and international social welfare.

At the center of Jewish communal service-delivery and planning, and in a real sense linking these disparate services at the *community* level, is the system of Jewish federations around the country. The federation, itself a model for the coordination of social services, originally (in the late nineteenth century) was developed in order to implement coordinated fundraising by a single entity on behalf of the social-service agencies in the community. The allocations function, and ultimately the function of social planning for the community, were taken on by federations in subsequent decades. The history and functioning of the federated system in the United States is the subject of Chapter 5 by Jewish communal official Donald Feldstein.

In addition to its array of social services, the Jewish community is permeated with a variety of formal and informal religious expression. It has been suggested that American Jewry is a community that is divided by a single religion. Indeed, the story of American Jewish religion is in large measure one of controversy, dissensus, occasional agreement, and often deep division. Jewish religion in America—specifically, Jewish "denominational" religion (i.e., the religious movements) as we approach the twenty-first century—is treated by Lawrence Grossman in Chapter 6. Grossman's unusually rich essay explores first the idea of "religion" as applied to the Jews; then extends the construct to the American Jewish community with a detailed historical analysis of American Jewish religion as a response to modernity; and finally offers a review and analysis of how the Jewish religious movements in America came to be and where they are headed.

If the concern for continuity is heightened due to the dissensus among the major religious denominations, it has been strained by the changing patterns and problems of the Jewish family. In Chapter 7, social scientist Sylvia Barack Fishman offers an approach to policy planning in this crucial area for Jewish communal organizations. Fishman's prescriptive analysis addresses *seriatim* the profound changes, and resultant problems, of "singles," diminished fertility, women in the workplace and dual-career families, Jewish education, divorce, abuse, the elderly, and couples with a non-Jewish spouse.[2]

Is the 1990s an era of an intermarriage "crisis"? Or are we viewing what has in fact been a consistent pattern over the past forty years—high numbers (steady at around 35 percent since the 1950s[3]) about which few are happy, but since there has been no great increase in this decade, it's therefore not a special "crisis"? This area, a "hot-button" for most Jews owing to fears about continuity and identity, deserves serious reexamination by social scientists and Jewish communal leaders.

Intermarriage as a distinct phenomenon is treated in Chapter 8 in roundtable format, with Jewish communal officials Steven Bayme and Dru Greenwood offering sharply contrasting perspectives in an area in which Jews are the last holdouts in American society. To Dru Greenwood, intermarriage is an inevitable downside of the American Jewish "success story," and the communal structures of the community (including the religious groups) need to be developing and implementing strategies of outreach to the intermarried. Steven Bayme's view differs sharply. To him, the central imperative for the Jewish community, in order to survive, is to retain its distinctiveness: "Intermarriage signals how profoundly the Jews have become like everyone else. . . . The Jewish community must remain honest about its values and maintain ideological clarity." The debate over intermarriage—exclusiveness versus inclusiveness—is but another iteration of the debate of the assimilationists and the transformationalists. Joel A. Block then describes the rationale and experience of his agency, the Suffolk Y Jewish Community Center, in providing services to intermarried couples and families.

Menachem Kellner's idiosyncratic chapter (Chapter 9) uses a central issue for American Jews—the State of Israel—as a vehicle for the analysis of a range of "boundary" issues: observant and nonobservant Jews, Israel and the *Golah*—Diaspora, Israel's present and Israel's future, universalism and particularism—and, most important, the present and future of Jews. Kellner's chapter is a fresh iteration of the assimilationist–transformationalist conversation, with a variety of new locutions.

As a "survival" issue for American Jews in the late 1990s, Israel recedes from American Jewish consciousness. Yet it remains a prime reality for American Jews, invoking a new set of "survival" issues having to do with continuity and identity. As such, Kellner's exploration of "Jewishness" complements Norman Linzer's chapter on Jewish identity and is a fitting sequence to the continuity and identity issues raised in the discussion on intermarriage and the family.

Federations are the bridge between the American Jewish polity and Israel. They must make the decisions on apportioning funds between Israel and domestic needs. Using continuity as a rationale, federations' recent decisions have lately inclined toward allocating more to domestic needs. Understanding the role of the federation is important not only substantively, in terms of its service function; more importantly, the federation is the best exemplar of a fundamental principle of communal organization in the Jewish community, that of *federalism*. Federalism, the covenantal relationship between agencies, in which agencies enter into contractually defined partnerships based on mutual obligations, informs a dynamic that flourishes in the United States. In the federal model, institutions and individuals are linked in contractual relationships designed to foster partnerships on any number of levels, and in which the integrity of the partners is maintained. These partnerships often take on a character of their own that is more than the sum of their constituent units.[4] The principle of federalism and coordinated activity plays out in other areas of Jewish communal activity as well.[5]

Federalism, voluntarism, and associationalism inform the ways in which American Jews address issues on the public-affairs agenda and in the realm of public policy. "Intergroup relations"—the ways in which Jews relate to the external world—are profoundly different in pluralistic America than they were in the organic Jewish societies of Europe in previous centuries. But even in America, as Jerome A. Chanes explores in Chapter 10, "Jewish Involvement in the American Public-Affairs Agenda," the agenda for decades was one of *defense*—against anti-Semitism, against discrimination, *for* acceptance of Jews and not merely tolerance of them. Only in the postwar period, with the diminution of many forms of anti-Semitism, has the agenda expanded in many different directions: Israel, the separation of church and state, the struggle for Soviet (and other "captive") Jews, social and economic justice, interreligious relationships. The criterion for being on the Jewish communal agenda, argues Chanes, is that the issue in some way implicates Jewish security.

The chapter (Chapter 11) by Mark Handelman on the resettlement of Soviet Jews beautifully illustrates how the expansion of the agenda, and how the agenda is modified, to address a serious issue. One begins reading this chapter with a basic premise: the issue of Soviet Jewry is no longer one of a *political advocacy* movement but of social-service delivery.[5] This sea change in the fundamental nature of the issue has profound implications in the way in which the issue is addressed by the American Jewish polity. Handelman recaps the history of Soviet-Jewish resettlement, reviews the range of the organizational response to resettlement needs, and, using Soviet Jews as an exemplar, develops a valuable analysis both of acculturation and the adjustment of the American Jewish community to the immigrants.

Whither direction is the Jewish community headed? In Chapter 12—an essay that serves as an epilogue and a peroration to the reader—sociologist Steven M. Cohen urges a "reengineering" model (implemented by many corporations) for Jewish communal structures as a vehicle for reinvigorating the Jewish voluntary sector. Centralization, interagency cooperation and communication, cross-disciplinary training, joint facilities—all will lead to a more efficient and effective voluntary organizational community, responsive to the needs of its grass-roots "consumers." By extension, argues Cohen, the community itself will become energized.

A number of analysts suggest that the reengineering approach—rooted conceptually in consolidation—will inform a trend of organizational shrinkage in which the competing voices of the community will be encouraged to become muted and even disappear. This notion runs diametrically counter to the fundamental pluralist principle on which the organizational structure of the polity (including the Jewish polity) is based. Shrinkage will lead to a weakening, rather than a strengthening, of the ability of the Jewish community to express itself and to act on issues of concern.

The issue is thus joined for present and future generations of American Jews. Whatever their flaws, are the guiding principles of the success story of American Jewish society—pluralism and voluntarism—to be yet regnant as American Jewry enters the twenty-first century? Or will the community, traumatized by the specter of assimilation, look toward other modalities and vehicles for organization and action?

Jerome A. Chanes
Norman Linzer
David J. Schnall
June, 1997

NOTES

1. Although, strictly speaking, the issues of Israel and "captive" Jewish communities come under the public-policy rubric as well.

2. The issues addressed in Fishman's chapter relate to those addressed throughout this volume. For example, with respect to continuity, ethnicity, and ethnic choice and religion, the reality among American Jews has become one in which Jews in previous times would say that they were Jewish because they had a Jewish mother; today they say that they are Jewish because they have Jewish children. In this regard, compare Norman Linzer's chapter, "The Changing Nature of Jewish Identity" (Chapter 1).

3. The 5–9 percent number offered as the intermarriage rate for the period 1950–1965 is based on very limited data. Many demographers and other social scientists suggest that the rate was 20–35 percent, and has remained more or less at that level.

4. For a detailed discussion of federalism in the organized Jewish community, see Daniel J. Elazar, *Community and Polity: The Organizational Dynamics of American Jewry* (Philadelphia: Jewish Publication Society, 1976).

5. See, for example, Jerome A. Chanes's discussion in his chapter (Chapter 10), "Jewish Involvement in the American Public-Affairs Agenda," of the conflicting tugs of American democratic pluralism and the need to act in a coordinated manner to address public-policy issues.

1

The Changing Nature of Jewish Identity

NORMAN LINZER

Jewish identity is an issue that has never been finally resolved, but rears its head in every generation in different forms. Its complexity stems from the fact that it is determined by the interface of religion, ethnicity, psychology, politics, and nationality in the context of social change. This chapter explores the changing nature of modern Jewish identity and its ramifications for the organized Jewish community.

Three concepts contribute to an understanding of the changing nature of Jewish identity: boundaries, dissonance, and choice. *Boundaries* refer to the physical and cultural separation between one ethnic group and another. The ethnic group that lowers its boundaries to permit members to leave and non-members to enter endangers its continuity as a viable group. *Dissonance* is necessary to preserve the distinctiveness of the group. If group members do not value their difference from others, the group will soon disappear. *Choice* of identity is a modern, ubiquitous phenomenon that is difficult for traditionalists to grasp. Identity is no longer perceived as ascribed but achieved; choices abound for the expression of Jewish identity. Traditionalists regard this tampering with traditional notions of Jewish identity as threatening to the continuity of the Jewish community.

When boundaries become permeable, when Jews do not experience dissonance from the values and culture of the greater society, when they express their autonomy in choosing to be Jewish, the consequences for the Jewish community are dire. The interrelated concepts of boundaries, dissonance, and choice comprise this analysis of modern Jewish identity.

JEWISH IDENTITY

Jewish identity is a great obsession and a great ambiguity in American Jewish life (London & Chazan, 1990). It is a great obsession because there is grave concern about the diminution of Jewish behaviors, intermarriages, and family size in the Jewish community (Kosman et al., 1991). The drive to preserve the Jewish community in the face of assimilationist forces is fueled by the weakening of Jewish identity across the age spectrum, but particularly among the young.

Jewish identity refers to Jewish feelings and affiliative behaviors. The call for strengthening Jewish identity is an exhortation to lead a life of greater commitment to Jewish acts and community. Jewish identity is a function of inwardness, a choice to focus on one's community, one's spiritual process, and the love of fellow Jews (*Jewish Week*, 1995, 8).

Jewish identity, according to Jewish law, is conferred through matrilineal descent or through conversion sanctioned by the Code of Jewish Law. The Reform and Reconstructionist movements have adopted the policy of patrilineal descent, which has conferred the status of Jew on the children of mixed-married spouses, and has caused severe strains in their relationship with the Orthodox and Conservative movements.

An important feature of Jewish identity can be traced to the Jews' "otherness": "Behold, this is a nation that lives alone and is not reckoned among the nations" (Numbers 23:9). Historically, the Jews' separateness was self-imposed but was reinforced by the nations among whom they lived. This separateness has been diminished in modern times with the Jewish community's greater acceptance into the mainstream of Western society.

Identity cannot long survive intact unless it is expressed through concrete behaviors. Levitz (1995), who distinguishes between *identity* and *identification*, defines identity as involving "a complex integration of values, attitudes, knowledge, content, skills, and beliefs that inform specific behaviors," which then reinforce those values and beliefs. Identification involves "taking on the admired attributes of another individual or idealized person whose characteristics are especially admired" (78). Identification is superficial; identity is deep. The focus in this study is on Jewish identity.

Components of Identity

According to Erikson (1974), identity is a "sense of being at one with oneself as one grows and develops, and a sense of affinity with a community's sense of being at one with its future, as well as its history or mythology" (27–28). The self concept includes belonging to a larger group.

The group has been identified as the "plausibility structure" (Berger & Kellner, 1972) that is indispensable for identity formation and continuity. Thus, the presence of significant others with whom one interacts in a social setting is required. Parents require interaction with their child to make the parental identity plausible. Jews require interaction with other Jews to make Jewish identity plausible. All people who occupy various roles need to confirm them socially in order for them to be incorporated into their total identity configuration. Consequently, Jews who are unaffiliated and who lack significant communication with other Jews would find it more difficult to maintain their Jewish identity over long periods of time.

The plausibility structure that most strengthens people's identity is the ethnic group to which they belong. The essential characteristic of ethnicity is the boundaries that separate one group from another, implied in the we–they phenomenon (Vincent, 1974; Pinderhughes, 1989). When the *we* is uttered by the ethnic group, the *they* implies boundaries and power.

THE FUNCTIONS OF BOUNDARIES

Boundaries have two essential functions: they keep members of the group in, and they keep nonmembers out. They thereby maintain the viability and distinctiveness of the group. Boundaries may take several forms. An obvious boundary is self-imposed geographic separation from other groups, as practiced by the Mennonites and Amish and among the Hasidim, the Skver, and Satmar. When an ethnic group closes its doors to the outside world and does not permit access to outsiders, it strives to *isolate* its members from external influences and preserve its unique culture. Geographic isolation is reinforced by prohibitions against television, movies, and newspapers. With geographic boundaries, ethnic identity tends to be solidly confirmed for group members.

A parallel boundary is social *insulation*. Though the group resides in a multiethnic urban environment, it stakes out a particular community that it saturates with the artifacts of its culture and religion. Social contacts are conducted almost exclusively with members of the ethnic group in the local community. Groups practicing social insulation in New York City include the Chinese in Chinatown, Muslims who have moved into Borough Park, Brooklyn, and among Hasidim, the Lubavitch, the Satmar, the Bobover, and other hasidic groups, also in Brooklyn.

Another boundary is language. When the ethnic group speaks its native dialect in public, it maintains cohesion within the group and excludes outsiders. Ritual and dress can also function in ways similar to language. These components of culture maintain the group's distinctiveness from other groups.

Some members of ethnic groups, however, wish to lower boundaries in the hope of reaping societal benefits. But groups that lower boundaries and appear to be no different from other groups pay a price for that acceptance by the larger society—the loss of a distinctive identity.

The higher, more impermeable the boundary, the greater the chance of preserving separateness and continuity. The lower, more permeable the boundary, the greater the chance for eliminating separateness and increasing assimilation.

Illustrations of lowered boundaries in the Jewish community abound, but they can be encapsulated in two statistics reported in the 1990 National Jewish Population Survey: the conversion of 210,000 Jews to other faiths, and the 52 percent intermarriage rate (Kosman et al., 1991). Conversion to other faiths and intermarriage with Gentiles reflect the ease with which Jews can leave the group and the ineffectiveness of the socialization industry—the federations, Jewish schools, and camps (Mason, 1991). Intermarriage also permits Gentiles to traverse the boundary of the Jewish community. Since only a small percentage of mixed-marrieds affiliate with the Jewish community, the loss of Jews is greater than the gain of Gentiles.

Outreach to mixed marrieds conveys the message that Gentiles can now be members of, and assume leadership roles in, synagogues. Thus the success of outreach can make it more difficult to discourage interfaith marriage by blurring the distinction between Jew and Gentile. The importance of conversion is de-emphasized.

Jews require much greater distinctiveness from American culture in order for Jewish identity to flourish. As long as the boundaries remain low and porous, Jews will exit the Jewish community and permit Gentiles to enter. The ebb and flow of the human traffic does not augur well for the continuity of a community whose existence was predicated on being "a nation that dwells alone."

Socializing Institutions

In order for a group to maintain boundaries and foster identity, it needs to develop and sustain socializing institutions. In the Jewish community, the family, religion, education, and social welfare are the major social institutions through which young and old are socialized into the traditions and culture of the Jewish people. Among the major socializing agencies are the federations, synagogues, Jewish schools and camps, Jewish family services, and Jewish community centers. Each is involved in reaffirming its mission to perpetuate the Jewish community through particular policies and programs. Except for the family, each institution is represented by lay and professional leaders who are presumably knowledgeable of, and committed to, transmitting Jewish culture and traditions. Ideally, when the institution's values and concerns are in accord with those of their representatives, the members' Jewish identity is deepened through shared study and practice.

Several social patterns threaten the successful performance of these socializing institutions. Jews reside in diverse rather than self-contained communities and are highly acculturated to American society. The high monetary cost of living Jewishly excludes many individuals and families from participating in Jewish communal life. Jewish distinctiveness is no longer valued as a viable alternative to assimilation. When Jews want to be like everyone else in public and private, socializing agencies struggle to maintain high boundaries and prevent the erosion of Jewish identity.

THE DECLINE OF DISSONANCE

A consequence of having permeable boundaries that permit easy access and egress is the decline of dissonance. Dissonance is the state of discomfort that results from the experience of difference. Throughout their history up until the modern era, Jews experienced dissonance because of their expression of their

Jewish identity. Dissonance was both a burden and an opportunity—a burden due to prejudice and persecution, and an opportunity for spiritual and intellectual growth through Torah study and the performance of *mitzvot*.

With large-scale acculturation and marital assimilation, dissonance has declined and is almost nonexistent in many sectors of Jewish society. On many levels Jews are not distinguishable from Gentiles, nor do they want to be. There are many Jews today who are both proud of their heritage and at the same time feel integrated into the American mainstream. One such group consists of young adults who experience the antithesis of dissonance, as they see no real conflict between their American and Jewish identities.

Dual Jewish Identity

Jewish young adults in America today are thoroughly acculturated to the American values and way of life. Eight of them were recently interviewed by the American Jewish Committee (AJC) to ascertain how they expressed their Jewish identities (Meir, 1993). The survey concluded that their Jewish identity is intertwined with their American identity. Neither excludes the other. If this group is paradigmatic of acculturated, young American Jews who have opted to actively pursue meaning in their Jewish identity, then being both Jewish and American are not seen as contradictory.

The study did not posit the necessity for dissonance in order for Jewishness to be salient. Neither did it ask about the primacy of American or Jewish identity. The likelihood is that for these young adults Jewish identity was secondary, though it seemed immaterial to them: their emphasis was on the importance of Jewishness in their lives, which makes them a growing minority in the Jewish community.

Klagsbrun (1995) corroborates this trend. She describes the hunger for spirituality and the study of Jewish texts by professional, educated men and women in their thirties, even as they pursue secular culture.

Dual identity was not the historic norm. In the traditional Jewish community—the East European shtetl, for example—the exclusive identity was Jewish. Excluded from dual citizenship, Jews sought the certainty of a Jewish identity through Torah study and *mitzvah* performance, buttressed by tradition, history, and community. Jewish identity was not a matter of choice but of birth, reinforced by the institutions of religion, family, education, law, and social welfare.

In America today some Jews can synthesize the duality of an American Jewish identity; some will not, as with Hasidim; others cannot and become marginal to Jewish life. Factors conducive to marginality include the lack of Jewish education, role models, ritual observance, and a Jewish ambience in the home. Assimilated peers play a significant role, as does the college environment.

The eight young adults in the AJC study regard themselves as full participants in American society, even those brought up in highly identified Jewish homes. They view their Jewish identity as a fulfillment of their American identity, rather than as a source of conflict (Meir, 1993).

When many of his generation were choosing not to be Jewish at all, one respondent attributes his decision to remain Jewish to his parents' decision to send their children to Jewish schools and provide a Jewish ambience at home. He learned that being Jewish and being American are not mutually exclusive, though they conflict in fundamental values. "Judaism emphasizes community and belonging; America extols individuality. . . . in America, the freedom to choose often operates to the detriment of the Jewish community" (Meir, 1993, 42). His dilemma was that "In San Francisco I had to choose to be Jewish or choose to let it go; there was no Judaism by diffusion" (58). This statement reflects a general trend that Jewish identity "is fully self-chosen, both in terms of the range of viable options available in American society and of the psychological autonomy of today's young Jews" (Reisman, 1992, 354).

In addition to the conscious choice of a Jewish identity, the young adults felt a strong need for religious/spiritual teachings and study, greater involvement in the Jewish community, a pluralistic approach to Judaism, and sharing the values of *tikkun olam*—repairing the world, *hesed*—loving kindness, family, and community.

The young adults' apparent integration of American and Jewish identities—their choice to be Jewish and to strengthen that identity through study and involvement in the community—seems to be a model for a distinctive American-Jewish identity that experiences no dissonance. This lack of dissonance flies in the face of traditional conceptions and experiences of identity. Dissonance has served as the spring of creativity in defining the Jewish experience, in searching for roots and uniqueness, and in relating Torah and *mitzvot* to the everyday life of Jews. Will the integrated identity survive the enticements of assimilation? Will it contribute to Jewish continuity? Does this new, modern form of identity bode well for the Jewish future? One wonders whether this group of eight young adults is representative of the Jewish young-adult population at large.

JEWISH IDENTITY BY CHOICE

A dual Jewish identity reflects a high degree of comfort with both being a Jew and an American. To attain inner compatibility, the individual must be selective in adopting values and behaviors from both systems that are compatible. This requires choosing among a plethora of ideologies that would fit the individual's personality and lifestyle—in other words, choosing who one wants to be.

Choosing an identity is a modern Western phenomenon. Traditionally, an individual's identity was ascribed by birth. It was then developed throughout the lifetime, but the core within is believed to be unchangeable. Jewish children were socialized into Jewish life by their parents, teachers, and rabbis, thus confirming their innate Jewish identities. "The community of belief constituted a *total system* (italics added) that controlled the individual's environment with a detailed pattern of prescribed actions and fixed roles. Group membership was thus clearly defined" (Medding et al., 1992, 16).

The total system was dominated by Judaism, which had the moral power to coerce individuals to follow certain patterns of prescribed behavior. Living in an institutionalized world with clearly prescribed norms of behavior enabled Jews to accept their clearly defined roles without having to think about what was expected of them. Hence they could be creative, turning their attention to other pursuits (Berger & Luckmann, 1967).

In the modern world, everything that was formerly in the institutionalized background has been shifted into the deinstitutionalized foreground (Berger & Luckmann, 1967). The traditional answer to the question "Why must we do it this way?"—because "We always did it this way"—no longer suffices. Traditional ways of doing things are no longer normative simply because they are tradition-al. The authority of tradition has diminished (Shils, 1981; Linzer, 1984):

The contemporary *community of shared individual feelings* (italics added) is a voluntary and partial community of personal choice, with unclear boundaries and undefined membership. It is characterized by emotions and attachments that, while often deep, are not always clearly articulated. (Medding et al., 1992, 16)

Group membership in the traditional Jewish community was different from a "community of shared individual feelings." The contrast is analogous to the difference between a group qua group and a group as an aggregate of individu-als. In the former, members identify with the group as a whole and defer their individual needs for the welfare of the group—the group transcends the individ-ual. In the latter, the group has not yet formed because the individuals do not share a common purpose; it is not an entity unto itself.

Group membership in the traditional Jewish community meant that individ-ual Jews identified with the goals and aspirations, the joys and travails, of the Jewish community as a whole. The success and failures of the community were felt by the members themselves. The destinies of individuals and the communi-ty were intertwined (Zborowski & Herzog, 1964):

To be a Jew means to belong to a very special family within the family of nations, to relive that family's joys and tragedies, and to build one's future upon the experiences of the past. To be a Jew means to be together even in a society where so many are alone, to derive security from deep roots even in a society where so many are struggling merely to remain afloat. (*Introduction to the Passover Haggadah*)

The metaphor of family is an apt description of the traditional Jewish communi-ty because it denotes a primary group in which membership is involuntary and relationships are intense, emotional, and interdependent.

In the modern community, relationships tend to be tenuous, superficial, and partial, and membership is undefined. The community resembles Soloveitchik's natural community—a community bent on biological survival and "doing"—rather than a covenantal faith community bent on spirituality and "being" (Soloveitchik, 1992). Today one *chooses* to belong, for *ascribed* belonging is devoid of meaning.

To the traditional Jew, choosing to belong is a puzzlement. How can one choose an identity that was already conferred at birth?

As our society becomes more and more multiethnic, we have reached an era of choices. We no longer define ourselves by what we are not, but by what we are . . . . The real choice is only in *how* we identify, how creatively, how whole or half-heartedly, how much weight in our self-concept we give our ethnicity. (Klein, 1989, 5–6)

Although Jewish identity may be conferred at birth it no longer suffices for many, nor does it inform future behaviors. The "contemporary community of shared individual feelings" (Medding et al., 1992) consists of isolated individuals who choose to express their Jewish identity in varying degrees of intensity and involvement. "Being a Jew is no longer settled by the fact of being born a Jew; Jewish identity now confers a range of choices and, consequently, confusion" (Klein, 1989, 7–8). Jewishness in America has become less a phenomenon defined by others through anti-Semitism and more of a subjective personal act. If identity requires an act of choice, then empirically at least many assimilated and unaffiliated Jews seem to have chosen *not* to belong.

In a pluralistic situation, the variety is there for the choosing. Choice is supported by the democratic ethos of autonomy, rights, and individualism. In the process, the individual is thrust back upon him or herself to decide how to live. Confusion ensues when knowledge and support are lacking and there is uncertainty about the validity and meaning of the choice.

Illustrations of such options abound. Under what circumstances would one choose to send one's child to a day school or public school? To Israel or to summer camp? To affiliate with a synagogue? To light candles on Friday night? To permit one's daughter to date a non-Jew? To give to United Jewish Appeal (UJA) or to the American Cancer Society? To postpone having children for the sake of a career? These questions evoke conflicting values. They challenge the individual to decide where his or her priorities are: In Jewish identity, commitment, continuity, and distinctiveness, or in American identity, commitment, equality, and integration. The resolution of this dilemma reveals the individual's confusion or clarity in ordering Jewish and American values. Since choosing a Jewish identity seems to be pervasive, it is incumbent upon the socializing agents in the Jewish community to influence choices and strengthen commitment.

JEWISH COMMUNAL RESPONSES

The issue of Jewish identity will not go away. As long as Jews struggle to reconcile conflicts between American and Jewish values and act them out in different ways, the organized Jewish community will need to confront this elusive issue and devise approaches to strengthen Jewish identity. A variety of efforts are already under way.

Commission on Continuity

In November, 1992, at its General Assembly, the Council of Jewish Federations established a Commission on Jewish Identity and Continuity to help reverse the trend of assimilation and intermarriage. The ultimate goal of the commission is "to make Judaism more central in the lives of more Jews, to nurture the desire and commitment to make Jewish choices and to live by Jewish values, to foster vibrant Jewish homes and families" (*Jewish Week* Nov. 12–18, 1993, 26). As a result, a large number of communities have undertaken various projects to deal with the issues of identity, continuity, and education.

The very nature of such a commission, however, will prevent it from taking the bold steps that need to be taken. This is because the problem of Jewish survival cannot be addressed without dealing with Judaism. Federation vocabulary speaks of committee, process, and consensus rather than Torah, covenant, and *mitzvot*. It is in the *mitzvot*—the repeated, concrete behaviors of daily Jewish living—that the tradition is perpetuated from parent to child, teacher to student, generation to generation.

Until Jews are ready to commit themselves to performing *mitzvot* on a daily basis, their Jewish identity will suffer from the infusion of secular culture. The continuity programs are valid in attracting the unaffiliated or marginally unaffiliated, but they only partially succeed in strengthening Jewish identity.

Programs and Services

In recent years federations have allocated considerable resources to both formal and informal Jewish education in Jewish schools and Jewish community centers. Federations and synagogues have been urged to cosponsor imaginative programs to combat the erosion of distinctive boundaries (Shrage, 1992).

Synagogues have instituted "Turn Friday Night into Shabbos" for individuals and families to experience traditional Shabbats. The concept is designed to convert a secular time frame into a meaningful, religious experience.

A recent survey of day-school graduates across denominational lines documents the value of day-school education. Jewish education was seen to have an overwhelmingly positive impact on adult Jewish identity and behavior, particularly on intermarriage rates. Only 4.5 percent of the respondents married non-Jews. The report reaffirms the need for Jewish communal agencies to support and provide opportunities for continued Jewish education (Schiff & Schneider, 1994).

At the 1994 General Assembly the call went forth to establish a new Jewish-continuity agenda that would include increased funding for: (1) Hillels on college campuses, (2) sending 50,000 Jewish teenagers to Israel annually, and (3) seeing to it "that every Jewish child who wants a Jewish education can get one regardless of ability to pay" (*Jewish Week*, Nov. 25–Dec. 1, 1994, 28).

Boards of Jewish Education have established the annual "March of the Living" trip in which thousands of teenagers visit the concentration camps in

Poland during *Yom Hashoa*—Holocaust Remembrance Day—and then travel to Israel to celebrate *Yom Haatzmaut*, Israel Independence Day. The scenes create indelible images and memories and serve to strengthen Jewish identity through the two most significant Jewish events in this century.

The buzzword of the nineties is "outreach." Jewish educational institutions have mounted extensive *kiruv*—outreach—activities to bring alienated Jews back into the Jewish community. The National Jewish Outreach Program is but one of the more prominent institutions that has concentrated mainly on teaching Jews to read Hebrew and become more literate in the language of the *Siddur*. In addition, Jewish family-education programs have invited entire families to participate in synagogue- or school-sponsored educational activities.

In recent years, upon the recommendations of the Mandell Commission (Chazan & Charendoff, 1994; Jewish Community Centers Association, 1995; Jewish Welfare Board, 1984), there has been a growing trend for Jewish community centers (JCCs) to hire Jewish educational specialists to provide formal, Jewish educational activities for all ages.

Religious institutions have taken up the cause of outreach by trying to combat interfaith marriages. Reform, Reconstructionist, and Conservative religious leaders have placed great faith in outreaching to intermarried couples to stem their alienation from the Jewish community, and to keep the children of these unions connected to Jewish life. One of the underlying functions of these outreach policies was to maintain the fiscal viability of synagogues and temples through increased membership rolls. Outreach efforts will not decrease despite Cohen's prediction that "by the year 2050, the American Jewish community may shrink numerically but be stronger qualitatively" (Cohen, 1994, 95).

Serious questions have been raised regarding outreach efforts to mixed marrieds. Does outreach make it difficult to discourage interfaith dating and marriage? Can Jewish identity be maintained in a home where one parent is a Gentile? Should funds for outreach be diverted from programs that serve active and involved Jews? (Bayme, 1992).

CONCLUSIONS

The complexity of defining modern Jewish identity is a function of its myriad expressions and the multiple factors that comprise its definition. Because Jews are a religious and ethnic group who are attempting to preserve their culture amid threatening assimilatory forces, Jewish identity is a dynamic phenomenon that is threatened by social change.

Three factors underlie the Jewish community's struggle to strengthen Jewish identity: (1) Policies that establish more impermeable boundaries are needed to entice Jews to remain within the fold, (2) to foster a greater sense of dissonance between Jewish and American values, and (3) to encourage limited choices. These are difficult to implement but indispensable if Jews are to remain a distinct group that is not swallowed up by the forces of assimilation.

The perceived weakening of Jewish identity—as indicated by the rates of intermarriage, synagogue attendance, Jewish education, ritual observance, fertility, philanthropy to Jewish causes, and visitations to Israel—has alarmed both lay and professional leaders in the organized Jewish community. Although these trends have been known for many years, they were highlighted by the 1990 National Jewish Population Survey. Serving American Jewish youth and their parents constitutes a priority in preventing the further erosion of Jewish identity and identification.

There are no quick solutions. The process is long and arduous. Ideologically, it requires a return to the study of ancient and contemporary Jewish texts—formal Torah study—and the performance of distinct Jewish behaviors, *mitzvot*. Jews have survived only because there were those who devoted their lives to Torah and *mitzvot* and taught them to their children. The Jewish community possesses the knowledge, talents, and resources to return to the old formula for survival, but how feasible is it? How serious are we about perpetuating Judaism and the Jewish community?

ACKNOWLEDGMENTS

The author wishes to thank Dr. Steven Bayme, director, Jewish Communal Affairs Department, American Jewish Committee, and Dr. David J. Schnall, professor, Herbert H. Schiff Chair in Management and Administration, Wurzweiler School of Social Work, for their critical comments on the original manuscript.

REFERENCES

Bayme, S. (1992). *Outreach to the unaffiliated: Communal context and policy direction.* New York: American Jewish Committee.

Berger, P., & Kellner, H. (1972). Marriage and the construction of reality. In H. P. Dreitzel (Ed.), *Recent sociology* (no. 2, pp. 49–72). New York: Macmillan.

Berger, P., & Luckmann, T. (1967). *The social construction of reality.* New York: Doubleday.

Chazan, B., & Charendoff, M. (Eds.). (1994). *Jewish education and the Jewish community center.* Jerusalem: JCC Association.

Cohen, S. M. (1994). Why intermarriage may not threaten Jewish continuity. *Moment, 19,5,* 54–57, 89, 95.

Erikson, E. H. (1974). *Dimensions of a new identity.* New York: Norton.

Jewish Community Centers Association. (1995, January). *Task force on reinforcing the effectiveness of Jewish education in JCCs* (Final Report). New York: JCC Association.

Jewish Week. (1993, November 12–18). 26.

Jewish Week. (1994, November 25–December 1). 28.

Jewish Week. (1995, February 17). 8.

Jewish Welfare Board. (1984). *Maximizing Jewish education in Jewish community centers* (Report of the Mandell Commission). New York: Jewish Welfare Board.

Klagsbrun, F. (1995, January 13). Coming home. *Jewish Week,* 8.

Klein, J. W. (1989). *Jewish identity and self-esteem.* New York: American Jewish Committee.

Kosman, B. A., et al. (1991). *Highlights of the CJF 1990 national Jewish population survey*. New York: Council of Jewish Federations.

Levitz, I. N. (1995). Jewish identity, assimilation, and intermarriage. In N. Linzer, I. N. Levitz, & D. S. Schnall (Eds.), *Crisis and continuity: The Jewish family in the 21st century*. Hoboken, NJ: KTAV.

Linzer, N. (1984). *The Jewish family: Authority and tradition in modern perspective*. New York: Human Sciences Press.

London, P., & Chazan, B. (1990). *Psychology and Jewish identity education*. New York: American Jewish Committee.

Mason, R. (1991). When Jews convert. *Reform Judaism, 20*(1), 4–6, 10.

Medding, P. Y., Tobin, G. A., Fishman, S. B., & Rimor, M. (1992). *Jewish identity in conversionary and mixed marriages*. New York: American Jewish Committee.

Meir, A. (Ed.). (1993). *Twenty something and Jewish*. New York: American Jewish Committee.

Pinderhughes, E. (1989). *Understanding race, ethnicity, and power*. New York: Free Press.

Reisman, B. (1992). The leadership implications of the National Jewish population survey. *Journal of Jewish Communal Service, 68*(4), 350–356.

Schiff, A., & Schneider, M. (1994). *Far-reaching effects of extensive Jewish day-school attendance*. New York: Yeshiva University.

Shils, E. (1981). *Tradition*. Chicago: University of Chicago Press.

Shrage, B. (1992). A communal response to the challenges of the 1990 CJF national Jewish population survey. *Journal of Jewish Communal Service, 68*(4), 321–330.

Soloveitchik, J. B. (1992). *The lonely man of faith*. New York: Doubleday.

Vincent, J. (1974, Winter). Brief communication. *Human Organization, 33*(4), 375–379.

Zborowski, M., & Herzog, E. (1964). *Life is with people*. New York: Schocken.

2

America's Challenge to Jewish Identity: A Historical Perspective on Voluntarism and Assimilation

JEFFREY GUROCK

In 1894, a year which witnessed approximately 55,000 Jews emigrate from Eastern Europe to the United States, Lithuanian Rabbi Israel Meir Ha-Kohen Kagan admonished his followers who lived under Czarist oppression against settling in the free world of America. In his *Niddehei Yisrael*, he railed against a libertine America that was inhospitable to the maintenance of traditional faith and Jewish identity, and stated decisively that "whoever wishes to live properly before God must not settle in those countries. Even if he had emigrated due to his economic distress, he must return to his home. The choice is given to the individual who truly fears the Lord to return to his homeland where he can inculcate his children with Torah values." [1]

Rabbi Kagan understood, and had his own ready answer for, the fundamental challenge and dilemma America had always posed to the perpetuation of Judaism. He recognized that from the beginnings of that group's settlement in America, this country had offered Jews unparalleled opportunities for personal and individual advancement and acceptance, largely unfettered by legal barriers or social discrimination. All that was implicitly requested of the Jews was that they be loyal to their new country and adapt themselves to the mores of their host society. In only the subtlest of ways, through informal proscriptions, had America ever prescribed that Jews live, work, or interact with one another. America left the decision of whether or not to identify with a voluntary Jewish community to the individual Jew, even as ideologies of Americanism advised that it would be best for all concerned for the Jew to assimilate. As Rabbi Kagan saw it, Jews in America had tragically always opted for advancement over affiliation, for integration over identification, and for mobility over the maintenance of an ancestral heritage. His view was that it was far better for Jews to continue to live as Jews under oppression than to risk the loss of Jewish continuity under freedom.

Unfortunately for this Russian Jewish sage, masses of European Jews either did not hear or chose to ignore his decree. In the very year following his book's appearance an additional 46,000 Jews arrived on these shores, all part of a forty-year period (circa 1881–1920) that witnessed over two million Jews seeking American borders and bounties. In so doing, they made the same fundamental judgments as had those who arrived here during the so-called Sephardic period (circa 1654–1830), a period that brought some five thousand Jews to these shores, and the era of central European migration (circa 1830–1880), which swelled American Jewish numbers to close to one-quarter million.[2] In each instance, in each period, European Jews made essential determinations about how important the Old World was to their lives and chose to move on to the "*trefa* land," where as Rabbi Jacob David Willowski, a contemporary of Kagan, once put it: "Even the stones are impure."[3]

To be sure, most Jewish immigrants, be they the Dutch or the English in the seventeenth through the early nineteenth centuries, the Germans, the Bohemians, or Poseners in the mid-nineteenth century, or the refugees from Romania or the Pale in the late nineteenth–twentieth centuries, did not abandon their Jewish identities with enthusiasm or extreme alacrity. Though the folklore of East European Jewish migration does speak, for example, of the Jew who, upon gazing for the first time at the Statue of Liberty, emerged from his steerage portal to cast his *tefillin*—phylacteries—overboard, the truth is that most Jews did not rush to sever their ties with other Jews.[4] Indeed, in a repeating pattern, elements within each migrating Jewish group did their utmost to transplant synagogue models and other forms of Jewish institutional life that they hoped would keep Jews together. But, in most instances, Jewish affiliation and identification foundered because immigrants, and most especially their children, wanted to advance and be accepted in America. The implicit requirements for success undermined religious and group allegiances.

During the earliest days of Jewish settlement in the United States, those who wanted themselves and their coreligionists to retain a group identity had to confront the reality that no power, temporal or ecclesiastical, could force American Jews to remain with their people. In colonial times, this endemic voluntarism was a direct result of the conditions that allowed for the very presence of Jews in seventeenth- and eighteenth-century America. It was only in those areas—principally in proprietary colonies—where no one church group held sway and did not control or dominate government that Jews were allowed to settle at all and advance their American agendas. But, if a colony like New York or Pennsylvania recognized no denomination and welcomed all who could contribute, leaving the decision to belong to a church largely up to individual conscience, it also, by extension, precluded the legal establishment of the synagogue and granted the Jewish settler freedom to dissociate himself from Judaism.[5]

With the founding of the United States, the legal disenfranchisement of religion became a national act of civic faith. From that point on, the Jews' right of settlement anywhere in this country was virtually assured. In short order, the several states, following the federal government's lead, removed almost all statutory barriers to Jewish integration in American society. Blessed now more than ever before with individual freedoms, American Jews were left largely to themselves to determine whether or not they wanted to remain tied to their ancestral group.[6]

To be sure, when synagogues were established in the eighteenth and early nineteenth centuries and assumed all the social, educational, and philanthropic functions of the traditional *Kehillah* (Jewish community), those in charge did have some influence over those Jews who might be interested in their services. For example, a synagogue might deny the most fundamental of Jewish religious privileges—the right to be buried in a Jewish cemetery—to intermarrieds. Likewise, since denominations, and not the government, were in charge of educating youngsters and succoring the poor, synagogues, at least in theory, could demand a degree of conformity to their rules from those who availed themselves of their basic services.[7]

What the synagogue-community lacked was the power of prior restraint or the ability to eliminate all other choices from those whom they hoped to lead. In the case of intermarriage, it could not forcibly prohibit a coreligionist from doing what he pleased; it could only punish after the fact, with sanctions that may or may not have troubled the resolute intermarrying Jew. As far as education and charity were concerned, although public schools and community chests were not yet in existence, Jews could turn to Christian schools and social-service systems for training and help if they were willing to ignore, or were unconcerned with, the subtle Christianizing messages that these agencies also proffered. Overall, for the early nineteenth-century community, which was small in numbers, unregenerated by new arrivals, isolated from Old World centers of Jewish knowledge, and bereft of rabbinic leadership, assimilation was an inevitable reality.[8]

CENTRAL EUROPEAN IMMIGRATION

Fortunately for the survival of Jewish life in this country, even as the early synagogue-centered community proved itself unable to overcome the indigenous group's drift towards disaffection, events in Europe stimulated a second epoch of Jewish immigration to these shores. These Jews, who hailed primarily from Central Europe, immediately gave strength to American Jewish numbers and reinvigorated communal life even as they too, inevitably, were challenged by the lures of assimilation.

Jews from Prussia, Bavaria, Austria, Bohemia, Posen, and other German, Austro-Hungarian, and Polish locales set out for America because of the economic deprivations, social dislocations, and political disabilities that vexed them in their homelands. One of the factors that had kept Jews at home in Central and Western Europe during the first decades of the nineteenth century was the optimism about the improvement in Jewish life and status engendered by the French Revolution and Napoleonic conquests. These hopes were dashed by the Congress of Vienna's return of the old order. The Jews' pessimism about their future inten-

sified further as the eras of reaction and Romanticism that followed forced them
to question deeply whether the bounties of emancipation would ever be theirs. For
some Jews the answer was alliance with the liberal forces within their countries
and the continued struggle for political freedom. For others, it was the reordering
of Jewish society and religion to prove—primarily to liberal friends—that the
Jews were worthy of emancipation. For still others, the ones who were most pessimistic about their Jewish future, conversion to Christianity for advancement into
society was the only solution. Then there were those who were less concerned
with the political value of emancipation and most interested in their own personal economic advancement. These latter were the ones who joined with Central
Europeans of other faiths in seeking out the benefits that America had to offer.[9]

Arriving in this expanding and expansive country, the so-called "German
Jews" sought out their fortune—or at least middle-class status—beginning either
as peddlers on the road leading West or as laborers who remained in the East.
Some progressed mightily and rapidly and were lionized and satirized for their
rags-to-riches successes. Many more achieved just enough to enter the lower
middle class of storekeepers, trades people, petty manufacturers, and entrepreneurs, thereby paving the way for their children to rise even further. In all events,
German-Jewish economic quests and accomplishments were not achieved without challenge or injury to their religious and ethnic identities. Jewish-peddler
memoirs are replete with the cries of those stranded from their communities,
complaining about their inability to remain true to their faith as they trudged
through the wilderness. The historical record is full of the difficulties urban-
based Jewish entrepreneurs faced in adjusting to the demands of the six-day
workweek in a world where the social, if not legal, seventh day of rest was
Sunday and not the Jewish Sabbath.[10]

The German-American synagogues of this period were not unresponsive to
their Jews' dilemmas. Though most began as immigrant congregations and thus
initially were dedicated to perpetuating Old World religious lifestyles here, as
these synagogues Americanized, efforts were made to make Jewish identification
both socially attractive and religiously convenient. In some instances that meant
that Orthodox synagogues were extremely tolerant of members' religious
deviances outside the synagogues' precincts. No one publicly criticized or cen-
sured those who opened their stores on Saturday afternoon after attending
prayers in the morning. Every effort was made to make the service more pre-
sentable to those concerned with American proprieties. Potential congregants
would be reassured that devotions and donations would be stripped of the "ori-
entalisms" that might embarrass rising Jews in front of the Gentile neighbors
whom they hoped to impress.[11]

Other, more religiously liberal congregations went even further in adjusting
the time and mode of services to meet American economic and social realities.
The most radical of Reform congregations went so far as to move the traditional day of rest to Sunday, both to bring American Judaism in line with America's
dominant religion and to make it possible for Jews to observe a Sabbath without
missing a day of work.[12]

In many instances immigrant rabbis from Central Europe who began arriving after 1840 were instrumental in leading synagogue adjustments, particularly in helping their laity articulate religious rationales for departures from traditional ways. In other cases, it was the laity that told their rabbis what they wanted to do, leaving them the choice of either conforming to their wishes—and maybe offer a religious apologia for what was to be done—or finding another post. In America, rabbis who dissented from congregational missions did not remain long in their pulpits.[13]

Even as these accommodating synagogues were striving to make religious identification easier, alternative forms of Jewish institutional life arose that attempted to strengthen the bonds linking Jews. Beginning in the 1850s, fraternal orders like the B'nai B'rith and literary, cultural, and recreational organizations like the Young Men's Hebrew Association (YMHA) offered men from varying walks of life congenial settings for sustained group interaction. The most affluent of Jews sometimes turned to private clubs to be with those of their own ethnic, economic, and social station. Jewish women found one another and interacted with Jewish men not only in the synagogue and in the Y's activities that were open to both sexes, but more impressively, they took extensive part in the good works of local Sisterhoods of Personal Services. Some of these organizations that worked among the poor were aligned with synagogues; others were linked to Jewish women's clubs. In all instances they provided Jewish women not only with the opportunity to come together in fulfilling a deeply felt Jewish mission to improve the world, but they also afforded them a chance at leadership in Jewish communal affairs.[14]

Of course, there were incalculable numbers of acculturating Jews who were manifestly disinterested in formal, organizational ties with other Jews. Though clearly they were prime candidates for assimilation, some remained tied to other Jews simply by demographic propinquity because they lived in their own ethnic enclaves within America's large cities. There they could not help but meet up with other Jews on a daily, ongoing basis. For other Jews, their drift away was mitigated by the rise of social anti-Semitism in the last quarter of the nineteenth century, which placed formal and informal barriers in the way Jews could live and hence integrate into a Gentile world.[15]

EAST EUROPEAN IMMIGRATION

As the 1880s began and German-American Jews continued to struggle with identity issues, a new mass immigration from Eastern Europe began arriving that rapidly increased American Jewish numbers and provided a new vitality to the community. However, as alluded to earlier, they too had to contend with the American challenges that threatened the Jewish values and identity brought with them from lands of oppression.

To some degree, the Russian, Polish, Hungarian, and Rumanian refugees wanting to maintain the staunchest of allegiances to the Jewish people and religion had a distinct advantage over the similarly minded Jews who had arrived in earlier migrations. By dint of their numbers and the poverty that caused them to settle together in urban ghettos, finding other Jews and being with other Jews was never a problem for them. Moreover, those who sought spiritual solace and social satisfaction could always turn to one of the hundreds of small, store-front landsmanshaft synagogues that dotted their neighborhood. Likewise, those who wanted intellectual stimulation of a different kind and political rhetoric of a very radical variety could always turn to the myriad Jewish workingmen's and socialist organizations in the ghetto. There were even Zionist groups for those who looked for new ideas and old friends within the Jewish national movement's downtown outposts. The transplanted institutions that were dedicated to preserve one or more forms of Jewish identity were always around for those who wanted them in the predominantly Jewish sections of the city. Indeed, places like the Lower East Side of New York City were in many ways so Jewish that it was almost impossible for resolutely disaffected Jews to achieve the goal of separating themselves from their brothers and sisters.[16]

Still, for all their strength in numbers, Jewish identification among both first-generation Jews and their children was under grievous attack from forces within and without their community.[17] East European Jews, like all immigrants of the time, were objects of strident debate within the United States. Racists, nativists, and restrictionists argued that these foreign masses were undermining the once-great America that they had known and that they were a breed of men and women that could not be assimilated into their idealized and declining white Anglo-Saxon Protestant society. Friends of the immigrants disdained this pessimistic view of newcomers even as they admitted that Russian Jews and all other newcomers had a long way to go before they could become 100 percent Americans. Rapid and aggressive Americanization was the answer these "melting pot" advocates offered to the antagonists' fears. To back up their position that immigrants could change, American progressives and German-American Jews worked hard to transform the linguistic, cultural, and behavioral outlooks of their clients. Institutionally that meant that great efforts were made in the public schools not only to teach the 3Rs (of reading, 'riting, 'rithmatic) but, just as important, to instill in pupils American values. After school, on weekends, and during the summer, in the large settlement houses that both Jewish and Gentile amateur social workers established and ran, every effort was made to intensify the efforts to provide immigrants and their children with new American identities.[18]

Implicit, when not totally explicit, in these calls to Americanization was the message that the culture and identities that Jews had brought with them from Europe were retrogressive and barriers against their full integration into their new American world. Clearly, in this view, the Yiddish jargon had to be forgotten. Likewise, the foreign social atmosphere of the old-style storefront synagogue had to be eliminated. Most certainly, the radical, secular identity harbored by so many Jews of socialist persuasion was frequently deemed inimical to good American citizenship.[19]

Most East European Jews were more than willing to conform to the prescriptions for acceptance and advancement articulated by these outsiders. For example, while Lower East Side Jews had the option, beginning in 1886, of sending their sons to a separatistic, all-day yeshiva instead of to the public schools, most downtowners, including most immigrant rabbis, chose to stick with the so-called "Temples of Americanization." There, disrespect for old Jewish ways and Yiddish means-of-expression were routinely inculcated. Occasionally, Christianizing messages were also subtly introduced into pupils' consciousness.[20]

Jewish socialists often had an even more difficult time with America's rules and ideologies. At several points before, during, and after World War I, identification with radical ideas was deemed unpatriotic. Jews of that political bent were then forced to either abandon their long-held beliefs or risk being read out of this country's mainstream.[21]

To be sure, downtown Jewish leaders, ably assisted by some of the more sensitive uptown ones, were not totally bereft of weapons in responding to attacks against Jewish values and traditions. On religious issues in particular, efforts were made to help the masses mediate between the calls of Jewish traditions and the demands of American society. The congregations for the acculturated that they established and the modern Talmud torahs they supported all argued strongly that the maintenance of the essence of ancient Jewish teachings and adherence to much of traditional rituals were not inconsistent with being a good American. These institutions would serve as the prototypes for this century's American Orthodox and Conservative synagogues and as centerpieces for a half century of supplementary Jewish education. On another front, some of the more outspoken communal spokesmen even advocated a role for Yiddish in Jewish settlement-house work. They argued logically that if social workers held out hope of reaching and influencing first-generation clients, they had better address them in their familiar foreign tongue. Ultimately, by the 1910s, these and other comparable plans for reconciling American and Jewish identities would find their greatest institutional expression in the New York-based Jewish community—*Kehillah*. There, uptown and downtown Jews adopted progressive methods to plan, experiment with, and execute strategies for meeting their communities' social, economic, and identity questions.[22]

Nonetheless, for all these efforts, the pressure upon Jews to assimilate remained strong and enduring. Indeed, on balance, possibly the greatest factor that restrained Jews from abandoning their community was the stark reality that the largest number of them and their children lacked the economic wherewithal to physically remove themselves from the proximity of their fellows. Graphically put, a resolute Jew bent on assimilation who had learned his American lessons well could stand proudly on a soapbox on Delancey Street and unabashedly declare in unaccented English that he had no further interest in anyone or anything Jewish. But unless he had the money to make his move he would, upon ending his brash remarks, still find himself trapped within the old ethnic enclave.

It was only in the 1920s that second-generation Jews in ever increasing numbers began to gain the economic means to choose where and with whom they would live and associate. But their integration and communal disintegration were slowed by individual proclivities to remain with their own kind and thus to move together to more favorable settings. Social anti-Semitism and prejudices of all kinds placed real external limits upon a Jew's disengagement from his people.[23]

The constricting powers of racist and restrictionist opinions confronted those Jews when they sought admission to this country's elite schools, to the most prestigious professions, and the best places to live. In each instance, quotas, social covenants, and "gentlemen's agreements" retarded Jewish integration into the Gentile world. Consequently, Jews continued to reside together. In New York, the Bronx's Grand Concourse was one of the neighborhoods that replaced the Lower East Side as a center of Jewish life. They attended together a less-select group of municipal and state colleges and universities. City College of New York was known as the "Jewish Harvard" or as "The Cheder on the Hill." Jews found each other in specific professional, trade, and social environments. Overall, regardless of whether Jews desired to stay with their own group and even if they chose not to formally affiliate with any synagogue, school, or other ethnic organization, they would continue to associate with other Jews for most of their lives on the streets of their Jewish neighborhood.[24]

For most American Jews the requisite confluence of acculturation, affluence, personal willingness, and social acceptance necessary for successful assimilation came together only in the third and fourth generations, starting after World War II. In the 1950s a combination of economic prosperity, the threat of Communism that commanded the use of the best and brightest (and that included Jews) to keep America great and safe, the more subtle ideology in emerging suburbia of "getting along," and ultimately the wide-spread acceptance of cultural pluralism as a value that everyone could believe in all joined to make Jews more widely accepted. It was then, with the Jew finally unshackled by the end of discrimination and no longer required to work, live, study, and play within his or her own group, that the essential crisis of Jewish survival became a permanent reality on the American scene.[25]

THE RISE OF JEWISH EDUCATION

Many of the descendants of the East European immigrants did not choose to abandon their ancestral associations, identities, and allegiances. Even as Jews after World War II joined with their Gentile neighbors in settling in a heterogeneous suburbia, they often chose to cluster in Jewish sections of suburban developments or towns, and most of their closest friends were Jews.[26] The same patterns frequently were repeated when Jews from the Northeast or Midwest sought new locales and homes in Sun-Belt communities.[27] There, away from Jewish metropolises, those intent on retaining and strengthening their identities more than ever before had to resort to and affiliate with formal Jewish religious and educational organizations. No longer could the Jewish neighborhood and tensions with the outside community be relied upon to retard assimilation. In this environment, Conservative synagogues—and to a lesser extent the Modern Orthodox congregations and Neo-Reform Temples against which they competed—were the places Jews turned to for ethnic and religious bonding. Concomitantly, Jewish education programs that were dedicated not only to educate youngsters but, more importantly, to strengthen their desire to be with other Jews became extremely important.[28]

In this regard the modern Jewish day-school system that began among the Orthodox but which eventually also emerged among Conservatives and some Reform Jews played a critical role. Its nuanced approach afforded pupils a subtle separatism from the Gentile environment, even as it was certain to inculcate respect for worldly knowledge and the skills requisite to live well in the outside world. Besides instilling in students a greater pride through knowledge of their Jewish heritage, day schools also created cohorts of similar-thinking alumni— ready candidates for endogamy and ongoing participation in Jewish life.[29]

As the post-war decades unfolded, Jewish education and survival found a new ally in a previously long-standing enemy—the American university. As noted above, during the interwar period America's most elite schools had quotas against Jews. Even those colleges that admitted Jews without questions were often inhospitable to Jewish practices and identification. Accommodations for Jewish holidays and observances were rare, even at open schools. Only a few universities, for their own reasons, taught Jewish culture, languages, and history as part of their academic programs. While some committed and ambitious Jewish students did establish societies, clubs, fraternities, and other informal venues for keeping Jews together and for teaching them about their past, until the 1960s the campus largely promoted assimilation.[30]

The efflorescence of Jewish studies in the contemporary era had much to do with the university's new openness to black, Hispanic, and all other ethnic-studies programs and a general awareness of cultural pluralism as a value that should be taught and extolled on campus. In all events, when universities offered Jewish and Gentile students these substantive programs and in fact recruited the best Jewish youngsters with offers of the availability of kosher foods on campus and that Jewish traditions would be honored, it became possible for those interested to both advance their Jewish knowledge and commitment while at school. The issue that would remain was whether these fully integrated American Jewish youngsters would choose to identify with their people instead of assimilating into the larger, accepting world around them.[31]

POST-WORLD WAR II IMMIGRATION

Even as the indigenous community dealt with the issues of voluntarism in a truly free society, the years after World War II also witnessed the arrival on the American shores of a fourth wave of immigrants, which possessed their own perspective on America's challenges. These were, primarily, the German and Austrian Jews who fled Hitler's threats and early persecutions of the 1930s and the Jewish survivors of the Holocaust from all over Europe who sought American sanctuary and freedom after their old worlds had been destroyed. They were joined by a less-readily noticed group of Sephardic Jews hailing predominantly from Syria who were fleeing repressive Arab regimes. Between 1945–1975 some 320,000 Jews immigrated to this country. The most Orthodox of these arrivals—most notably those from Eastern Europe—were essentially the descendants of those who had harkened to Rabbi Kagan's admonition of some fifty-years earlier. Others, including those from Germany, Austria, and Western European countries, had never before considered America because they had been comfortable, acculturated, and satisfied as emancipated Jews in their own home countries until Nazism revoked their freedoms and threatened their lives. These victims of the Third Reich were joined in the early 1950s by Syrian Jews who foresaw no safe future for themselves under the Ba'athist government, and in the late 1950s by Hungarian Jews escaping the terror of Russian tanks and Communist oppression.[32]

In several significant ways these immigrants' experiences as new Americans in confronting the issues of transplantion and adjustment have been much different from all earlier migrants. Arriving as they did into an American environment that had come to respect the values of cultural pluralism and ethnic diversity, the pressure upon them to rapidly acculturate was much less than in earlier periods. In addition, those who would most resolutely resist Americanization came to this country with the strongest sense of their own cultural superiority. In many instances they settled in this country with and around charismatic, traditional leaders who helped strengthen their commitments to transplanting and preserving the traditions of the past. Whether it was Rabbi Joseph Breuer in Washington Heights, the Lubavitcher Rebbe in Crown Heights, or Rabbi Aaron Kotler in Lakewood, New Jersey or others of comparative stature in the new Sephardic communities, their consistent message always was that what they had salvaged and brought with them to the United States was far greater and dearer than anything the American dream had to offer. Needless to say, the very visible fidelity of Hasidim and others to the oldest of Jewish ways has had a noticeable impact upon the indigenous American Orthodox group. This group had always made the types of social adjustments they perceived as requisite to maintain the core of traditional belief and practice within an open society. These accommodators have frequently been regarded as weak in resisting America as increasingly the values of stalwart defenders of the faith have impacted much of the larger Orthodox community.[33]

While much can be made of the successes and the impact of the transplanters who have resisted, the fact is that this heterogeneous group of immigrants, refugees, and survivors also includes significant numbers who have chosen to pursue acculturated American lifestyles. Not unlike all other Jews who preceded them here, they have sought the American dream with zeal and determination and now, well into their second generation, have seen themselves and their children integrated into contemporary society. While these children of refugees and survivors may possess a strong rootedness to their parents' past and present than had earlier groups, their future horizons are comparable to those of other Americanized Jews. They too deal with the questions of whether and how to identify with their community instead of assimilating into the accepting world around them.[34]

Today the American Jewish community is also in the process of absorbing elements from the fifth, most recent phase of immigration: that of settlers from the former Soviet Union. This wave, which numbered as of 1994 approximately 280,000, reached its apogee in 1992 when some 46,000 Jews immigrated.[35] They arrived in this country with many of the same dreams of success and economic mobility that had characterized earlier Jewish immigrants.[36] However, their identity issues are fundamentally different from those who preceeded them. Living as they did under atheistic Communism for more than fifty years, and isolated as they were from Jews elsewhere in the world, they were bereft of the types of traditional Jewish identities that both the early East European immigrants and the later Holocaust survivors had cherished. For these newest arrivals, the issues of voluntarism and identification began with the question of whether they would choose in this land the freedom to acquire a sense of belonging to the Jewish community.[37]

CONCLUSIONS

It remains to be seen if this latest group of Jewish newcomers to America will opt to avail itself of the network of Jewish social services that were organized, tried, tested, and transformed by earlier attempts to meet the identity needs of preceding groups of Jewish immigrants. But if they do respond affirmatively to those who reach out to them, then, ironically, these refugees from the former Soviet Union will prove to be the first wave of migrants to experience an intensification in Jewish identification within their community as they move from their first to their second generation.

NOTES

1. For statistics on East European migration to the United States in 1894, see Moses Rischin, *The Promised City* (Cambridge, MA: Harvard University Press, 1962), p. 270. For Rabbi Kagan's statement see, Israel Meir Ha-Kohen, *Niddehei Yisrael,* Warsaw, 1894), pp. 129–130 quoted in translation in Aaron Rakeffet-Rothkoff, *The Silver Era: Rabbi Eliezer Silver and his Generation* (Jerusalem/New York: Yeshiva University Press and Feldheim Publishers, 1981), pp. 118–119.

2. For a basic periodization of American Jewish history, see Jacob Rader Marcus, "The Periodization of American Jewish History," *Publications of the American Jewish Historical Society* (hereinafter *PAJHS*) (March 1958) pp. 125–133. See below for my comments on the Jewish multiethnic nature of these several periods.

3. For a discussion of Willowski's statements and career in the United States, see Aaron Rothkoff, "The American Sojourn of Ridbaz: Religious Problems within the Immigrant Community," *American Jewish Historical Quarterly* (hereinafter *AJHQ*) (June 1968), pp. 557–572.

4. Obviously, at most, only half of the Jewish population—Jewish men—could have made that symbolic, dramatic break with Judaism by throwing their *tefillin* overboard. Women would have no phylacteries to get rid of. Perhaps they could have thrown their candlesticks overboard, but such an act did not enter into the folklore of migration history.

5. For a complete discussion, colony by colony, of the presence of American Jews and their level of emancipation up to the Revolutionary period, see Marcus's massive, *The Colonial American Jew, 3 Vols.* (Detroit: Wayne State University Press, 1970).

6. For a survey of the processes of removal of legal barriers against Jews, state by state, see Stanley F. Chyet, "The Political Rights of the Jews in the United States, 1776–1840," *American Jewish Archives* (hereinafter *AJA*) (April 1958): 14–75. For a description of Jewish life at the close of this period, see Malcolm Stern, "The 1820s: American Jewry Comes of Age," *A Bicentennial Festschrift for Jacob Rader Marcus* (New York: KTAV, 1976), pp. 539–561.

7. For discussions of the problem of intermarriage and the role the synagogue played in philanthropic and educational matters, as well as the pressures leaders tried to place on Jews to conform, see Hyman B. Grinstein, *The Rise of the Jewish Community of New York* (Philadelphia: Jewish Publication Society, 1946), pp. 137–150, 225–235, 377–378. For another important discussion of the phenomenon of intermarriage in the Nineteenth Century that notes the role synagogue rules played in the decline of Jewish numbers, see Moshe Davis, "Mixed Marriage in Western Jewry," *Jewish Journal of Sociology, 15*(2) (1968), pp. 180–181.

8. For a discussion of the American synagogue's lack of prior restraint, see Jeffrey S. Gurock, "The Orthodox Synagogue," in *The American Synagogue: A Sanctuary Transformed* (Cambridge, UK: Cambridge University Press, 1987), pp. 37–39. On the question of Christianizing against Jews in the early nineteenth century, see Jonathan D. Sarna, "The American Jewish Response to Nineteenth Century Christian Missions," *Journal of American History* (June 1981), pp. 35–51.

9. On the motivations and processes of Central European migration to America see, Bertram W. Korn, "Jewish 48ers in America," *AJA* (June 1949), pp. 3–20; Rudolf Glanz, "The German Jewish Mass Emigration, 1820–1880," *AJA* (April 1970), pp. 49–66; and A. Barkai, "On German Jewish Migration in Nineteenth Century America," *Leo Baeck Year Book* (1985), pp. 301–318.

10. On the economic rise of these Jews both on the frontier and in the cities, see Allan Tarshish, "The Economic Life of the American Jew in the MiddleNineteenth Century," in *Essays in American Jewish History to Commemorate the Tenth Anniversary of the Founding of the American Jewish Archives under the Direction of Jacob Rader Marcus,* ed. *Jacob Rader Marcus* (Cincinnati, OH: AJA, 1958), pp. 263–295; Elliot Ashkenazi, "Jewish Commercial Interests Between North and South: The Case of the Lehmans and the Seligmans," *AJA* (Spring/Summer 1991), pp. 25–40; Stephen Mostov, "A Sociological Portrait of German Jewish Immigrants in Boston, 1845–1861," *AJS Review* (1978), pp. 121–152. For an examination of a peddler's diary that underscores the immigrants trials and travails, see Abraham Vossen Goodman, "A Jewish Peddler's Diary, 1841–1843," *AJA* (June 1951), pp. 81–111.

11. On the behavior of German-American synagogues, particularly those that remained Orthodox, towards their membership's laxity of observance, see Gurock (cited above [8]), pp. 43–47.

12. On the processes of Americanization and liberalization of services in the nineteenth century, see Leon Jick, *The Americanization of the Synagogue, 1820–1870* (Hanover, NH: University Press of New England, 1976). On the Sunday-Sabbath movement in

Reform Judaism, see Kerry Olitzky, "The Sunday-Sabbath Movement in American Reform Judaism: Strategy or Evolution?" *AJA* (April 1982), pp. 75–88.

13. The American careers of some important Jewish rabbis and other clergy are described and capsulized in Moshe Davis, *The Emergence of Conservative Judaism: The Historical School in Nineteenth Century America* (Philadelphia: Jewish Publication Society, 1963).

14. On the history of B'nai B'rith, see Deborah Dash Moore, *B'nai B'rith and the Challenge of Ethnic Leadership* (Albany, NY: State University of New York Press, 1981). On Women's activities during this same time period and beyond see, Beth Wenger, "Jewish Women and Volunteerism: Beyond the Myth of Enablers," *AJHQ* (Autumn 1989), pp. 16–36.

15. On the phenomenon of social anti-Semitism in the late nineteenth century and beyond, see John Higham, "Social Discrimination against Jews in America, 1830–1930," *PAJHS* (September 1957), pp. 1–33. This is an excellent exemplar of the vast literature on the subject.

16. For the best study of the conditions of settlement and the ideological groups that informed the culture of transplantation on the Lower East Side, see Moses Rischin, *The Promised City* (Cambridge, MA: Harvard University Press, 1962), especially chapters 4, 5, and 7.

17. It should be noted that during the period of large-scale East European immigration to America, this country also witnessed the arrival of some ten thousand or more Levantine Jews, primarily those who fled the unrest in the Turkish empire. They lived a somewhat separate existence from the Russian immigrants, as noted in Rischin, cited above [16], pp. 107–108.

18. On the battle over immigration restriction, see Esther Panitz, "Polarity of Jewish Attitudes to Immigration," *AJHQ 53* (December 1963), pp. 99–110; and idem. "In Defense of the Jewish Immigrant (1891–1924)," *AJHQ 55* (September 1965), pp. 57–97. On Americanization efforts of German Jews and others among the new arrivals, see Myron Berman, "A New Spirit on the East Side: The Early History of the Emanuel Brotherhood, 1903–1920," *AJHQ* (September 1964), pp. 53–81. On the life of Jewish children in public school, see Stephan F. Brumberg, "Going to America, Going to School: The Immigrant-Public School Encounter in Turn of the Century New York City," *AJA* (November 1984), pp. 86–135.

19. On the fate of transplanted Old World ideologies in America, see Gurock, "Change to Survive: The Common Experience of Two Transplanted Jewish Identities in America," in *What is American about the American Jewish Experience*, Marc Lee Raphael (Ed.) (Williamsburg, VA: The College of William and Mary, 1993), pp. 54–69.

20. On the founding of an all-day yeshiva for boys on the Lower East Side, see Gurock, *The Men and Women of Yeshiva: Orthodoxy, Higher Education and American Judaism* (New York: Columbia University Press, 1988), especially chapter 2.

21. On the particular problems Jewish socialists faced in maintaining their views in an often antagonistic United States, see Gurock, "Change to Survive . . .," cited above [19], pp. 64–69.

22. On the efforts in the religious realm before World War I to modernize the synagogue that brought German and acculturated East European leaders together, see Gurock, "A Generation Unaccounted for in American Judaism" *AJHQ* (December 1987), pp. 247–259. The history of the *Kehillah* is discussed in Arthur A. Goren, *New York Jews and the Quest for Community: The Kehillah Experiment, 1908–1922* (New York: Columbia University Press, 1970).

23. See Nathan Goldberg, "Occupational Patterns of American Jews," *Jewish Review* (January 1946), pp. 262–290, for an early yet still useful study of Jewish economic mobility of this period.

24. Deborah Dash Moore has argued convincingly that at least in New York during the 1920s, Jews moved together to new neighborhoods not only because of social barriers elsewhere, but more importantly, because they wanted to live together, and that in this most ethnic of cities, other ethnic and religious groups continued to live within their own enclaves. In other words, New York City had few WASP neighborhoods into which Jews might even think of settling. In addition, she argues that the nature of Jewish neighborhood life encouraged ethnic persistence. She also notes the institutional developments and activities that helped maximize ethnic persistence. See Deborah Dash Moore, *At Home in America: Second-Generation New York Jews* (New York: Columbia University Press, 1981). For an overview of the barriers and successes of Jewish nationally during this period, see Henry L. Feingold, *A Time for Searching: Entering the Mainstream, 1920–1945* (Baltimore: Johns Hopkins University Press, 1992).

25. For a general overview of the 1945–1990 period in American Jewish history, see Edward Shapiro, *A Time for Healing: American Jewry Since World War II* (Baltimore: Johns Hopkins University Press, 1992).

26. For an example of a Midwestern Jewish community where the Jewish residents were highly acculturated and yet most Jews (and Gentiles) tended to associate with their own kind, see Benjamin Ringer, *The Edge of Friendliness: A Study of Jewish–Gentile Relations* (New York: Basic Books, 1967).

27. Deborah Dash Moore, *To the Golden Cities: Pursuing the American Jewish Dream in Miami and L.A.* (New York: Free Press, 1994).

28. For an analysis of the important leadership role and hegemony achieved by Conservative Judaism in the early postwar period, see Marshall Sklare, *Conservative Judaism: An American Religious Movement* (Glencoe, IL: University of Chicago Press, 1955).

29. For an overview survey of the rise of Jewish day schools in the early postwar period, see Alvin I. Schiff, *The Jewish Day School in America* (New York: Jewish Education Committee Press, 1966). For a study of the ideology and alumni profile of one leading day school during this time period, see Gurock, *Ramaz: School, Community, Scholarship, and Orthodoxy* (Hoboken, NJ: KTAV, 1989).

30. For examinations of the changing attitudes of American universities towards Jews and Judaic studies on their campuses, see Harold S. Wechsler, *The Qualified Student: A History of Selective College Admission in America* (New York: John Wiley, 1977), and Paul Ritterband and H. S. Wechsler, *Jewish Learning in American Universities: The First Century* (Bloomington & Indianapolis: Indiana University Press, 1994).

31. For an examination of changes at Princeton University away from restriction and towards that of welcoming Jews of all commitments to its campus, see Marianne Sanua, "Stages in the Development of Jewish Life at Princeton University," *AJHQ* (June 1987), pp. 391–415.

32. See Howard M. Sachar, *A History of the Jews in America* (New York: Alfred A. Knopf, 1992), pp. 898–899, for the estimate that 321,000 "legal" Jewish immigrants arrived from the close of World War II to 1975. He also notes correctly that these figures include Cuban Jews who fled Castro and Canadian Jews who left Montreal and other areas where Canadian Separatism had anti-Jewish implications.

33. For a discussion of the resettlement of what I have called "leader-oriented" Askenazic refgee and survivor Orthodox communities, which should include the

Sephardim as well, and their impact on the indigenous Orthodox community, see Gurock, "Resisters and Accommodators: Varieties of Orthodox Rabbis in America, 1886–1983," *AJA* (November 1983), pp. 150–159.

34. On the acculturation processes and degree of assimilation of children of German refugees, Holocaust survivors, and Syrian immigrants see, respectively, Steven Lowenstein, *Frankfurt on the Hudson: The German-Jewish Community of Washington Heights, 1933–1983, its Structure and Culture* (Detroit: Wayne State University Press, 1989), pp. 254–264; William Helmreich, *Against All Odds: Holocaust Survivors and the Successful Lives They Made in America* (New York: Simon & Schuster, 1992), pp. 66–68, 216; and Joseph A. D. Sutton, *Magic Carpet: Aleppo-in-Flatbush: The Story of a Unique Ethnic Jewish Community* (New York: Thayer-Jacoby, 1979), pp. 149–152, 228, which looks somwhat uncritically at Syrian Jews' "unique" level of avoidance of assimilation while accepting acculturation.

35. Steven J. Gold, "Soviet Jews in the United States," (*American Jewish Year Book,* 1994), 3–57.

36. During the period of Soviet immigration, Jews from Iran also fled to the United States to escape the Khomeini regime. Sachar, *A History of the Jews in America,* pp. 899–900, notes this. Concomitantly, Israeli Jews also came to America in significant numbers. As of 1986, estimates as to the number of Israelis who had moved to the United States ranged from 100,000 to a half-million. See Zvi Sobel, *Migrants from the Promised Land* (New Brunswick, NJ: Transactions Books, 1986), p. 11.

37. An analysis of this phase of Jewish migration to America will be found in Dr. Mark Handelman's contribution to this volume (Chapter 11).

3

The 1990 National Jewish Population Survey: Impact and Implications

JEFFREY SCHECKNER

In the six years since the release of the Council of Jewish Federation's (CJF's)[1] landmark "1990 National Jewish Population Survey (NJPS),"[2] the organized Jewish community on both the local and national levels has undergone a radical shift in both its mood and outlook. The primary cause for this developing concern is the now-famous NJPS figure of 52 percent: the proportion of born Jews who married non-Jewish partners in the period 1985–1990. No longer comfortable about its present nor upbeat about its future, both professional and lay leaders in the Jewish community have paused to reflect on why assimilation has occurred to such an extent. Most of the concern centers around the concept known as "Jewish continuity." Many leaders have approached the problem of assimilation and continuity with caution and have acknowledged that the NJPS has served as the spark for the plethora of Jewish-continuity projects. Incoming CJF President Conrad L. Giles has on several occasions publicly stated that virtually every major national Jewish organization and agency has been impacted in one way or another by this study.

One editor defines Jewish continuity as "the need to maintain Jewish culture and identity and pass them down to succeeding generations. It stands for saving Jewish souls from the evils of Americanization" (Rubin, 1995). Another source suggests that Jewish continuity is "the process through which successive generations of Jews develop and express a connectedness to their fellow Jews, Jewish culture, and a tradition that informs their lifestyles, life choices and life decisions" (JESNA, 1995). Intensified Jewish education has become the centerpiece of any continuity effort, and in this regard the rabbinate as well as Jewish educators have not let the impact of NJPS go unnoticed. According to one rabbi, "The 1990 NJPS jarred our community into reassessing our priorities and approaches. 'Continuity' became our rallying cry and educators began to enjoy a heightened status as crucial players on the community's agenda" (Levinson,

1996). While strengthening and expanding Jewish education are central to any notion of Jewish continuity, continuity could also involve a broader vision of organizing the Jewish community so that it enriches the lives of individual Jews. In order to achieve this, Jewish-continuity efforts may need to involve all Jews, regardless of affiliation. Since the advent of NJPS and its impact, the term "Jewish continuity" has come to mean the reinvention of a Jewish community. Ongoing Jewish learning that leads to a deepening of personal Jewishness and a richer, more vibrant, more spiritual and community-conscious life has been suggested by rabbis and lay leaders alike. Along with Jewish education, membership and participation in a synagogue are seen as vital parts of this equation. Rabbi Alexander Schindler, former head of the Union of American Hebrew Congregations (UAHC) has stated, "The new realities are reflected in the Council of Jewish Federations' own 1990 NJPS, which reveals how much more deeply committed to Jewish life are synagogue-affiliated Jews than those who belong to no congregation. Their attachment to Israel is more intense, their attitude toward intermarriage more wholesome from a communal perspective, and their being Jewish feels more impassioned" (Schindler, 1992).

With Jewish continuity as the principal focus, thousands of articles and books, magazines, journals, newsletters, and newspapers and other media have discussed extensively or at least made mention of the "1990 NJPS." At the end of this chapter is a select bibliography of published papers that are based on NJPS data. Before further considering the obvious impact of the NJPS in both the world of print as well as in the context of invigorating continuity, I will first explore eight key areas in the NJPS and review the salient points in the context of periodic changes.

WHAT THE DATA SHOW—THE KEY FINDINGS

Marriage and Intermarriage

We know from the NJPS that 62 percent of the adult Jewish population age 18 and over are currently married, 8 percent are divorced or separated, 7 percent are widowed, and 23 percent have never married. By age 45, 89 percent of Jews will have been married at least once. Of those that are currently married, 1.8 million (68 percent) are married to another Jew, 105,000 (4 percent) are married to a Jew by choice, and 739,000 (28 percent) are married to a non-Jew. For Jews who married prior to 1965, only 9 percent married a non-Jew. For those who married between 1965 and 1974, 25 percent married non-Jews. During the next decade this rose to 44 percent and, as we have stated, for the final five years covered by the NJPS this figure rose to 52 percent. Finally, the Jewish divorce rate, long believed to be below that of other religious groups in America, is now on par with them.

Jewish Identity and Assimilation

With regard to this complex topic the NJPS presented both positive and negative results from a Jewish-affiliation perspective, although most other indicators of Jewish attachment had shown a decline. Compared with the 1970 NJPS, smaller proportions of Jews were members of Jewish organizations, gave to Jewish charities, observed the High Holidays, attended religious services, or lived in Jewish neighborhoods. On the attitudinal level, NJPS respondents indicated less attachment to Israel, greater acceptance of intermarriage, and did not feel as strongly that being Jewish was very important in their lives.

On the contrary, the 1990 NJPS indicated that observance of Purim, Passover, and Chanukah were still very widely practiced and that Yom Hatzmaut had become a newly significant holiday. Data from other sources have shown that Holocaust commemoration is more widely observed now than in the recent past. Jewish education for children is at higher levels than ever before and day-school education, which had participation of only a few thousand children annually in the years after World War II, now has over 70,000 children attending.

We had mentioned that the rate of intermarriage had surged and that attachment to Jewish organizations and institutions have also weakened. These and other findings from the NJPS point towards increased assimilation. We know too that the percentage was over 20 percent of NJPS respondents who reported that their denominational background while growing up was Orthodox, while only 7 percent of respondents indicated that they are now Orthodox. Similarly, while the percentage of those reporting Reform observance was higher than in the past, those reporting "secular" or "no denomination" had increased most significantly. While the NJPS found that there were 185,000 persons not born of Jewish parentage who had converted to Judaism, a slightly higher amount of 210,000 had been born Jewish but switched to another religion.

Population and Age Profile

The "1990 NJPS" revealed that the Jewish population in the United States in 1990 was 5,515,000, up slightly from around 5.4 million in 1970. Had it not been for immigration from the former Soviet Union, Israel, and other places, the number would have declined slightly. The post-World War II baby-boom generation had ended by the mid-1960s, and from the late 1960s to about 1980 the rate of Jewish births in the United States was far below replacement level; but starting in the early 1980s the baby-boom generation began producing offspring approaching replacement level.

While showing a generally older profile than other Americans, the Jewish population was found to be dominated by the baby-boom generation, as one-third of all American Jews were born between 1946 and 1964. While there were relatively many children under age 10, there was a dearth of persons in their teenage years, as well as those in their fifties. About 18 percent of American

Jews are age 65 and over, compared with only 13 percent of all Americans in this age group.

Age Differentials

Age is one attribute that is strongly associated with differences in the level of Jewish connection. Overall, the older Jewish age groups show deeper levels of Jewish commitment and behavior; however, some aspects of Jewish identity are equally as strong in the younger age categories.

Membership in Jewish organizations, doing Jewish volunteer work, serving on the Board of a Jewish organization, and donating to Jewish charities were all stronger for those age 45 and over. In terms of attitude and connectedness, those 45 and over were also more likely to report that being Jewish was very important in their lives; they were more likely to report that all or mostly all of their friends were Jewish; and they were more likely to feel that it was important to live in a Jewish neighborhood. Moreover, those age 45 and over had a greater likelihood of having visited Israel. Stronger emotional ties to Israel were also more apparent in this group. However, some behaviors are equally strong in the younger age groups. Some of these reflect on child-centered activities such as celebrating Chanukah and Purim and having attended a Jewish camp; however, being a member of a synagogue, attending a Passover Seder, belonging to a Jewish community center (JCC), and having received a Jewish education are all more widespread in younger age groups than just child-centered activities.

Philanthropy and Communal Participation

Along with the various components of Jewish identity showing decline over the last few generations, philanthropic behavior as it relates to Jewish giving and volunteer work in Jewish organizations have shown less and less participation. In 1970, approximately two-thirds of adult Jews gave to Jewish causes, whereby today only 59 percent give. Referring to age groups, we know from the NJPS that for Jews age 65 and over nearly three-quarters give to a Jewish charity, while do only 40 percent of those under age 45. For comparative purposes, of the older age group, two-thirds gave to a secular charity, while about 60 percent of the younger group did so. This small difference indicates that giving priorities have indeed shifted.

Mobility and Migration

A shift in the Jewish population to the South and West and away from concentrations in the Northeast and Midwest has occurred over the last several generations. South Florida and the West Coast are now significant centers of Jewish population, while many older urban centers in the Northeast and Midwest have declined and numerous smaller cities in these regions no longer have a Jewish community. Further, the NJPS found that over half of all Jews move to new residences within six years.

Geographic Aspects

There are significant differences in Jewish behavior and practices based not only on geographic location but also size of the Jewish community. As for region of the country, synagogue membership is strongest in the Northeast and Midwest. Jewish educational achievement is equally strong in these regions. Having been to Israel and keeping kosher are as likely in the South as these two other regions, which leaves the West as usually the weakest in most measures of Jewish communal participation and Jewish practice.

In terms of size of community, those places that have a Jewish population of between 25,000 and 100,000 tend to have the strongest levels of Jewish behavior and association. It is my observation that communities that are very large in size often lack the ability to bring people together as a community. A case in point might be the relatively low levels of donating to Jewish federations in Manhattan. In big cities it is easy to be anonymous and not be approached to join, to give, or to participate. On the other hand, some very small communities simply lack the communal infrastructure needed to foster certain Jewish commitments. For example, a critical mass is required to sustain a Jewish day school or a kosher butcher.

Household Structure, Education, and Income

The nuclear two-parent family with children and all members Jewish now describes only 17 percent of core Jewish households found in the NJPS. If we include interfaith households, these nuclear families still comprise only 32 percent of households. One person living alone, which described 23 percent of households, was the most common type of household found in the NJPS. Single-parent households now comprise nearly 14 percent of all Jewish households with children. Some 50,000 children in Jewish homes, nearly 3 percent, are adopted. Of these, a significant number was born in Asia and Latin America.

Income from American Jewish households was nearly $40,000 in 1990, and in comparison with other religious groups,[3] this places Jews among those with the highest income levels. Educational attainment for American Jews also exceeds that of national norms. For example, Jewish men were twice as likely as other American whites to have attained post-graduate degrees; however, on the other hand, Jewish women were three times as likely to have attained this level as women in general in the United States.

Gender Differentials

From a Jewish communal perspective, the NJPS did not indicate significant differences between men and women in key areas. However, two important issues were revealed in relation to intermarriage and Jewish education as it relates to gender. Our data on Jewish education show that in the past, males were more likely to have received a Jewish education, but by the 1980s a balance was achieved. Our data also find that while Jewish men and women were as likely to intermarry, intermarried Jewish women were more likely to convert out of Judaism than Jewish men after marrying a person of another faith. Further, non-Jewish women who married a Jewish man were more likely to convert to Judaism than non-Jewish men who married a Jewish woman. Interfaith couples were less likely to provide their children with a Jewish education than endogamous couples, but our data show that intermarried Jewish women were more likely than intermarried Jewish men to provide their children with a Jewish education.

Jewish Education

Jewish education is often considered the key mechanism for identity formation and socialization into Judaism. The NJPS provided details on the type of Jewish education and number of years. This information has been cross-tabulated to portray the association that Jewish education has with other Jewish behavioral and associational patterns.

Our basic finding is that about three-quarters of adult men have had some Jewish education, and close to 60 percent of adult women have had a Jewish education. Gender differences have vanished for children. Overwhelmingly, there was a strong association between the amount of Jewish education and Jewish behaviors; in other words, the more Jewish education generally, the more Jewishly connected. However, we need to realize that participation in Jewish education does not occur in a vacuum. When a family is already Jewishly active, there is a higher likelihood that these children will receive a Jewish education. A Jewishly committed family is thus predisposed to providing for Jewish education.

WHAT THE DATA REVEAL—THE IMPLICATIONS

Intermarriage

From a Jewish communal perspective, much of the NJPS data convey bad news. One example of this might be the rapid rise in the rate of intermarriage. Intermarriage in itself may not necessarily be the cause for concern within some circles of the Jewish community; however, we know from our data that the participation of the intermarried couple and the likelihood of their children being Jewishly connected are lessened. These have become the real issues, particularly for Jewish federations. Our data show that for exogamous couples, only 12 percent donate to a Jewish federation or United Jewish Appeal (UJA) campaign, while 45 percent of endogamous couples do so. It is true that philanthropic giving is just one, narrowly defined area; however, if we were to measure the success and effectiveness of Jewish organizational life, support for Israel, and other Jewish social services, then the giving levels of interfaith couples should be cause for concern, especially since these entities depend on Jewish dollars. One related concern is that for the children in these households, just under one-third are being raised as Jews; a third are being raised in another religion (including mixed religions); and just over a third are not being raised in any religion at all. The number of children of interfaith couples who are being raised with some Jewish identity, either as a Jew by religion or as secular Jews (in no religion), is growing faster than the children born of two Jewish parents; if present trends continue, their numbers will be even greater in the near future. According to the sociologist Egon Mayer, "There is little doubt that two generations of intermarriage will produce a third generation in which Jewishness is highly attenuated if it survives at all" (Mayer, 1994, p. 78). Therefore it is believed that intermarriage will lead to growing intergenerational losses to the Jewish population.

Overall, the conversion rate of non-Jewish partners in intermarriages is only between 5 and 10 percent, according to evidence shown in the NJPS. We have indicated that women are more likely to convert, but this includes converting *out* of Judaism. Other research suggests that if a formal conversion to Judaism has occurred, the non-Jewish partner and children are as likely to be Jewishly connected as if the marriage were between two born Jews. We need to ask the question: How should intermarriage be viewed as an element in the broader context of Jewish identity and continuity? We also question: What modes of outreach are acceptable and effective in ways that are welcoming and not threatening to the non-Jewish partner? We also need to consider allocating our limited resources into this effort, and additionally consider what institutions within the Jewish communal system (synagogues, federations, JCCs, or others) need to take the impetus for appropriate action.

Jewish Identity and Assimilation

The substantial increase in the proportion of Jews who are secular or do not practice the religion as opposed to those who are Jewish by religion presents several problematic issues for the Jewish community. Should current trends continue, some residual Jewish practices and observances exhibited by secular Jews may not be enough to sustain Jewish institutions such as synagogues, JCCs, and a whole array of Jewish community services. We also need to consider their ability to transmit Jewish behaviors and practices to future generations.

While only 37 percent of American Jewish households belong to a synagogue at any one time, close to 80 percent have been or will be members at some time in their lives. The NJPS and local Jewish-population-study evidence suggest that households are most likely to join synagogues to meet the Jewish educational needs of children and/or the preparation for a Bar or Bat Mitzvah. Therefore synagogues are probably *the* Jewish institutions that touch more Jews at some point in their lives than any other. We need to ask how being Jewish in America can be made more relevant and more of a priority in people's lives; and further, what role does Jewish education play in emphasizing Jewish life-cycle events, Jewish holidays, and religious observance or practice. Also, how can strong, positive Jewish associations be created within the structure of community planning? As many small communities lack the infrastructure to support such resources as full-time Jewish education or kosher food products, how can this impediment be overcome? The same holds true for regions of the country where Jewish identity and affiliation are seen as weak. More research is needed though to develop an understanding of what works to sustain Jewish identity and thus transmit it to successive generations. Specific modes of Jewish-identity outreach to subpopulations like the intermarried need to be considered in any approach. The role that Jewish education and religious practice plays in all aspects of outreach cannot be overlooked.

Philanthropy and Volunteer Behavior

We discussed the eroding base of Jewish philanthropic giving among those in the younger age groups. This diminution is partially apparent in the multi-purpose or umbrella campaigns: Namely, the UJA and Federation. We should note that special campaigns and endowment contributions have increased; but still, only a small fraction of gifts continue to account for the vast share of dollars raised in campaigns. For example, according to CJF data, of the 870,000 donors who gave to a Jewish federation campaign in 1990, only 1.6 percent of households contributed 58 percent of the total dollars. A greater concern is the fact that in 1972, two-thirds of Jewish philanthropic giving went to Jewish causes, while in 1990 less than half did. We need to explore the challenge of entering into untapped markets and broadening the base of giving by increasing the development of sophisticated data on the donor base. Population segmentation and more effective target-marketing are needed to optimize the number of donors. With smaller numbers of Jewish households contributing to Jewish charities, ways must be found to reach the larger numbers of potential givers. Jewish giving and volunteering needs to be made more appealing and rewarding.

Population and Age Profiles

The current age profile suggests that as we approach the year 2000 and into the early years of the next century, there will be increasing numbers of Jewish teens and college students. Although the number of Jews age 65 and over will remain about the same, the proportion of elderly who are age 75 and over will increase. This will translate into a greater need for youth groups, Jewish college-student groups, and nursing homes. We acknowledge that there are certain points within the life-cycle at which people call upon institutions and resources in the Jewish community; for example, birth (circumcision or baby-naming ceremony), Bar or Bat Mitzvah, marriage, and death. At these significant points of contact we need to find a way of reaching out to people and encourage their involvement. We have already indicated that the population under age 45 is comparatively weak in their Jewish associational and religious patterns, and therefore if we wish for a Jewish future, any outreach must target this age group. If the approach of the organized Jewish community is optimal, life-cycle-associated activities such as child care, teen youth groups, camping experiences, college groups, services for singles, and senior adult groups can be effectively targeted by the Jewish-communal system. Such points of entry can be made where people can easily fit into the Jewish community by means of seeking these services.

HOW THE DATA ARE BEING UTILIZED—THE IMPACT

After the initial reactions of alarm to the foreboding findings of the NJPS had subsided, many communities began working intensively on projects to deal with the rising intermarriage rates and trends toward assimilation. In order to address these and other issues, the approach in most communities has centered around the themes of strengthening Jewish identity to ensure Jewish continuity.

Upon the release of the NJPS in the Spring of 1991, CJF broadcast several satellite programs to the network of its constituent communities to begin disseminating the information. In July 1991 approximately 100 lay leaders and professionals from across the United States took part in the three-day Sidney Hollander Memorial Colloquium at the University of Judaism's Wilstein Institute on Jewish Policy Studies. At this event, a first step was made to develop community priorities with regard to the NJPS findings. A monograph series was established to create close to 20 reports on specific detailed subjects emanating from the 1990 the NJPS data. A Jewish Environmental Scan was developed to serve as a tool for social planners and others in the field of Jewish communal service. Council of Jewish Federation staff, NJPS data-users, monograph writers, and others associated with the NJPS began going to communities throughout the country to report on the findings and discuss their impact and implications. Most major Jewish organizations and institutions that had assembled for major gatherings began featuring the findings of the NJPS prominently in their agendas. For example, at the 1991 Union of American Hebrew Congregations' General Assembly, Rabbi Schindler delivered a lengthy speech on the present state of the Jewish community, the major theme being about what the NJPS data revealed. The American Jewish Committee, the Jewish Community Centers Association, the Association of Jewish Family and Children's Agencies, the National Jewish Community Relations Advisory Council, and others included the NJPS data as the focus of their conferences during the 1991–1992 period. At the 1992 CJF General Assembly, for the first time a full day of programming was devoted to the issues raised by the NJPS, with particular focus on Jewish identity, education, and continuity.

I have laid out the initial impetus taken up by national Jewish organizations and how these issues have been given attention, and will next report on how this information has filtered down to the local communities.

By mid-1993 a significant number of local Jewish federations had established task forces on continuity, Jewish identity, or related themes. As common denominators, all focused on outreach, educational programs, and intensive Jewish experiences. The motivation was to create a community of Jews that is consciously Jewish, knowledgeable on Judaism, and committed to Jewish values and practices. Other aspects have included participation in synagogue life, Jewish communal and cultural life, and prioritizing Jewishness in lifestyle and life-commitments. The centrality of Israel and feeling for the Jewish Holy Land are further illustrations of such efforts. The following is a select but somewhat representative list of programs that were established in the five years following the release of the 1990 NJPS data—developed primarily in response to addressing what some are calling the "crisis in continuity."

1. Boston, MA—A program titled *Sha'Arim-Gateways to Jewish Living* is a collaboration between the Federation and its agencies, the Synagogue Council of Massachusetts, and the denominational movements. The initiative provided congregations with matching funds to hire family educators to give in-depth interviews to each incoming family and develop personalized opportunities for learning Jewish history, values, and traditions. For all parents who enroll a child in the Hebrew school, a representative will help them strengthen or initiate Jewish practice and observance in their home.

2. Cleveland, OH—A program cosponsored by the Federation and Congregational Plenum includes a broad array of new programs to deepen Jewish identity and revitalize Jewish education. This program focused on extracurricular-educational goals, raising professional standards for teachers, and increasing family involvement and hiring Jewish educators.

3. Houston, TX—"*Yom Limmud*—A Day of Learning," is a yearly event designed for family studying and learning. The 1994 program theme was geared to teaching about mitzvot, healing, and sacred texts.

4. Kansas City, KS—The Federation Commission on Jewish Continuity, Identity, and Affiliation has initiated a program in which several synagogues jointly participate in a Jewish education program for parents with children aged 9–13 years. Joint parent–child activities are also featured.

5. Lexington, MA—A synagogue features a parallel-study session for parents and children; for example, the children learn about Cain and Abel while the parents learn about sibling relationships. At home, the families are encouraged to discuss what they have learned.

6. Los Angeles, CA—The Council on Jewish Life's Refugee Acculturation works with synagogues to match Russian immigrants with families for Passover and the High

Holidays. Another component of this program is classes designed to develop leadership roles and learn more about Judaism.

7. Los Angeles, CA—An online home page on the Internet called *ACCESS* was created that provided Jewish activities for a variety of subgroups in the population; for example, for singles, the elderly, the young, and parents. Also, online chat rooms for Jewish singles are a principal feature.

8. MetroWest (Morris–Essex Counties, NJ)—A program titled *Pathways* is designed for unaffiliated individuals, particularly those in interfaith marriages. One target group is Jewish grandparents of interfaith grandchildren to help them instill a sense of Jewish connection and identity transmission.

9. New Haven, CT—The TIES (The Israel Experience Savings) program offers creative ways of funding for teens who want to visit Israel. The family and the federation place money into interest-bearing accounts over the course of eight years. Southern New Jersey, Canton, Ohio, and other communities have developed similar savings programs that allow for teens to visit Israel.

10. New York, NY—UJA Federation's Jewish Continuity Commission is awarding grants to Jewish community centers, synagogues, camps, and other institutions that have specific goals relating to enhancing Jewish identity. These grants are mainly for the creation of Jewish educational programs for families.

11. Philadelphia, PA—The Mandel Campus sent its Jewish educators on a larger, organized trip to Israel during the summer of '96 to help convey the message that Judaism belongs to a people whose past, present, and future are tied to the land of Israel.

12. Portland, OR—The Jewish Federation accepted grant applications from projects that support Jewish education and community building and a broad spectrum of Jewish educational opportunities.

13. Rochester, NY—A day-long event called *Project Machon* featured 50 workshops on Jewish topics and celebrated Jewish learning, attracting 500 people. Workshops included such diverse topics as the Jewish thoughts on reincarnation and Jewish approaches to environmental issues.

14. San Diego, CA—The "Making Jewish Memories" program reaches out to marginally affiliated, single-parent, and intermarried families with hands-on educational programs. Activities focus on holidays, food, and storytelling.

15. Southern NJ—A full-time position of family educator was created. The person in this position will act as a consultant, resource person, facilitator, and program creator.

16. Stamford, CT—The Bi-Cultural Day School boasts an innovative program whereby eighth graders spend a month in Israel and reinforces these field experiences through in-class lessons.

17. Worcester, MA—The Jewish Federation, in conjunction with the Rabbinical Association of Central Massachusetts, held several day-long, community-wide, Jewish-learning series of workshops called *Torahthon*.

While these are just a small sampling of local efforts, we need to acknowledge that virtually all of the denominational movements, Jewish organizations, Jewish agencies, and other institutions in the Jewish community have added new elements to programs that have been in existence for many years whose goal is to cultivate a positive Jewish identity. National organizations (e.g., the Jewish Community Centers Association, Union of American Hebrew Congregations, etc.) have adjusted policy on the national level to reflect the intensification of Jewish content in programming, and these changes have filtered down to the local level, affecting most community efforts. The Bronfman Foundation has made a major effort to send Jewish teens to Israel, and the Jewish Outreach Institute in New York has created national and local resources for interfaith households. Independent operations like the National Jewish Outreach Program (NJOP) and the Center for Learning and Leadership (CLAL) also contribute to continuity efforts by bringing Jewish educational programs to thousands of people each year at both Jewish and secular facilities. Jewish foundations such as AVI CHAI have been instrumental in providing funds for creating and supporting Jewish day schools.

For most communities that have absorbed Russian immigrants, resettlement programs that incorporate Jewish acculturation as a key element have become commonplace.

In 1993 the Council of Jewish Federations convened the North American Commission on Jewish Identity and Continuity, which was comprised of top lay leadership and professionals. After two years of meetings this commission produced a report whose major concluding points were as follows:

1. Jewish growth should be promoted in order to strengthen Jewish continuity, and the Jewish people must increase their knowledge of Jewish history, Jewish religion, and Jewish culture and incorporate it into their lives.

2. Unconnected populations must be engaged. The organized Jewish community must reach out to unengaged segments of the populations outside the affiliated core and embrace them.

3. Jewish institutions must be strengthened; the way we support these institutions and the people that devote their professional lives to serving in these facilities must be positively reinforced.

4. We need to create continental partnerships and strategies for promoting cooperative action to address centennial issues.

Referring to the multitude of projects that have risen as a result of the NJPS, one former federation executive said, "Where there was inertia, there is movement. While it may be necessary to multiply these investments many times to see a community level of impact, we believe that we are witnessing early steps in a movement toward a culture of continuity" (*National Jewish Post and Opinion*, 1996). The NJPS confirmed that there have been drastic changes in the

American Jewish community over the last generation. The organized Jewish world's job is to consider how these changes impact upon Jewish community life. It is also necessary to harness the energy made apparent in the local program models described here and use that impetus to help shape the American Jewish community in the twenty-first century. If anything, the NJPS clearly indicates that being born of Jewish parents is no longer an assurance of a life of Jewish practice and commitment. The place to begin inculcation to Judaism had traditionally been in the home through a process we know as "socialization." The reality though is that Jewish socialization no longer occurs automatically. Changes in lifestyle and household structure has placed the family in a situation in which transmission of Jewish practice is less automatic than in the past. All of the available choices and competition from a market-driven society has placed Judaism and Jewish culture in a less-exclusive role than in past generations. According to Barry Shrage (1995), "If being Jewish is to regain its meaning for Jews today, the Jewish community must be transformed. While it is impossible to know the exact shape the new paradigm will take, we must begin with humility and respect for alternative proposals" (91).

We must not forget that the cost of living Jewishly precludes involvement for some. A lack of action in addressing this issue will mean that for many, Jewish cultural participation and economic deprivation will be highly correlated.

CONCLUSIONS

Each of the 18 local-program models presented in this chapter provides creative approaches towards helping Jews affiliate. One cannot determine the long-term effect of such efforts; however, in research done by the CJF, the denominational movements, and others, the impact that the Israel experience has in bringing about increased involvement and commitment should not be understated. Research also indicates that there is a positive effect for related experiences (e.g., informal Jewish education, Jewish youth groups, etc.); however, measuring this impact is not an exact science. We don't know what will happen 10 and 20 years from the point of the experience or the results other experiences will produce. Some believe that the only thing that can bring about a change away from assimilation is the return to tradition; that is, learning Torah, performing mitzvahs, accepting the sanctity of Shabbat, and revering other aspects of traditional Judaism. While there is current debate as to whether an emphasis on religious tradition, as opposed to Jewish culture and peoplehood or some combination thereof, works best, we need to find the route that is most likely to ensure a Jewish future. We know that different approaches work for different populations; it is simply a matter of finding the best means for outreach and specifically tailoring or marketing it to the respective population. Realistically, numerous approaches are needed.

As an intelligent and well-organized Jewish community, we have now heeded the wake-up call that was so clearly prompted by the NJPS. I am optimistic, but from having been in the field of Jewish communal service for over a decade and having seen those changes already in progress designed to promote a Jewish life, it is easy to feel this way. However, I live in a real community comprised of people of all backgrounds, including both affiliated and non-affiliated Jews. From interacting with my secular friends and neighbors, my own observation is that they are not necessarily disinterested in their Jewish background; rather, they have not been given a good-enough reason to make Judaism central to their lives. With some of the approaches outlined here and others, it is indeed possible that these last Jews will be touched in a way that they have not been before. It is simply a matter of outreaching with the right message.

My own guess is that we have turned the corner and reached a "saturation level" of the rate of intermarriage. However, I believe that certain aspects of Judaism will continue to be less meaningful in people's lives, but others will become more significant. Yom Ha'Atzmaut and Yom Hashoah were barely acknowledged just 20 years ago, and today they have gained wide participation. Sociologist Sylvia Barack Fishman believes that new observances such as Rosh Chodesh and other women's rituals have breathed new life into Judaism. The 40 or so gay and lesbian synagogues and Jewish organizations are reaching people who generally have felt disenfranchisement from Judaism. Twenty-five years ago such groups did not exist.

As stated above, participation in Jewish education is at an all-time high. With so much good news, we need to be reminded of the negative trends that were established in the 1990 NJPS. The NJPS helped us realize the bad news; now that we know this, we as a Jewish community can move forward and harness the energy from the positive and build upon it.

As we approach the twenty-first century the American Jewish community faces the challenges of transmitting their Jewish heritage to successive generations. Secular culture is highly seductive and it is for this reason that every means possible are needed to stimulate Jewish involvement both on a personal and global level. It is my belief that the impact of the NJPS has already commenced this process.

NOTES

1. The Council of Jewish Federations (CJF) is the continental association of 190 Jewish federations in the United States and Canada.

2. The 1990 National Jewish Population Survey (NJPS) was released in the Spring of 1991 and was based on a sample of 2,500 qualified Jewishly identified households in the United States contacted through Random Digit Dialing.

3. The National Survey of Religious Identity (NSRI) was produced as a result of the screening phase of the 1990 NJPS. Some basic household-demographic characteristics were ascertained in this exercise.

REFERENCES

Levinson, A. J. (1996, March 28). Changing our leadership culture. *Jewish Exponent, 18.*
National Jewish Post and Opinion. (1996, June 12). Continuity is winning an impressive status, *4,*
Rubin, N. (1995, July 14). The continuity sham. *Jewish Times, 8.*
Schindler, A. (1992, November 6). It's time to pool resources and energies. *The Jewish Week, 16.*
Shrage, B. (1995). Building community of Torah and Zedek: A new paradigm for the Jewish community of the twenty-first century. In *At the Crossroads: Shaping Our Jewish Future.* Boston: The Combined Jewish Philanthropies and the Wilstein Institute of Jewish Policy Studies.

ADDITIONAL READINGS

Abramowitz, Y. (1996, August 2). Where will American Jewish life be in fifty years?: Is there a demographic time bomb? *Florida Jewish Heritage News, 39.*
————. (1996, September 20). Reach out, a reborn Jewish community on the horizon. *The Jewish Advocate, 1.*
Ain, S. (1995, March 15). Assimilation reversing study finds. *Jewish Week, 16.*
CJF. (1993). *Strengthening Jewish Identity and Continuity: The Challenge to the North American Jewish Federation System.* New York: Council of Jewish Federations.
————. (1995). *The Report of the North American Commission on Jewish Identity and Continuity—To Renew and Sanctify.* New York: Council of Jewish Federations.
————. (Summer 1996, Spring 1996, Summer 1993, Winter, 1994). *What's New at Federations?* New York: Council of Jewish federations.
Fishel, J. (1996, March 15). Accessing community. *Jewish Journal of Greater Los Angeles, 5.*
Goldstein, S. (1992). Profile of American Jewry: Insights from the 1990 NJPS. In David Singer (Ed.), *American Jewish Year Book.* New York: American Jewish Committee and The Jewish Publication Society.
Harris, D. (1996, August 28). Time to stop talking about continuity. *National Jewish Post and Opinion, 9.*
JESNA. (1995). *Planning for Jewish Continuity: Synagogue, Federation, Collaboration—A Handbook.* New York: Jewish Education Service of North America, 7.
Kanter, A. B. (1996, September 12). Grandparents can be role models for children in interfaith marriages. *MetroWest Jewish News* (Whippany, NJ), 8.
Kosmin, B., Nava, L., Keysar, A., Goldstein, S., Waksberg, J., & Scheckner, J. (1991). *Highlights of the CJF 1990 National Jewish Population Survey.* New York: Council of Jewish Federations.
London, A. (1996, January 25). Herman: Serious issues confront the Jewish community. *The American Israelite, 1.*
Mayer, E. (1994, April). Will the grandchildren of intermarrieds be Jewish? The chances are greater than you think. *Moment, 78.*
Menashe, E. (1995, March). Federation facilitates communal cooperation. *The Jewish Review, 11.*
Olshansky, B. (1992). *Consultation on Policy Implications of the 1990 CJF and NJPS.* New York: Council of Jewish Federations.

Reisman, B. (1995). An agenda for a watershed change. In *At the Crossroads: Shaping Our Jewish Future.* Boston: The Combined Jewish Philanthropies and the Wilstein Institute of Jewish Policy Studies.

Saperstein, D. (1995). Jewish continuity and social action. In *At the Crossroads: Shaping Our Jewish Future.* Boston: The Combined Jewish Philanthropies and the Wilstein Institute of Jewish Policy Studies.

4

The Jewish Communal-Service Arena

DAVID J. SCHNALL AND
SHELDON R. GELMAN

Today's Jewish communal-service activities emerge from a religious and social tradition rooted in Scripture, Talmud, and rabbinic dicta. Jewish religious practice is defined by *mitzvot*, literally, commandments. These are broadly divided between those that are largely ritual and ecclesiastical and those that define a vast array of social relations, including marriage, economic pursuit, childrearing, and care for the widow, the orphan, and the stranger (Cover, 1987; Schnall, 1997; Schreiber, 1979). Judaism looks upon personal charity as part of a systematic network of social obligations rather than as voluntary acts of kindness (Bernstein, 1965).

As an example, the Bible enjoins that crops forgotten in the field or inadvertently left standing after the harvest remain for the poor. In addition, a corner of one's field must be purposefully left uncut so that the needy might glean in private. Such prescriptions stand side-by-side with those that require employers to pay workers punctually and those that restrict creditors in their demands upon debtors (Schnall, 1993; 1995a; 1997), as well as those that specify the obligations of adult children to their aged and infirm parents (Schnall, 1995b; 1996).

Two themes have remained constant over the years: One who extends a hand for assistance must never be turned away, and second, in so doing, the benefactor follows in the paths of righteousness and sanctity that characterize the Lord. In sum, while numerous Hebrew terms connote philanthropy and voluntary service, *tzedakah,* the most popular usage, derives from a root more accurately described as "justice." This epitomizes the classic Jewish attitude toward such undertaking.

Fundamental sources regarding personal obligations to the needy and dependent gave rise to discussions of the organization and structure of community services. This grew in importance as largely autonomous Jewish communities emerged, first as part of a centralized monarchy in ancient Israel, and later as Jews were dispersed throughout the Near East, North Africa, and Europe. By Talmudic times, that is, during the first centuries of the Common Era, Jewish communities were required to maintain systems of assessment and collection, with detailed prescriptions for the oversight and accountability of those who were trustees and administrators. Food was disbursed through the *tamhuy* or community kitchen, while cash was available from a community fund known as a *kupah.*

The dignity and self-respect of those who were recipients of communal beneficence was given primacy. Thus the highest form of *tzedakah,* ruled Maimonides, a twelfth-century Jewish philosopher and jurist, is that which provides the poor with the wherewithal to become productive and self-sufficient, for example, by extending loans, providing assistance in finding a job, or beginning a business (Maimonides, 1965). Second in order is a system of completely anonymous philanthropy in which neither recipient nor donor can be directly identified. This reduces embarrassment on the one side, and arrogance on the other. He suggested that the goal is best facilitated through a central *kupah* in which the process of donation is separated from disbursement.

Given the heavy emphasis upon religious education as equivalent to all other *mitzvot* combined, it is no surprise to find that public education was an area of special concern to these early Jewish communities. The Talmud warns that a town in which no facilities for primary education are provided deserves to be destroyed. Medieval authorities established detailed principles regarding educational method, the structure of the curriculum, teacher training and certification, and appropriate remuneration. These were included as part of the basic documents of local governance in Jewish communities throughout the Middle Ages and early modern era.

Today, Jewish education is provided by a broad network of day schools, known as *Yeshivot,* and supplementary schools that typically meet six to ten hours each week. Each form of schooling provides religious instruction that extends from early childhood to mid-adolescence, with advanced studies available for the serious scholar and professional. Recent data indicate that exposure to some form of Jewish education is nearly universal among younger American Jews, and day-school education is highly correlated with various indicators of Jewish social and religious identification. These programs of formal study are buttressed by an array of summer camps, study tours to Israel, and informal religious/cultural adventures (Schiff & Schneider, 1994).

In addition to caring for the needy (i.e., widows, orphans, the frail, and the elderly) and seeing to public education, classic Jewish sources established the communal obligation to create local structures of governance and to provide for refugee aid, hospitality for the wayfarer, funeral and bereavement assistance, and the mediation of civil and domestic disputes (Schnall, 1995a). The scholarly literature of the period records active debates over public participation and the scope of the franchise in communal decisions, including the choice of leadership.

Communities typically had a board of governors, known as *parnassim,* who worked alongside the rabbi and other religious functionaries to oversee the social and spiritual needs of their constituents (Gelman et al. 1996). Beyond their local bounds, they represented their people before Gentile overlords and at meetings of loose confederations of Jewish communities. By the Middle Ages, these boards were invested with quasi-judicial authority. They established tribunals for mediation, assessed taxes in support of public services, placed liens on private property, and used a variety of bans and social sanctions to enforce their decisions.

It is against this backdrop that Jewish communities were founded in the New World, as early as the mid-seventeenth century. From the first, they attempted to maintain linkages with these religious and social obligations while integrating new patterns of democracy and voluntary association. This dynamic continues to inform much of what they have established in the United States over the past three-and-a-half centuries (Elazar, 1995; Elazar & Cohen, 1985).

The pattern of Jewish welfare organizations, while rooted in Scripture, is distinctively different from that of other sectarian groups. For the most part, Jewish social services have developed apart from the synagogue. They have been the response of the Jewish community to the special needs of its members. Although the beginning of American Jewish philanthropy took place in the synagogue, the sudden and massive influx of Jewish immigrants created needs for which a synagogue alone could not provide (Reid & Stimpson, 1987). Jewish immigrants formed literary societies for recreation and "landsmanchaften" for mutual aid and self-help. These organizations facilitated the acculturation of émigrés to their new land and assisted in caring for those in need, facilitating their independence and self-sufficiency.

It is estimated that 5.8 million Jews live in the United States today. As their numbers have increased from the original twenty-three who debarked in New Amsterdam in 1654 (with special permission from the Dutch West India Company, so long as "the poor among them shall be supported by their own nation"), so too have the social organizations that provide for their health, welfare, recreational, and spiritual needs (Berger, 1980). According to Teicher (1997): "Jews have been ever mindful of the stranger, but we do not discharge our Jewish obligations merely by quoting biblical, rabbinical or Talmudic texts. We prize good works above good words. Our faith and our belief—our morality and our values—require deeds and acts."

Demographic changes and the complexity and scope of service needs required by those identifying themselves as Jews have over time resulted in the development of a comprehensive, coordinated, and evolving service network that today provides a wide array of services to the Jewish and general communities.

THE ROLE OF COMMUNAL-SERVICE AGENCIES

According to Steinitz (1995/96), Jewish-communal agencies through much of their history have focused on four primary goals:

- to deliver basic social services to indigent members of the Jewish community,
- to resettle refugees and help Americanize both the immigrant and second generations,
- to respond to international crises,
- to fight anti-Semitism.

However, beginning in the 1960s, because of changing demographics, identification with the developing State of Israel, newly established governmental-funding streams designed to expand service options and opportunities, and interest in specialized therapeutic interventions delivered by highly trained professional personnel led to a reordering of organizational priorities. The overview provided by Graenum Berger in 1980 (p. 77) is enlightening:

The headlong shift to seek government support for sectarian agencies was marked by some of these factors: (1) Agencies, unhappy with the modest increases received annually from Jewish federations, saw an opportunity for dramatically enriching and widening their services. (2) Federations unable to meet the demands of their societies encouraged their affiliates to seek such help. (3) Agencies had become enamored of "big" business attitudes: planning, expansion, computerization, executive suites, use of government consultants, and so forth. There was a definite power shift toward the professional with expertise in government contacts. (4) There was a widespread acceptance of the rationalized social-welfare principle which mixed public and private welfare as a boon to experimentation, efficiency, economy and expansion. (5) New services in mental health, in work with the retarded, the aged, those in need of rehabilitation, in drug addiction, in research, and, of course, service to the poor, could now be funded in a way undreamed of by private Jewish philanthropy.

These changes not only resulted in the dramatic expansion of social services provided under Jewish auspices (Blum & Naparstek, 1987; Smith & Lipsky, 1993; Gibelman, 1995), but also led to a real blurring of what had been the historical distinction between sectarian and nonsectarian agencies (Levine, 1997; Ortiz, 1995). Jewish agencies today exhibit a great degree of autonomy from religious authority, are largely nonsectarian in intake, and compete in the marketplace for service contracts.

THE JEWISH FEDERATIONS

The 200 Jewish federations in the United States are autonomous, voluntary organizations that engage in or provide a series of functions for communal affiliates, which include:

- joint or coordinated fundraising,
- allocations and central budgeting,
- centralized research and community planning,
- leadership development and training services,
- initiation of new services.

Federations developed in the United States beginning in 1895 and exist today in communities where there is a significant Jewish presence. The Council of Jewish Federations (CJF), which was founded in 1932, represents the local Jewish federations of the United States and Canada on issues of public social-policy nationally and internationally.

Today, the federations and/or the United Jewish Appeal are the central fundraising organization(s) within the Jewish community, raising and distributing hundreds of millions of dollars to local community agencies and to Jewish communities around the world and in Israel.

According to Dubin (1994), Jewish communal agencies have historically been dependent on federation and United Way allocations for significant support. The federations were the conduit and authority for the planning, initiation, and in some instances for the initial operation of needed community services. Increasingly, the support and development of expanded service commitments abroad, particularly the rescue and resettlement of refugees and declines in campaign growth, have impacted on the level of support available to a range of communal-service agencies. This phenomenon has resulted in the need to identify other funding streams such as membership dues, contributions, endowments and planned gifts, fee-for-service and government contacts, blurring the Jewish identity of many agencies.

In addition to their annual fundraising campaign, federation-network agencies receive more than 41 percent of their total budget from federal, state, and local government sources, an amount in excess of 3.67 billion dollars (The Council of Jewish Federations, 1995). UJA-Federation of New York, which is the largest of the federation campaigns, raising more than $200 million annually, received $2.45 billion, approximately 62 percent of its budget in 1993 from government sources (UJA-Federation, 1994).

Jewish agencies have learned to apply for, receive, and use public funding for the benefit of the Jewish and general community. Although one can debate the nature of the change created by the acceptance of public funds by these historically sectarian agencies, it is clear that the number of units of services delivered to the Jewish community, as well as the general community, has increased dramatically as a result of the acceptance of this support. (Solomon, 1995/96)

The following examples of Jewish communal-service agencies are presented to provide a sense of the mission, scope, and involvement. The examples are not all-inclusive and the authors apologize in advance for not providing a more extensive listing of Jewish communal agencies that play important roles in the community with youth, families, college students, volunteer, and specialized health and research programs. In addition, it should be noted that several denominations also have affiliated agencies and programs that provide education, youth services, and gerontological care for their membership.

REFUGEE SERVICES

The primary mission of the Hebrew Immigrant Aid Society (HIAS) is to help Jews whose lives and freedom are endangered. Since 1880, HIAS has been the worldwide arm of the American Jewish community for the rescue, relocation, family reunification, and resettlement of refugees and other migrants. Its mission is derived from the Biblical teaching, *Kol Yisrael Arevim Ze Ba Ze*—all Jews are responsible, one for the other.

During 1995 HIAS resettled 21,967 migrants into 125 communities throughout the United States, including 21,659 Jewish refugees from the former Soviet Union. Its annual budget exceeds 37 million dollars, with more than 80 percent of its funding coming from contracts with the United States government. Since the mid-1970s, when barriers to immigration were eased in the former Soviet Union, HIAS has assisted in the resettlement of almost 400,000 Jewish refugees in the United States (Hebrew Immigrant Aid Society, 1996).

The American Joint Distribution Committee (JDC) was formed as a merger of three agencies in 1914. Over the course of its history it has assisted hundreds of thousands of Jews and non-Jews in Europe, Israel, the former Soviet Union, the Middle East, Asia, and Africa through humanitarian and development efforts. Its goal is "to develop systematic solutions to social problems through research and development, pilot demonstration projects and strategic interventions" (Schneider, 1994). The JDC's activities take place in various areas of the world where war or natural disasters occur and where populations have been displaced. It is currently training lay Jewish leaders in former Soviet-block countries and has formed a coalition with 35 other Jewish agencies to mobilize emergency relief in response to the Rwandan tragedy. The coalition works collaboratively with the United Nations, the U.S. Agency for International Development, the U.S Department of Agriculture, and the World Bank.

COMMUNITY CENTERS

The Jewish community centers (JCCs) as we know them today originated with the Young Men's Hebrew Associations of the mid-nineteenth century whose purpose was to improve the social, moral, and mental conditions of young Hebrew men (Kraft, 1967). Assisting immigrants in acclimating to life in America occupied the YMHAs through the first two decades of the twentieth century. Their strength lay in their ability to change priorities as new needs emerged (Kosansky, 1978).

Today, the Jewish community centers and Young Men's and Young Women's Hebrew Associations provide cultural, recreational, educational, and social opportunities for members of the community. Even though they operate under Jewish auspice, these community-based centers serve populations that are ethnically diverse, fall along a continuum of religious observance, and vary by age from nursery school to senior citizens. The centers embody in their mission and functioning the notions of "citizenship responsibility," "social concern," and "community relatedness" (Dubin, 1987; Linzer, 1987). While the centers traditionally were group-work-focused agencies that employed a range of programs designed to facilitate the socialization of their members, this focus declined during the seventies and eighties as the range of disciplines employed in the centers increased and emphasis shifted toward Jewish programming (Birnbaum & Pine, 1997; Reisman, 1972). Efforts to revive the group-work focus of these agencies are reflected in a set of model standards for social-group-work student internships in Jewish community centers that were developed and field-tested by a working committee of the Jewish Community Centers Association and the Wurzweiler School of Social Work, Yeshiva University. The standards represent a series of expectations and obligations for agencies, students, and schools of social work and serve as a model of cooperation and professional development (Aronowitz & Birnbaum, 1992; Birnbaum & Pine, 1997). Unlike the services provided by Jewish family-service agencies that have a sliding-fee scale for services, the centers are membership agencies.

The centers are affiliated with the Jewish Community Centers Association (JCCA), the successor organization to the Jewish Welfare Board (JWB) that came into being during World War I to provide welfare, morale, and religious services to men and women in the armed forces.

FAMILY SERVICE

Jewish family-service (JFS) agencies have been a mainstay of the Jewish communal network since the last century. They are affiliated with the Association of Jewish Family and Children's Agencies (AJFCA) and employ trained social workers and other professionally trained personnel that specialize in clinical work and case management. The Jewish family-service agencies are recognized for their clinical expertise and innovative approaches with the more challenging mental-health issues of today (Abramson, 1994). Many of these agencies provide adoption services, foster care, group homes for the developmentally disabled, and geriatric services under contract with governmental agencies. Services address individual and family concerns, including the mental-health needs of recent immigrants. Jewish family services provides the Jewish and non-Jewish community with high-quality mental-health services sanctioned by the Jewish community. The New York-based Jewish Board of Family and Children's Services, a UJA-Federation network agency, is reputed to be the largest nonprofit mental-health and social-service organization in the nation and has an annual budget in excess of $80 million, 82 percent of which is provided by government (The Council of Jewish Federations, 1995). This agency has taken a leadership role in responding to the new "managed-care" environment.

HOSPITALS AND SERVICE FOR THE AGED

The development of sectarian hospitals, nursing homes, and specialized geriatric facilities in American communities is a tradition that dates back to the last century. Homes for the aged have been the primary source of service to the Jewish elderly since early in this century. Since the 1930s, Jewish geriatric facilities have innovated in providing a range of community-based services. According to Shore (1995/96), these innovations include the provision of meals-on-wheels, independent- and assisted-living arrangements, health services, and the introduction of outpatient physical occupational and speech therapies. The Jewish community has also been instrumental in the development of hospice-based care for those who are in the final stages of terminal illnesses. In addition to their humanitarian purpose, these facilities were established so as to provide kosher food for patients or residents who observe traditional dietary laws. While these facilities have historically received support from benefactors, self-pay, third-party sources, and federation subsidies, they are increasingly dependent on governmental Medicare and Medicaid reimbursement for the services they provide. More than $2.5 billion was provided to Jewish-supported hospitals by Medicare and Medicaid in 1994 (The Council of Jewish Federations, 1995). An additional $500 million of Medicare and Medicaid funds provided support to Jewish-geriatric facilities (The Council of Jewish Federations, 1995). It should be noted that the services of these organizations are available to all regardless of race, ethnicity, or religious affiliation. In spite of their long history of service to the Jewish community, many of these sectarian agencies are being acquired by for-profit managed-care organizations.

VOCATIONAL SERVICES

Jewish vocational-services (JVS) agencies were founded by Federations to address specific communal needs in the areas of employment. Founded on the concept of *parnosah*—income, JVS agencies had an obligation to help Jews secure a source of income so they could raise a family, remain independent, live in dignity, and continue to be a vital and productive part of the Jewish community (Miller, 1995/96). They supplement the efforts of public employment services, with special assistance being provided to physically and mentally handicapped individuals and to recent émigrés in need of retraining. Services include vocational testing, individual and group counseling, job placement, educational support, training programs for the developmentally disabled, mentally ill and dually diagnosed, and economic-development services. These programs are designed to assist individuals in becoming self-sufficient. Federation-supported Jewish vocational services receive approximately 77 percent of their $180 million annual budgets from governmental services (The Council of Jewish Federations, 1995).

COMMUNITY RELATIONS

Community relations are an integral part of the Jewish communal-service agenda, reflected in the work of the Anti-Defamation League, The American Jewish Committee, The American Jewish Congress, and the national and local Community Relations Councils. These agencies are concerned with issues of "church–state" separation, anti-Semitism, human and civil rights, immigration, equality of women, cultural relations, and the relationship between various religious and ethnic groups.

JEWISH COMMUNAL SERVICE ASSOCIATION

Today's Jewish Communal Service Association (JCSA) was founded in 1899 as the National Conference of Jewish Charities. It is the primary professional association for a wide range of professionals employed in Jewish-communal agencies. It publishes the major quarterly journal in the field, the *Journal of Jewish Communal-Service.* Affiliated professional associations include:

- Association of Jewish Center Professionals
- Association of Jewish Community Organization Personnel
- Association of Jewish Community Relations Workers
- Association of Jewish Vocational Service Professionals
- Council for Jewish Education
- Jewish Family and Children's Professionals' Association
- North American Association of Jewish Homes and Housing for the Aging.

In additon to these groups whose primary concern is Jewish communal service, in recent years a group of Jewish social-work educators has come together under the auspices of the Council on Social Work Education to address issues of curriculum, anti-Semitism, and ethnic understanding.

EDUCATION FOR JEWISH COMMUNAL SERVICE

According to Teicher (1996), efforts to educate professional personnel for Jewish communal service began in 1890 when scholarships were offered to college graduates who expressed a desire to prepare for service in Jewish agencies. In 1902, the National Conference of Jewish Charities made three such scholarship grants available. Lack of interest quickly led to the program's demise. During the next ten years, "earn while you learn" courses were provided in Baltimore, Chicago, and New York, where under the auspices of the Jewish Chautauqua Society, communal workers took courses to improve their skills.

The first Jewish school of social work was formally established in 1913 by the Jewish Settlement, a social agency affiliated with the Federation of Jewish Charities in Cincinnati. This pioneering institution was abandoned a year-and-a-half later because it was unable to attract students. The New York *Kehillah,* which opened its offices in the Spring of 1909, organized a School for Jewish Communal Work in October 1916. This School closed in its third year, partly because military conscription for World War I made it difficult to find students. The Graduate School for Jewish Social Work, sponsored by the National Conference of Jewish Charities, opened in 1925. It operated until 1940, when lack of funds caused it to close its doors.

The Training Bureau for Jewish Communal Service was launched in 1947 by five major agencies—the American Association for Jewish Education, National Community Relations Advisory Council, the National Jewish Welfare Board, the American Jewish Joint Distribution Committee, and the Council of Jewish Federations and Welfare Funds. It closed in 1951. The first attempt to pre-pare Jewish communal workers in a university setting occurred at Yeshiva University in 1957 with the founding of what was to become the Wurzweiler School of Social Work. Wurzweiler, which celebrated its 40th anniversary in 1997, has continued to serve the Jewish and general community in the prepara-tion of masters- and doctoral-level social workers.

There has been an ongoing dialogue over the last twenty-five years as to whether Jewish communal service is a field of service (Pins & Ginsburg, 1971), a profession (Reisman, 1972), or both (Bubis, 1976, 1994; Bubis & Reisman, 1995/96). Currently, there are eleven different programs in North America that specifically train individuals for careers in Jewish communal-service agencies, nine of which are linked to the Federation Executive Recruitment and Education Program (FEREP) of the Council of Jewish Federations. Several are housed in or affiliated with schools of social work granting the MSW plus a certificate in Jewish communal service; graduates of one program receive two masters—one in social work and the other in Jewish communal service; others stand alone, awarding a master's degree in Jewish communal service, reflecting the belief that Jewish communal service is a distinct profession, separate from social work that had provided requisite professional preparation to the Jewish community for the preceding 50 years (Reisman, 1972). Jewish communal service is not a unitary profession, but a field of practice bound by a series of shared attributes in which workers are personally committed and responsible for:

- developing and deepening Jewish consciousness based on knowledge and emotional commitment,
- excellence in professional competence, management, interpretation, and planning,
- leadership through initiative and service as educators and models for emulations and inspiration,
- participation of laypersons,
- effective use of human and financial community resources (Goldman, 1981).

The commitment to these principles and the diversity of programs preparing both Jewish professional and lay leadership were reflected at the 1997 Paris Meeting on Training for Jewish Leadership that took place under the auspice of the European Center for Jewish Leadership and the American Joint Distribution Committee.

THE JEWISH POPULATION SURVEY

Over the past three decades Jewish communal organizations have attempted to better understand their constituencies, evaluate their services, and plan for future needs through a series of systematic statistical profiles and community surveys. The most ambitious and influential of these surveys to date is the 1990 National Jewish Population Survey (NJPS), sponsored by the Council of Jewish Federations through the North American Jewish Data Bank (NAJDB) housed at the City University of New York.

Such analyses have been part of Jewish communal activity since the late fifties, though their role in planning and evaluation was limited and largely academic. These efforts were hampered by the absence of any questions regarding religion in the U.S. Census and by the small number of Jewish respondents included in more general marketing or public-opinion surveys.

The 1990 National Jewish Population Study, based on a sample of some 2,500 households, yielded important findings about how American Jews live, what they think and believe, and how they behave as both Jews and Americans. Despite limitations of definition and sampling procedure, its data are the most comprehensive and authoritative gathered to date (Kosmin et al. 1991).

The study served as a testament to the geographic mobility of the American Jewish community. It also confirmed social patterns with which American Jews have long been associated. It found that regardless of gender, the core Jewish population tended to be older, better-educated, more likely to hold professional or managerial positions, and to express politically liberal values than their white, Gentile neighbors. It also found that Jewish marital and fertility rates had declined. Most dramatic of all were data regarding Jewish identity, ritual behavior, and patterns of intermarriage. The latter had always been of particular concern among communal leaders as a final mark of self-exclusion and the ultimate loss of a household from Jewish affiliation. The study showed that rates of intermarriage have increased with each generation, with some 90 percent of those married before 1965 choosing a born or converted Jew as a marital partner, as compared to only 48 percent of those married between 1985–1990. In addition, when asked if they would oppose a marriage between their child and a non-Jew, only 22 percent of Jews-by-religion answered in the affirmative, while some three-quarters said they would "support" or "accept" such a union. Data regarding strength of identification and ritual behavior indicated high levels of secularism and indifference to Jewish affiliations and creed (Medding et al., 1992). Similar findings were also evident in regard to patterns of communal affiliation. Even among those identifying themselves as Jews-by-religion, only 38 percent held synagogue membership, 33 percent belonged to a Jewish organization, and 31 percent had ever visited Israel. Among "secular" respondents, the percentages dropped to 10 percent or less (Goldstein, 1992; Rimor & Katz, 1993).

JEWISH CONTINUITY

Against the backdrop of the 1990 NJPS and its evidence of waning levels of Jewish affiliation and dramatic increases in intermarriage rates, the delegates to the 1992 General Assembly of the Council of Jewish Federations declared "Jewish continuity" to be the primary and foremost mission of Jewish communal and social-services efforts. The call was to "reinvent" community and create a strategic vision of Jewish life that accounted for the realities of its constituents, actual and potential. The 1990 NJPS made it clear that most Jews in the United States considered themselves well-accepted in the general society, and operated within a largely secular arena. The community would have to prove "worthy" of their support by providing initiatives that instill a sense of belonging and affiliation beyond and independent from those of their ancestors.

In response, local Jewish federations, especially those from larger cities with substantial Jewish populations, established "continuity commissions." These undertook to identify goals and objectives for this mission, with particular focus upon Jewish education, the vitality of the Jewish community, and individual Jewish identity (Dashefsky & Bacon, 1994). Community endowments were created to support new programs of outreach, family education, professional training, and study or travel in Israel. Collaborations have been encouraged between local institutions already involved in such activities, and efforts have been made to win support from donors and activists for this redirection of communal priorities (Dashefsky & Bacon, 1994).

In addition to the issues raised by the National Jewish Population Survey, other scholars have identified additional concerns that have become the focus of Jewish communal agencies. These include spousal and child battering, substance abuse, the changing role of women, outreach to intermarried couples, abortion, and the needs of populations at risk (e.g., those afflicted with HIV–AIDS) (Bayme & Rosen, 1994; Dubin, 1996; Linzer, 1996; Linzer, Levitz, & Schnall, 1995). While some of these relate specifically to the Jewish community, they are similar, if not identical, to concerns being addressed by other sectarian organizations and by social-service agencies in general.

It is far too early to evaluate the success of these efforts in facilitating Jewish continuity, affiliation, and support. It has been suggested, however, that such programs have not inspired great confidence among supporters of Jewish causes. For example, a recent study of Jewish philanthropic patterns indicates that despite their genuine concern for the future of the Jewish community, donors:

1. are skeptical about the role of the fundraising system to address the continuity issue effectively;

2. prefer specific proposals that achieve commonly understood goals, rather than a broad "continuity" agenda;

3. support continuity programs only if they are convinced that the needs of the elderly, the hungry, the homeless, and the unemployed within the Jewish community are adequately financed (Tobin & Tobin, 1995).

TRENDS IN JEWISH COMMUNAL SERVICE

The future of Jewish communal service is intertwined with efforts at assuring Jewish continuity in the United States. In addition to the growth in formal Jewish day-school education, alternatives for enhancing Jewish social and religious culture are being developed. In particular, various programs of informal Jewish education have been launched.

For example, Jewish summer camps and touring programs have been designed to create a "total environment" for young people to explore their heritage with carefully trained advisors and staff. Linkage is maintained through campus and youth programming that support these objectives during the course of the school year.

Jewish community centers have undertaken early childhood, after-school, and weekend programs of family education. These engage parents and children in religious ritual and tradition through family and community participation. Such programs have also focused on outreach to "special" client groups; for example, recent immigrants from Eastern Europe or the Middle East, single-parent families, or the intermarried.

Some communities have created a "Jewish communal campus," that is, one large facility housing the community center, day school, museum and cultural agency, home for the aged, and other arms of the organized Jewish community. This allows intergenerational and multidisciplinary activities and coordinated efforts at fundraising and planned change. However, it presumes the physical stability of a community better known for its demographic and residential mobility.

Much has also been done with study tours to Israel. Aside from generating political and fiscal support for the Jewish homeland, these are intended to spark and reinforce Jewish identity. Family tours, Bar/Bat Mitzvah celebrations, summer courses, archaeological digs, accredited academic programs, and study at religious academies all have been promoted as ancillaries to synagogue or community-center activities. The March of the Living is an international program designed for high-school students. Comprised of a week-long visit to the remains of the death camps in Poland, followed by a week in Jerusalem, its timing coincides with Holocaust Memorial Day and Israel Independence Day.

As evidenced in the preceding description, Jewish communal services have emerged from and been supported by a set of social obligations that has as its root the concept of *tzedakah,* or "justice." While these services and the agencies that provide them are sectarian and derive ongoing support from the Jewish community, their specialized services are available to members of both the Jewish and general communities. Today, the Jewish community and Jewish communal agencies are struggling with the specific issue of Jewish continuity and the broader issues raised by the emerging managed-care environment in which all social services operate. "Jewish communal workers are a powerful link in the chain that binds Jewish legacy to the Jewish posterity" (Teicher, 1997).

REFERENCES

Abramson, G. (1994). Doing the job in difficult times: An appreciation of Jewish family service. *Journal of Jewish Communal Service, 70*(4), 248–252.

Aronowitz, E., & Birnbaum, M. (1992). *Field work standards for group work students in Jewish community centers.* New York: Association of Jewish Center Professionals— Eastern Region.

Bayme, S., & Rosen, G. (1994). *The Jewish family and Jewish continuity.* Hoboken, NJ: KTAV Publishing.

Berger, G. (1980). *The turbulent decades.* New York: Conference of Jewish Communal Service.

Bernstein, P. (1965). *Jewish social services.* In H. L. Lurie (Ed.), *Encyclopedia of social work* (15th ed., pp. 418–428). New York: National Association of Social Workers.

Birnbaum, M. L., & Pine, B. (1997). *Reviving group work in Jewish community centers.* Unpublished manuscript.

Blum, A., & Naparstek, A. J. (1987). The changing environment and Jewish communal services. *Journal of Jewish Communal Service, 63*(3), 204–211.

Bubis, G. (1976). Professional education for the Jewish component in casework practice. *Journal of Jewish Communal Service, 52*(3), 270–277.

———. (1994). Jewish communal service today: Paradoxes and problems. *Journal of Jewish Communal Service, 71*(1), 6–12.

———, & Reisman, B. (1995/96). Jewish communal service training programs and the federation system. *Journal of Jewish Communal Service, 72*(1/2), 102–109.

Council of Jewish Federations. (1995). *Government funding for human services in the Jewish community.* Revised working draft.

Cover, R. (1987). Obligation: A Jewish jurisprudence of the social order. *Journal of Law and Religion, 5,* 65–90.

Dashefsky, A., & Bacon, A. (1994). The meaning of Jewish continuity in the North American community: A preliminary assessment. *Agenda: Jewish Education, 4,* 22–28.

Dubin, D. (1987). Ethical dilemmas in the Jewish community center. *Journal of Jewish Communal Service, 64*(1), 23–31.

———. (1994). The liberation of the constituent agency. *Journal of Jewish Communal Service, 70*(4), 226–231.

———. (1996). *"I witness": Comments on continuity by a Jewish communal profession- al.* Floral Park, NJ: Association of Jewish Center Professionals and the Jewish Community Centers Association.

Elazar, D. (1995). *Community and polity.* Philadelphia: Jewish Publication Society.

———, & Cohen, S. (1985). *The Jewish polity.* Bloomington: Indiana University Press.

Gelman, S. R., Gibelman, M., Pollack, D., & Schnall, D. (1996). Philanthropic boards of directors on the line: Roles, realities and prospects. *Journal of Jewish Communal Service, 72*(3), 185–194.

Gibelman, M. (1995). Purchasing social services. In R. L. Edwards (Ed.), *Encyclopedia of social work: Vol. 3* (19th ed., pp. 1998–2007). Washington, DC: NASW Press.

Goldman, R. (1981). The role of the professional in developing and shaping Jewish com- munal policies and strategies. *Proceedings of the International Conference of Jewish Communal Service,* 5–36.

Goldstein, S. (1992). Profile of American Jewry: Insights from the 1990 National Jewish

Population Survey. In *The American Jewish Yearbook 1992* (pp. 77–173). New York: The American Jewish Committee.

Hebrew Immigrant Aid Society. (1996). *Rescue, hope, freedom.* New York: Hebrew Immigrant Aid Society.

Kosansky, H. (1978). The Jewish community center: We may not be unique but we are very special. *Journal of Jewish Communal Service, 54*(4), 303–308.

Kosmin, B. A., Goldstein, S., Waksberg, J., Lerer, N., Keysar, A., & Scheckner, J. (1991). *Highlights of the CJF 1990 National Jewish Population Survey.* New York: Council of Jewish Federations.

Kraft, L. (1967). *The development of the Jewish Community Center: Purpose, principles, and practice.* New York: The National Association of Jewish Center Workers.

Levine, E. M. (1998). Church, state and social welfare: Purchase of service and the sectarian agency. In M. Gibelman and H. Demore (Eds.), *The Privatization of Human Services: Policy and Practice Issues* (pp. 117–154). New York: Springer Publishing.

Linzer, N. (1987). Resolving ethical dilemmas in the Jewish community center. *Journal of Jewish Communal Service, 64*(2), 145–155.

———. (1996). *Ethical dilemmas in Jewish communal service.* Hoboken, NJ: KTAV Publishing.

———, Levitz, I., & Schnall, D. (1995). *Crisis and continuity: The Jewish family in the 21st century.* Hoboken, NJ: KTAV Publishing.

Maimonides, M. (1965). *Yad HaHazakah: Hilchot Matanot Le Aniyim.* New York: Moznaim Press.

Medding, P., Tobin, G. A., Fishman, S. B., & Rimor, M. (1992). Jewish identity in conversionary and mixed marriages. In *The American Jewish Yearbook 1992* (pp. 3–76). New York: The American Jewish Committee.

Miller, A. P. (1995/96). Jewish vocational service and the federations. *Journal of Jewish Communal Service, 72*(1/2), 87–90.

Ortiz, L. P. (1995). Sectarian agencies. In R. L. Edwards (Ed.), *Encyclopedia of Social Work: Vol. 3* (19th ed., pp. 2109–2116). Washington, DC: NASW Press.

Pins, A. M., & Ginsburg, L. (1971). New developments in social work and their impact on Jewish center and communal service workers. *Journal of Jewish Communal Service, 48*(1), 60–71.

Reid, W. J., & Stimpson, P. K. (1987). Sectarian agencies. In A. Minahan (Ed.), *Encyclopedia of Social Work: Vol. 2* (18th ed., pp. 545–556). Silver Spring, MD: NASW Press.

Reisman, B. (1972). Social work education and Jewish communal service and JCCs: Time for a change. *Journal of Jewish Communal Service, 48*(4), 384–395.

Rimor, M., & Katz, E. (1993). United States National Jewish Population Survey: A first report. In *The American Jewish Yearbook 1973* (pp. 264–306). New York: The American Jewish Committee.

Schiff, A., & Schneider, M. (1994). *Far-reaching effects of extensive Jewish day-school attendance: The impact of Jewish education on Jewish behavior and attitudes.* New York: Yeshiva University, David J. Azrieli: Graduate Institute of Jewish Education and Administration.

Schnall, D. J. (1993). Exploratory notes on employee productivity and accountability in classic Jewish sources. *Journal of Business Ethics, 12,* 485–491.

———. (1995a). Faithfully occupied with the public need. *Journal of Jewish Communal Service, 71*(4), 315–324.

————. (1995b). Filial responsibility in Judaism. *Jewish Journal of Sociology, 37*(2), 112–118.

————. (1996). Care for the incapacitated parent: A case study in classic Jewish family norms. *Journal of Religious Gerontology, 9*(4), 27–41.

————. (1997). An alternative source for contemporary public administration: Aspects of public service employment in classic Jewish tradition. *Administration and Society, 29*(1), 3–17.

Schneider, M. (1994, July). *Weathering the storms of a changing world.* (Speech given at Wurzweiler School of Social Work, Block Commencement.)

Schreiber, A. M. (1979). *Jewish law and decision-making: A study through time.* Philadelphia: Temple University Press.

Shore, H. (1995/96). Jewish homes and housing for the aging: Relating to the federation. *Journal of Jewish Communal Service, 72*(1/2), 91–95.

Smith, R., & Lipsky, M. (1993). *Nonprofits for hire: The welfare state in the age of contracting.* Cambridge, MA: Harvard University Press.

Solomon, J. R. (1995/96). Evolving models of federation-agency cooperation. *Journal of Jewish Communal Service, 72*(1/2), 60–65.

Steinitz, L. Y. (1995/96). It's all in the family: Jewish family services and the federation. *Journal of Jewish Communal Service, 72*(1/2), 70–76.

Teicher, M. (letter, 1996). *Journal of Jewish Communal Service, 73*(1), 91–92.

————. (lecture, March 13, 1997). Samuel Belkin Memorial Lecture, Yeshiva University.

Tobin, G., & Tobin, A. (1995). *American Jewish philanthropies in the 1990s.* Boston: Brandeis University.

UJA-Federation of New York. (1994). *Report to the community 1993–1994.* New York: UJA-Federation of New York.

5

The Jewish Federation: The First Hundred Years

DONALD FELDSTEIN

INTRODUCTION

For all we know, Jews may have accompanied Columbus on his voyages; most likely, some Jews found their way to the New World during the sixteenth and the early part of the seventeenth centuries. Yet historians of the Jewish community in the United States generally commence with the first communal band of Jewish settlers in what was then New Amsterdam (New York) in 1654. The Governor, Peter Stuyvesant, did not want to receive these guests but was eventually overruled, and so the first organized Jewish settlement in the United States began. For almost 250 years Jewish settlement continued and grew in what became the United States. Jewish communities established synagogues, burial societies, credit unions, and Hebrew youth societies in dozens of cities before there was a single federation. From the start, the Jewish community promised local governments that they would take care of their own people and that Jews would not become a burden to the community. Soon after the first Jewish federation in the United States was founded in Boston in 1895, another was organized in Cincinnati, Ohio, and within several years federations sprung up around the country wherever there were significant Jewish communities.

WHAT IS THE JEWISH FEDERATION?

Secular Jews who never committed themselves to the observance of Biblical law and Jewish tradition were the primary founders of the federations. In spite of this, consciously or unconsciously, the founding and philosophies of the federations were very deeply influenced by Jewish tradition and law. In some ways they were similar to the *Kehilla,* the communal organization that existed in many parts of Eastern Europe for many years, in their attempt to be comprehensive and inclusive of Jewish organizations and in their concern for meeting the welfare needs of Jews in their respective communities. But the Kehilla was usually formed by local governments, subject to their authority, to collect taxes from the Jewish community to support their programs and services. The essential difference between the *Kehilla* and the Jewish federation is that the latter is ultimately fully autonomous. *Hesed*—lovingkindness—was very much in the minds of the founders of Jewish federations, though they were unaware that this was following in Jewish tradition. Thus, as God clothed Adam and Eve, federations were concerned about clothing the naked; as Abraham cared for strangers, federations cared for strangers; as God buried Moses, Jewish federations supported Jewish burial societies.

The phenomenon of unconscious re-creation of a tradition is not unique. Anthropologists have taught us that certain Native Americans, generations removed from their tribal practices, once permitted to establish self-government, sometimes reinvented or re-created certain practices and customs that had been observed by their forebearers generations earlier, of which they had no conscious memory. It seemed like the right thing to do.

There is no single source where one can find a comprehensive history of the Jewish federation in North America. The best sources are Philip Bernstein (1983; 1994) and Charles Miller (1985). Using different categories and titles, one can cull-out four primary principles and characteristics of the Jewish federation in North America.

Autonomy

Although federations are very similar across North America, each one insists that it makes its own autonomous decisions and prides itself on its differences from the others. "You have to understand," a visitor will be told, "that this federation is unique and not like all the others." In fact, in the ways that federations allocate their funds, giving priority to different causes, one can discern significant differences one from another.

Localism

Federations traditionally insist on their own local characteristics and the fact that they make policy only for their own catchment areas. Too much localism can weaken any kind of governing structure, and the federations have sometimes been hurt by an excess of localism. But when overriding crises or causes appear, the degree of unity that is achievable among the federations is also remarkable. The characteristic of localism has been significantly modified in recent years, to be described more fully later. Both autonomy and localism are related to what Daniel Elazar (1976) calls "federalism" as a primary characteristic of the federations.

Americanism

Since the "to bigotry no sanction" letter of George Washington, the American Jewish community has been engaged in a shameless love affair with the values, traditions, and customs of the United States. The Jewish community tends to mirror or follow general American trends in geography, population, etc., and sometimes is even in the vanguard of these trends, such as in the aging of the American population.

Communalism

Carmi Schwartz, former chief executive of the Council of Jewish Federations, has pointed out that Judaism may perhaps be unique among the great religions in making a commandment of the need to communalize—to form a community. Almost from the beginning of their founding, the federations ultimately saw the needs of the communities as their targets for service, rather than the needs of individual Jews. No one is exempt from contributing to the community, not even the very poor.

Autonomy, localism, Americanism, and communalism are the central characteristics or guiding principles of the Jewish federations in North America. What follows are some additional activities of federations, derived from the writings of Bernstein and Miller.

Joint Fundraising, Allocating, and Central Budgeting

The idea is deceptively simple: As large Jewish communities began to develop a plethora of Jewish institutions to meet various needs with their own fundraising campaigns, it appeared that it might be more efficient to aid these institutions through one appeal and one gift by donors. The central appeal could allocate the funds to its member agencies in some equitable manner, and to the federation for its own needs as well as the needs of its agencies. The idea was so simple and successful that it was copied by many communities. Communities did, in fact, raise more money in a single campaign than had previously been raised. The first federations were followed in 1913 by the first community chest in the United States in Cleveland, Ohio, the forerunner of the contemporary United Way.

Community Planning

Although joint fundraising and allocations were very central to the federation, this innovation was almost immediately followed by a desire to plan for the communities' needs. Community planning has now become a central part of the federations in the United States and Canada.

Central Services

Federations vary widely in the amount of central services they provide for their agencies and communities. There are those that simply do some bookkeeping for agencies, and those that provide research, demographic information, statistical, and central-accounting data as well. Sometimes the federation itself provides community relations rather than through a separate agency dealing with government relations and with the larger philanthropic community.

Agency Benefits

Not only did the campaign provide more financial support to the agencies than they could have received separately, but federations also provided legitimacy and power through their reputation for doing professional works.

Inclusion

Federations try to include services and agencies to meet emerging common needs. They aim to be inclusive rather than exclusive, even while trying to come to grips with the reality that no federation can meet every possible need. Limitation and expansion are twin pillars of the federation concept of inclusiveness.

Governance

Federations differ in their governance structures but each one is accountable to the Jewish community through some kind of elected board of directors or trustees who are ultimately responsible for the operations of the federation. Further, all federations now devote some resources and energy to locating, attracting, and developing new or young lay leadership.

Leadership

At first, federations were led by volunteers, but soon they needed to engage paid executive secretaries, financial officers, and other staff. Before long, federations became complex organizations with various departments that employed various skills. Between the 1930s and 1950s federations developed a strong marriage bond between Jewish communal service and the emerging profession of social work. Federations and Jewish Community Centers (JCCs) vied with each other as to which employed the most masters of social work (MSWs). But the major policy decisions of the federations were always made by volunteer citizens of the Jewish community.

Council of Jewish Federations and Other National Agencies

Since its inception in 1932 the Council of Jewish Federations (CJF) (formerly "and Welfare Fund") has represented the Jewish federations in the United States and Canada in a continental network. CJF was a leader in the efforts to help federations secure public support for housing for the elderly (along with B'nai B'rith); it was also key in promoting legislation to helping resettle Russian Jews in the United States, for which hundreds of millions of dollars have been spent.

Since the birth of Israel, the United Jewish Appeal has been a vital partner in the work of federations. Local welfare funds and the United Jewish Appeal have merged, locality by locality.

Finally, CJF was instrumental in founding several national agencies to serve distinctive needs such as the National Jewish Community Relations Advisory Council and the National Foundation for Jewish Culture. National agencies are now a small but essential part of the concerns of Jewish federations.

Changes in Services

Jewish federations are broadly based and therefore tend to be somewhat conservative and slow to change—but change is a constant. In the early twentieth century Jewish orphanages were vital institutions. Now they have largely disappeared. On the other hand, publicly supported residential facilities for the elderly have grown as a major service in most large and large–intermediate Jewish communities. These are just minor examples of the fact that the services of the federations and their agencies have changed considerably over a century of development.

Public Social Policy

Public policy and advocacy (tax-deductible groups avoid the word "lobbying") have become increasingly important to the federations and CJF. At this time, fifteen states maintain associations of federations that focus on public-policy issues being debated in the respective state capitals.

Community Chests

Almost since their inception, community chests, United Ways, and federations under other religious auspices have worked closely together with the Jewish federations. United Ways allocate over $15 million annually to the agencies of the federations. This is but one example of the Jewish federations' concern with and relationship to larger nonprofit community.

Unity

Broad representativeness is characteristic of the Jewish federation. Almost any constituency can find representation on its board of directors. Occasionally, a group is seen as being so far to the right or left that it is denied membership in the local Jewish federation or community council. But with rare exceptions, the federation is committed to including every group and thereby unity on consensus issues.

Social Justice, Ethical Values

The Jewish community in the United States has never been solely concerned with Jewish issues: It has worked at promoting democracy for all—for freer immigration and a just society. Writers debate how central the social-justice agenda should be in the Jewish community, but it is certainly still there.

No institution can guarantee the ethical behavior of every one of its members. Federations have noted the importance of individual ethical behavior but have concentrated on ensuring the institutional behavior of the organization and its accountability to its community of contributors.

Creativity and Excellence

Almost from the start, Jewish federations expected the agencies they supported to be the finest. Federation agencies have pioneered in residential child care, in developing professionalism in family agencies, and in creating a wide array of services for the elderly. Some of the world's finest medical centers and nursing homes are federation agencies.

Maximum Feasible Participation

Long before maximum feasible participation was a slogan in the United States' War on Poverty in the 1960s, it was a principle guiding the Jewish federation—a commitment to plan *with* rather than *for* the members of the community.

Sanctity of Life and Dignity of Each Person

These ancient elements of Jewish tradition were incorporated into Jewish-federation philosophy and practice and continue to be part of the ethical framework of everything that federations strived to do.

The above characteristics are at the heart of what federations do and inform the vast array of services that they provide. These characteristics should enhance our understanding of the history of the Jewish federation in the United States.

WHAT DO FEDERATIONS DO AND WHAT SERVICES DO THEY PROVIDE?

It would take at least another chapter to adequately describe the services provided by or supported by Jewish federations. What can be offered here is only the briefest of summaries of some of the major agencies and services.

The title "human services" is probably the best available for the package of activities and services described below. These include services to the poor, services to the aging, resettlement services, and a variety of other services. The federations like to describe themselves as "the central address" of the Jewish community and to varying degrees this is true. Over 30 percent of the Jewish households in North America contribute annually to their federations, or through their federations to the United Jewish Appeal. In smaller communities this percentage can become a good deal higher, sometimes even greater than 50 percent. In a small number of the very largest communities the percentage may be lower. Jewish federations have received as many as a million contributions to their annual campaigns. The number today is somewhat smaller, about 850,000, but the number of participants is certainly greater than in any other philanthropic activity of the Jewish community. The dollars raised are significantly more than any other fundraising institutions, in spite of the greater percentage gains made by universities and hospitals in Israel and other institutions in recent years.

Each year federations raise something like $800 million for their various causes. Less than half of that amount makes its way to Israel by way of the United Israel Appeal, which provides tax deductibility. The funds earmarked for overseas are also shared with the American Jewish Joint Distribution Committee, an organization that provides innovative services in Israel and aid to Jewish communities around the world needing assistance in education and social services. Slightly more than 50 percent of the funds are allocated each year to the various local agencies of the Jewish federation, with a small percentage—under 2 percent—allocated to national organizations such as the American Jewish Committee, the American Jewish Congress, the Anti-Defamation League of B'nai B'rith, the Jewish Community Centers Association, etc. The federations actually created some of the national agencies and agreed to continue to provide some support in return for small constraints on the fundraising of the national agencies. The support for national agencies has shrunk in recent years from about 3 percent of domestic allocations to under 2 percent.

Within each community the federation distributes its allocations to a variety of constituent agencies. In recent years the largest single local allocation is to Jewish education. This includes Boards or Bureaus of Jewish Education, day schools, the congregational schools, adult Jewish education in the JCC, and other specialized programs. These funds account for about 25 percent of the domestic allocation from the Jewish federations of the United States. Close behind are the allocations to the local JCCs. The JCCs have always faced the question of why the community should be supporting them since they serve a cross-section of

Jews, including those who could pay the full membership fees. In fact, the attempt to recoup costs from users and members does take place and is sometimes successful in specialized areas such as day camps and early childhood-education programs, but the general programs of the JCCs still need communal support to survive.

The other long-standing debate concerning JCCs has been regarding support of "basketball palaces," as opposed to services for people with special needs such as the disabled, elderly, etc. JCCs try to strike a balance and purport at least to serve people of all kinds and needs within the Jewish community. Very few JCCs are exclusively sectarian in their clientele, but the day has long passed when many JCCs were concerned about "tipping" because of a large percentage of non-Jewish members. By choice or public regulation most of the agencies of Jewish federations are open to all, though they primarily serve the Jewish community.

Sometimes in third place, sometimes in second in domestic allocations is the Jewish Family and Children Service of the local community, providing a wide range of services to individuals, families, and groups such as counseling and often highly specialized psychotherapeutic services and a variety of others. A few of the large cities also maintain group homes for child care. These child-care institutions are shrinking because there seems to be a shrinking Jewish base for them and increasingly they are dependent upon public support, which has been declining.

There was a time when providing adoption services for prospective adoptive families was part of the basic operations and services of the Jewish Family and Children's Services, but this function has largely been transferred to lawyers. Jews' demand for adoptive children is so disproportionate to their percentage of the total population that some Jewish Family and Children's Service agencies have begun to rediscover adoption services and have learned that adoptive children can be found if the right methods are used.

The Jewish Family and Children's Services, more often than any other institution, is the agency chosen by the local Jewish federation to provide resettlement services for new Jewish immigrants within the community. There was a time when this was a very small and insignificant service, but has increasingly grown with some federal financial support because in recent years 40,000 Jews from the former Soviet Union have been annually admitted into the United States. Providing a variety of resettlement services in each community is a major undertaking of the Jewish family agency.

Before the advent of Medicare and Medicaid in the mid-1960s, the largest domestic recipients of Jewish federation funds in many of the large cities were Jewish hospitals. These hospitals were originally created because Jews were not welcomed in medical schools, internships, and residencies. Jews have made such vast strides in the medical profession in recent decades that the very validity of allocations to Jewish hospitals has come into question. In fact, allocations are now a very small fraction of the total Jewish-federation allocation to its domestic agencies. In one case a Jewish hospital was actually sold, and in other cases Jewish hospitals have merged with other general medical institutions. There continue to be major hospitals under Jewish auspices in some of the largest cities in the United States; the likelihood is that they will continue under Jewish sponsorship in the foreseeable future. But the allocations will continue to shrink to a smaller percentage of the total budget. Where the federations *do* make allocations to Jewish hospitals, they tend to do so for specific programs.

Many Jewish communities and their federations also count among their member agencies Jewish Homes for the Aged. This is usually a skilled-nursing facility, sometimes affiliated with an intensive-care unit. These homes include some of the finest nursing homes in the United States and are a source of great pride to the Jewish community. When federations do their annual fundraising, they find that support for Israel and the aged are the easiest sells.

Perhaps equally as important is the large number of residences for the elderly, built under Jewish auspices or sponsorship, primarily from the Jewish federation system. B'nai B'rith International was also an early entrant into the effort to receive federal support for residences for the elderly. In the last thirty years or so, the federations have become by far the largest player in this field of Jewish communal service.

There are often a number of other Jewish social services that are provided by the federation, usually with a smaller allocation than the ones mentioned above. The federations have become major supporters of the B'nai B'rith Hillel Foundations in the United States, providing services for Jewish youth on the college campus. They may also support group homes for developmentally disabled youth or adults. A score or so of Jewish federations help to support a Jewish Vocational Services agency, providing a variety of services concerned with job-seeking and training. Some of these agencies have melded into those serving the general population because their clientele ceased to be primarily Jewish.

There also tends to be some special allocations made by the federation to some specialized service or to deal with problems of which the community has become aware. The large and growing endowment funds of the Jewish federations are usually the source of these particular grants and will be discussed below in the final section of this chapter.

Community Relations

Some federations have among their members a separate, independent agency—a Community Relations Council. In other federations the council is an arm of the federation. Either way, the vast majority of federations have some body that is charged with responsibility for local Jewish community relations. These Community Relations Councils or committees not only deal with local outbreaks of anti-Semitism (as do the large community-relations agencies: the Anti-Defamation League of B'nai B'rith, the American Jewish Committee, and the American Jewish Congress), but they also tend to support Jewish education in their communities regarding the Holocaust, sponsor interreligious or interracial committees promoting goodwill and democracy, and perform a number of other community-relations tasks.

Other Specialized Services of the Federation

Various federations provide a variety of other services in addition to the above list. A few, large Jewish communities still sponsor Jewish child-care agencies. Sometimes federations sponsor or own group homes for people with special needs or handicaps. There are often federation programs aimed at AIDS, Alzheimer's disease, and others.

We have been able to give here only the briefest possible introduction to the encyclopedic nature of the services of the modern Jewish federation. Its range is quite remarkable.

HISTORY OF THE JEWISH FEDERATION

The history of the Jewish Federation may be divided into four periods, given below.

Period of Jewish Integration: 1895–1945

The first half-century of the Jewish federation movement in the United States was largely devoted to what might be described as welfare—meeting the health, social, and welfare needs of individual Jews. During this period the federations expanded in number and function as they served more people in the growing Jewish population in the United States.

Most services were available to all Americans, although they were primarily addressed to the needs and interests of the Jewish community. (That condition of being interested primarily in the Jewish community but serving all people to some degree continues to this day.) Federation agencies have always been simultaneously sectarian and universal.

It would not be far from the truth to say that the goal of the Jewish federation and Jewish social-service agencies during this period was actually assimilation, by helping Jews integrate into the United States: learning its language, culture, and values. That goal was openly expressed by the Jewish settlement houses in New York City, and more subtly in other agencies. The goal was to eliminate barriers to the full Jewish participation in the American dream.

Period of Integration of Welfare and Israel: 1948–1967

With the establishment of the modern State of Israel many elements of the federations changed dramatically. The United Jewish Appeal became a much more important institution nationally. Speakers from Israel were much in demand at major fundraising functions of the local federations. Gradually, communities began to integrate their welfare funds, which focused on social services in the local area, with the needs of the Jews in Israel and other places overseas. A symptom of this was the gradual beginning of joint campaigns of the federations for local and Israel/overseas needs. The entire American Jewish community was witnessing a very gradual and inevitable marriage between their two major concerns: providing for the welfare of Jews in the United States, and providing aid to Jews in the rest of the world and, in particular, Israel.

Period of Israel-Centric and Holocaust-Centric Judaism: 1967–1990

The Six-Day War of 1967 was a watershed event for Jews around the world and particularly in North America. After Israel's dramatic victory, simple pride in the Jewish state became a major foundation of Jewish identity. After the capture and trial of Adolph Eichmann in Jerusalem there was an awakening to the Holocaust. Holocaust awareness became a second pillar of Jewish faith, along with pride in Israel. That movement did not peak until the 1990s with the opening of the Holocaust Museum in Washington, D.C.

Two other developments also characterize this period in Jewish federation history. First, the integration of the local federation and the United Jewish Appeal was completed. The last and largest community to effect this integration was the UJA-Federation in New York, which did so in the mid-1980s.

The second development was a major increase in funds allocated to Jewish education. Federations in varying degrees had always supported Jewish education. Larger federations had boards/bureaus of Jewish education, and some had colleges of Jewish studies supported by the federation. A very small amount of support from the federations had even been given to specific Jewish-educational institutions, but that support was minimal. Most Jews believed that all-day Jewish schools were either somehow un-American or, at least, not worthy of specific support. This attitude, too, began to change dramatically after 1967. The year 1969 marked a student rebellion at CJF's General Assembly in Boston, where student activists demanded that federations support Jewish education more fully. This set off a chain of small and large changes, from providing kosher food at General Assembly functions to making direct support of Jewish education the largest single component of local allocations in the federations of North America. It now totals about 25 percent of the federations' local allocations.

Period of Emphasis on the Future of Judaism: 1990–Onward

Only several years after the National Jewish Population Survey (NJPS) of 1990 did the findings of this study begin to make an impact. In one such impact, 1995 saw a major increase in the number of young Jews given an opportunity for an extended visitation in Israel, a number that is likely to increase in the next several years. However, immediately after its release in 1990, the NJPS set off a wave of concerned meetings, institutes, and follow-ups. These were provoked by the shocking realization to most American Jews that the intermarriage rate of 52 percent threatened the Jewish future in the United States in the long-term, and that even concerns for Israel and awareness of the Holocaust were not sufficient by themselves to guarantee Jewish continuity and survival. Since 1990 support has been increased for Jewish education, particularly among those who believe strongly that Jewish education for an extended period of years in all-day Jewish schools is the best ensurer of intramarriage; others feel equally strongly that associational correlations, participation in the Hillel Foundations on campus, attendance at Jewish summer camps, or even taking a Jewish-studies course while at college are the most important ensurers of Jewish continuity and intramarriage.

All of these responses are attempts to answer the fundamental question: Can the Jewish community, which has successfully survived and usually grown in environments of persecution and discrimination, survive in a climate of complete freedom, autonomy, and choice, where Jews are welcome not only in medical schools and country clubs but also among the families of the larger general community? The answers to this question are being studied and written about and will continue to be so in the coming years. By the time of the next National Jewish Population Study it may even be possible to see whether certain specific programs such as visitation to Israel, greater support for the Hillel Foundations and the like do indeed have some positive effect on continuity. The attempt to answer this question definitively will go on well into the twenty-first century when, most likely, Israel will replace the United States as having the largest Jewish population of any country in the world.

The period since 1990 in Jewish federation history is primarily characterized by an emphasis on the search for ways to ensure Jewish continuity and survival in North America in an environment of freedom and with relative prosperity.

One other characteristic of the current period is the emergence of a continental Jewish community. The wealthy Jewish contributor in Scarsdale, New York or Skokie, Illinois has always been concerned for the poor Jew in the Bronx or the southside of Chicago; he or she has always been concerned for the poor, oppressed Jew in Russia, Ethiopia, or Israel. Yet traditionally that same Jew has had very little concern for the Jew in Albany, Georgia or Albuquerque, New Mexico. The responsibility for that Jew was thought to rest in his or her community. However, there has been a sea change in the sense of Jewish community concerning continental issues, as manifested by the following developments:

• The Jewish community taxed itself to support Jews from the former Soviet Union as they arrived in each community in the United States.

• The Jewish community, through the federations, taxed themselves to guarantee loans for Jews from the former Soviet Union settling in Israel, in a mini-version of the $10 billion loan guarantee from the United States to Israel.

• The Jewish federations voted to accept a new governing structure for CJF in which certain decisions made by a super-majority might be binding on the federations despite the tradition of autonomy.

- The Jewish federations are maintaining a revolving fund for emergency disaster relief to be made available to any community needing it.

- Federations voted to develop a special fund to augment support for the Hillel Foundations in the United States, and for Jews on the college campus.

Thus an awareness of the needs of the continental Jewish community, along with the growing emphasis on Jewish education and continuity, are the hallmarks of the current period in the history of the Jewish federations.

THE JEWISH FEDERATION IN THE TWENTY-FIRST CENTURY

Some of the important trends likely to impact the federations in the coming years are described below.

Jewish Continuity

The federations will continue to increase their support for programs to strengthen Jewish identity and continuity in the United States. They will develop programs to support formal Jewish education, primarily in day schools, and for strengthening Jewish associational activities. In some communities, federations will strengthen their relationships with synagogues, including the funding of synagogue staff members. A somewhat different approach, which is also gathering strength, is increased outreach to marginally affiliated Jews and even to those individuals who are part of intermarried households. There is little hard evidence that these approaches have produced significant results, but the impetus is there to make the attempt, along with a countertrend of concentrating all or most activities on the core Jewish community.

Fundraising

Increasing attention will be paid to the fundraising efforts of federations. Contributions to the federation/UJA system have generally not increased in recent years and not kept pace with inflation. Three signs of a crisis have appeared in the organized Jewish community: 1) The bottom line is relatively flat and not keeping pace with inflation. 2) The number of donors has declined from its peak and will continue to shrink as a result of assimilation and intermarriage. 3) Jews remain as philanthropic as ever, perhaps the most philanthropic group in the United States except possibly for the Mormons. However, they are now dividing their philanthropic contributions evenly between Jewish and general causes, where they used to provide at least two-thirds of their philanthropy to Jewish institutions. This is a direct result of Jews being welcomed and courted by institutions from which they were formerly excluded—symphonies, university boards, etc. There is also hard evidence that fundraising from the organized Jewish community has the potential of growing apace.

For a number of years the organized Jewish community dreamed of a $1 billion annual campaign. Yet they never seemed able to achieve it: The campaigns generally tended to hover at around $800 million per year. But for two years, when Operation Exodus was at its height, focusing on the rescue of Jews from the former Soviet Union and their resettlement in Israel, the regular campaign and Operation Exodus raised $1.2 billion per year. There are no reports that as a result of this level of giving there were wholesale bankruptcies within the Jewish community. The capacity is obviously there, waiting to be tapped.

Critics of the fundraising efforts of the organized Jewish community tend to overlook the growing impact of the endowment funds of the federations and their agencies. While CJF and the federations began rather late to pursue this avenue of support, the endowments in the federations today are in excess of $3 billion, and the income from these endowments now provides over 15 percent of agency support.

Along with the growth of endowment funds there has been an explosion in family and other special foundations. The largest of these is the Weinberg Foundation, centered in Baltimore. No one has a complete list of the Jewish foundations and the amounts generated by them at this point, but they are growing rapidly. The Wexner Foundation has made a tremendous difference in the support for education and training of young Jewish men and women for Jewish communal service, Jewish education, and the rabbinate. The CRB Foundation has supported visitations to Israel by larger numbers of Jewish young people than ever before. The Mandel Family Foundation supports new initiatives in Jewish education. This is just a sampling of the dozens of Jewish family foundations that have sprang up recently; others are foundations by the Gruss, Brookdale, and Cummings families.

There is adequate evidence that the wealth that exists in the Jewish community, since Jews have turned increasingly to investment banking and other business opportunities, is more than enough to permit the annual federation/UJA campaign to meet its goals. There was a fear in the 1970s that Jews were turning away from business, and that the daughters and sons of Jewish business people were entering the professions instead. But the career-attractiveness of business, banking, and finance has grown greatly since the 1980s.

In sum, it is clear that there is a crisis in fundraising in the organized Jewish philanthropic system and in the federation/UJA system in particular. The problem is one of inspiring enough Jews to identify with these special needs; when that occurs, the funds will follow. The system needs to find a moral equivalent to war or rescue.

Mergers

There is an important trend towards merger and consolidation in the organized Jewish community. We now face the possibility that the two giant, national agencies, the Council of Jewish Federations and the United Jewish Appeal, may merge into one body. Other mergers may follow, and certain small and marginal Jewish organizations may simply have to go out of business, as did the

Synagogue Council of America not too long ago. But the merger of CJF and UJA would be a major and radical change for a system that generally moves very incrementally and conservatively.

Leadership Opportunities for Women

As in general society, there has been a great increase in consciousness among Jewish women about achieving equality of opportunity in the leadership of the Jewish federations. In the last 15 years much progress has been made and most of the large-city Jewish federations and national organizations outside the federation have had at least one female president or chief voluntary officer. The same degree of progress has not yet been made on the professional side. There has never been a female chief executive of any large Jewish federation in the United States. One may expect that in the coming decade some breakthroughs will take place because of the degree of ferment on this issue.

CONCLUSIONS

Partly as a result of the alarming aspects of the 1990 NJPS findings, there is some feeling among a number of lay leaders in the Jewish community that a greater percentage of funds should be used for Jewish continuity at home instead of being sent to Israel. In support of this argument, as Israel's GNP grows and if peace becomes more secure, the emphasis on fundraising for Israel may be diminished, whereas the emphasis on Israel's economic development may be increased.

One conclusion is fairly certain: The Jewish federations are 100 years *young*. The most important and most glorious chapters in the Jewish federation history in the United States are yet to be written. Those of us who will be privileged to participate in the developments and changes that are anticipated are in for an exciting and fulfilling time.

REFERENCES

Bernstein, P. (1983). *To dwell in unity*. Philadelphia: Jewish Publication Society.
————. (1994). *The principles of Jewish federations*. New York: Council of Jewish Federations.
Elazar, D. J. (1976). *Community and polity: The organizational dynamics of American Jewry*. Philadelphia: Jewish Publication Society.
Miller, C. (1985). *An introduction to the Jewish federation*. New York: Council of Jewish Federations.

6

Jewish Religion in America

LAWRENCE GROSSMAN

The complex patterns of Jewish religious life in America at the end of the twentieth century are the product of confrontation between beliefs, attitudes, and practices that developed over millennia, with the forces of modernity as experienced in a distinctive American milieu. The challenges of modernity began to affect preexisting patterns of Jewish life in the West some 200 years ago—just around the time that the United States gained its independence—and today, on the eve of a new century, they show no sign of abating.

Premodern Judaism was based on traditions originating in the Hebrew Bible (canonized some 2000 years ago but containing material much older), as interpreted and developed over the centuries in rabbinic literature. Until the late-eighteenth century in Western and Central Europe, the mid-nineteenth century in Eastern Europe, and into the twentieth century in Islamic lands, the rabbis were the virtually undisputed religious authorities in the Jewish community, and Jews understood Judaism through the prism of rabbinic thought. Wherever Jews lived, they shared a number of common assumptions, values, and behavior patterns.[1]

JEWS AS EXTENDED FAMILY

Judaism is not simply a "religion" on the model of Christianity, Islam, or Buddhism. In addition to its theological and spiritual essence, it also has a national or ethnic dimension, which today is often characterized as "secular"—though the very concept of secularity is itself modern and would have had no meaning during Judaism's formative period. This national/ethnic component is an essential element of biblical theology: God promises Abraham, the first Jew, not that he will attain salvation, but that "I will make you a great nation" (Genesis XII, 2). The Bible portrays the Israelite people as the descendants of Abraham. Over the centuries, converts to Judaism came to be seen as "honorary" scions of the patriarchal clan: Jews-by-choice even today are called in Hebrew "son of Abraham" and "daughter of Sarah." Jews, then, constitute an extended family. Important practical implications flow from this fact.

Like members of a family, Jews are required to feel a sense of mutual obligation—thus the ramified network of Jewish philanthropic agencies that are, at one and the same time, the envy of other groups, but also the basis for the charge that Jews are "clannish."

Also, like members of a family, Jews who reject traditions of the group cannot be disowned; medieval rabbis, faced with the reality of Jewish converts to Christianity, decided: "Even though he has sinned, he remains a Jew." An echo of this is still felt today: While a Christian who denies Jesus or a Muslim who rejects the Koran can no longer be considered a member of the original faith, there are many "secular Jews" whose commitment is not to a God or a religious way of life but to the warmth and heritage of the "family."

Before the advent of modernity, with its novel emphasis on individual self-fulfillment, the existence of tightly knit Jewish communities cut off from social relations with the outside world reinforced the Jewish predilection to value kinship. Jews generally dressed in distinctively "Jewish" garb and spoke a "Jewish" dialect (the nature of which varied from region to region) among themselves. The threat of excommunication for deviant behavior (those excommunicated were still, of course, considered Jewish) was effective in maintaining community discipline, since the threat of social isolation from the community—in an age when there was no "nonsectarian" alternative—was almost unbearable.

COVENANT, HOLY PEOPLE, HOLY LAND

A central theme of the Hebrew Bible is that God made a series of covenants with Abraham and his descendants. Over and over, the patriarchs, and then the Israelites, are promised that if they fulfill certain conditions they will be blessed. The conditions are clear: Obedience to the moral and ritual laws of God. The blessing was equally clear, at least in biblical times: Possession of the Land of Israel, which will enjoy fruitfulness and peace. While the Bible never indicates why God selected this particular extended family, by entering into a covenant with this group, God made Israel his "chosen people." Premodern Jews were utterly untroubled by this expression, which they took literally. Many modern Jews have reinterpreted it to refer to a special Jewish mission to redeem the world.

In line with covenant theology, the destruction of the Holy Temple in Jerusalem by the Babylonians in 586 BCE and the exile of the Jews from the Land were interpreted as divine punishment for breaking the covenant, just as the return from exile 70 years later was understood as the divine response to Jewish repentance. The Roman destruction of the Second Temple in 70 CE was viewed as another manifestation of God's wrath at Israel's disobedience, and mourning over the Temple became a central theme of Judaism. Jewish liturgy, with its numerous pleas to God to restore His people to its ancient homeland, indicates that premodern Jews considered themselves only temporary residents in the countries where they lived. While religiously obligated to be loyal to the sovereign, these Jews had no conception of themselves as "Englishmen," for example, but as Jewish exiles residing in England on sufferance.

MESSIAH

The idea that history is not merely a series of endlessly repeating cycles but rather a cosmic drama that will come to a final climax was apparently first suggested by Judaism. In the later prophetic books of the Bible there are predictions of the coming of a messiah (literally, annointed one) descended from the royal house of David, who will gather all the exiled Jews back to their land, defeat Israel's enemies, and inaugurate a new era of peace and justice in the world. Tied in with this messianic coming will be a Judgment Day when the righteous will be rewarded and the wicked punished, and a resurrection of the dead.

While the influence of this Jewish eschatology on early Christian thought is unmistakable, Jewish speculation regarding the "end of days" was never as dogmatically formalized as it came to be in Christianity. Nevertheless, premodern Judaism would be unthinkable without it. The yearning for the messiah—understood literally by most Jews—combined with the promised return to the Holy Land is found in many classic Jewish prayers. So great was the messianic expectation that numerous "false messiahs" made claims to be the anticipated savior, only to end up disappointing their followers. The most famous was Shabbetai Zevi in the seventeenth century, whose ultimate conversion to Islam had a profoundly devastating effect on his many followers.

LAW AND STUDY

As noted above, Jews were obligated, under the covenant with God, to observe His laws. There are numerous such laws mentioned in the biblical books of Exodus, Leviticus, Numbers, and Deuteronomy; later rabbinic tradition had it that they totaled 613. Some of the Jewish regulations are common to most civilized peoples: Not to murder, steal, or oppress widows and orphans, to love one's neighbor, to act justly. Others commemorate momentous events in biblical history, such as the Sabbath, marking the culmination of God's creation of the world, and the Passover seder, signifying God's redemption of His people from bondage in Egypt. Yet other laws have to do with ritual—the kosher food regulations, laws of impurity, rules for the sacrifices in the desert tabernacle and later in the Temple.

The Bible prescribes that these laws must be studied. Though the precise historical details of the process remain hazy, the imperative of Jewish study grew in significance with the end of the Temple cult, as rabbinic culture supplanted priestly activity. Around the year 200 CE, rabbinic legal traditions were brought together in the form of the Mishnah, which then became the focus of attention for generations of scholars. The Talmud (the Palestinian version dates to about 400 CE, the Babylonian version a century later) is a voluminous and discursive commentary on the Mishnah, with a heavy admixture of homiletics, legends, and folklore. This genre of literature—to the virtual exclusion of all others—would occupy the minds of male Jews (women were excluded from formal study) for well over a thousand years, a situation that continues today in much of the Orthodox community.

This traditional Jewish commitment to learning was more than simply knowing the ritual or moral law in order to fulfill it properly. Study of sacred texts came to be seen as a religious value in itself, a primary means for attaining closeness to God. Over the years the corpus of the sacred literature grew, with commentaries and supercommentaries on Bible and Talmud, law codes and their commentaries, mystical works, and ethical treatises. And as long as Jews maintained their traditional society, the acquisition of Jewish learning gave a man status in the community.

THE SHOCK OF MODERNITY

Beginning imperceptibly in the seventeenth century and accelerating in the eighteenth—exactly when the colonies that would become the United States were being established—intellectual, economic, and social changes in Western and Central Europe undermined the Jewish status quo and set in motion the forces that would produce modern forms of Judaism. While these same shifts affected Christianity as well, the Jewish religion faced a unique challenge. Members of a ghettoized minority faith historically denigrated by the majority, Jews were sorely tempted to jettison large parts or even all of their religious heritage in order to share in a new world-view that seemed to break down barriers between peoples and open up unprecedented opportunities.[2]

For many educated people scientific explanation replaced theology. The great discoveries of the scientific revolution suggested that human reason, empirical inquiry, and mathematical analysis could account for the world we experience without recourse to the supernatural. And the critical approach to evidence that characterized the scientific method also began to be used to cast doubt upon the divine origin of the Bible. The fall-back position for many Christians was Deism, the belief that God rules through the means of the laws of nature and of reason. While there was a tradition of philosophic rationalism in Judaism, and Benedict Spinoza, an excommunicated Jew, was an intellectual godfather of Deism, traditional Judaism could hardly be reconciled with it. Neither the complex and seemingly arbitrary dictates of Jewish law nor the imaginative renderings of Jewish mysticism and legend fit easily into a religion of reason. And the traditional insistence that Jews shall be a "people that dwells alone" seemed to make little sense in a world governed by universal reason.

Economic change reinforced the breakdown of sharp distinctions between Jews and others. The localized economy of the Middle Ages gradually gave way to modern capitalism, which in theory—and to a great extent in practice—recognized no ethnic or religious barriers to the free flow of money and credit. The theory of liberal capitalism, that wealth is most efficiently created for society by the free enterprise of individual businessmen maximizing their profits, encouraged Jewish entrepreneurs to participate in the national economy on a par with others. That these Jews and their families came to see themselves as more and more akin to their Gentile counterparts, and less and less part of a distinctive Jewish community, was not surprising. They learned to speak the native language, dress in local costume, and appreciate the majority, non-Jewish culture.

The new intellectual atmosphere and changed economic circumstances set the stage for political innovations. Enlightenment thought, with its emphasis on reason and natural law, led political philosophers like John Locke to suggest that non-Christians, by virtue of their possession of reasoning powers, should be given political rights. (Locke, by the way, wrote a constitution for the colony of Carolina that indeed granted equality for Jews.) The increasing participation of Jewish businessmen in the economies of Western Europe added another incentive for the political emancipation of the Jews: By proving themselves useful to the larger society and willing to conform to at least some of its behavior standards, why bar them from citizenship? To be sure, centuries of Christian-inspired suspicion of Jews remained, and even many of the secularized, enlightened thinkers—Voltaire, for example—still harbored anti-Semitic stereotypes, but the general thrust of modernity was clear: Equality under the law for all people.

JEWS COME TO AMERICA

While the formal implementation of Jewish emancipation would not begin in Europe until the French Revolution of 1789 and the Napoleonic conquests that followed, Jews arriving in the North American colonies beginning in the mid-seventeenth century enjoyed a considerable degree of equality because in much of this new, sparsely settled frontier society there were too many different sects and denominations for any single one to establish authority. Early attempts to restrict Jewish economic activity and religious practice in some colonies proved futile. A number of the colonies had laws on the books restricting citizenship and voting rights to Christians (or even more strictly to Protestants) but these were rarely enforced with any rigor. The U.S. Constitution of 1787 barred any religious tests for federal officeholding, and the First Amendment to the Constitution guaranteed freedom of religion and—in a profound departure from European precedent—barred the new national government from establishing an official religion. Over time, restrictive state laws still on the books were removed. Jews in America, then, unlike their European cousins, did not require political emancipation. They were "born free," a fact that would profoundly affect the development of American Judaism.[3]

The earliest settlers were mostly Sephardi Jews (tracing back their ancestry to Spain or Portugal, often to families that had been forcibly converted to Catholicism). By the early eighteenth century these were outnumbered by Ashkenazi Jews (from German-speaking lands), but the newcomers assimilated to the Sephardi style of Judaism. Synagogue ritual was meticulously traditional, but individual religious behavior varied widely. In keeping with European precedent, each American community maintained only one official synagogue, run by a lay board. Since there were no ordained rabbis in the country, knowledgeable congregants conducted services.

It became evident quite early that the tightly knit, traditional form of Jewish community could not be transplanted to America. Fines and penalties meted out by communal authorities had no power to enforce standards of behavior in a land where freedom was an everyday reality even for Jews, and the openness of the larger society, where a Jew could blend-in without his religion even being noticed, rendered the threat of excommunication by the synagogue meaningless. And when the communal leadership attempted to assert the kind of monopolistic powers it had in Europe—preventing the establishment of new synagogues or asserting sole power over kashrut supervision, for example—the courts made it plain that separation of church and state meant that religious authority could not use the American legal system to stop anyone from doing anything.

The resulting paradox would recur repeatedly in the history of American Judaism, becoming in fact its central theme: The freedom that was so beneficial for Jews could be deadly for Judaism. True enough, synagogues sprouted in new areas of settlement as the frontier advanced and new synagogues multiplied in the older communities as Jews acted out their penchant for "breaking away" for social or political reasons and forming their own splinter congregations. At the same time, the individualism of American life in the early nineteenth century and the concomitant weakening of Jewish institutions brought a drastic decline in religious observance. This tendency was reinforced by the growing popularity of the American public school. The availability of free public education led to the demise of the Jewish schools previously supported by some of the larger congregations. Judaic literacy—taken for granted in traditional Judaism—became increasingly rare. Avid participants in the great American experiment, Jews sloughed off much of their Jewish identity. Disaffiliation escalated, and marriage to non-Jews became commonplace.

AMERICAN REFORM

A stream of Jewish immigrants from German-speaking lands, beginning in the 1820s and continuing until the Civil War, had a profound impact on American Judaism. First, it provided a demographic boost to a community that seemed on its way to extinction. Second, while it was the established Sephardi congregation of Charleston, South Carolina that first espoused "Reform" Judaism in the 1820s, it would be the German newcomers who would make this form of Judaism the primary American expression of the religion until well into the twentieth century.

Reform Judaism began in German cities that had been occupied by Napoleon, whose armies had broken down ghetto walls and granted Jews equality. Eager to retain their rights under the restored German regimes, early Jewish advocates of reform sought to bring Jewish life—and particularly the synagogue service—in line with contemporary notions of reverence and deportment. To merit full emancipation, they felt, Jews would have to shed the premodern habits that had developed in the ghetto: Decorum must replace informality during worship; German must take its place alongside Hebrew as a language of prayer and replace Yiddish—condemned as a mere "jargon"—as the language of conversation; organ music and regular sermons in German must become part of the services; and secular and vocational education must take priority over the study of religious texts. The reformers did not see themselves as distorting Judaism; on the contrary, they believed they were purifying the religion, enabling it to flourish under modern circumstances.[4]

Changes in practice were followed by criticism of the prayer book, and this in turn entailed challenges to doctrine. Virtually every principle of traditional Jewish theology was reexamined and revised. The old ghetto assumption that Judaism had an ethnic/national dimension was dropped or subordinated, since Jews were now—or, in some countries soon would be—equal citizens. Judaism came to be seen simply as a religion, and Jews were Germans, or Frenchmen, or Americans "of the Mosaic persuasion." Furthermore, the biblical covenant of God with the Israelites was reinterpreted to deemphasize traditional religious observances and highlight instead the mission of the Jews to spread monotheism and prophetic ethics to the world. Traditional Jewish law that had guided Jewish communities through centuries of exile was now superseded by the law of the land. And as good citizens, many Jews gave up any interest in an ultimate messianic "redemption" that included a return to the Holy Land; messianism was now to be understood, in line with the liberalism of the time, as a process whereby mankind progresses toward a future of peace and harmony.

In America, where most Jews had already shaken off the obligations of ritual observance, where there was no traditional rabbinic establishment that could counter innovation, and where—unlike Germany—Jews were accepted unreservedly as bona fide citizens, Reform Judaism enjoyed its greatest successes. Under the energetic leadership of Isaac Mayer Wise (1819–1900), who arrived in the United States from Bohemia in 1846 and served as rabbi in Cincinnati from 1854 until his death, an Americanized version of Reform spread rapidly, especially in the West and South. And Wise built institutions that he hoped would eventually represent all of American Jewry (hence the word "Reform" does not appear in their names): The Union of American Hebrew Congregations (UAHC) (1873); Hebrew Union College (HUC), a rabbinical seminary (1875); and the Central Conference of American Rabbis (1889).[5]

The first official theological pronouncement of American Reform—the work not of Wise, who was rather indifferent to theology, but of Rabbi Kaufmann Kohler of New York—came in 1885. Known as the Pittsburgh Platform because it emerged from a rabbinical conference in that city, it described Judaism as "the highest conception of the God-idea," a "progressive religion ever striving to be in accord with the postulates of reason." Biblical law—called "Mosaic legislation"—was understood as "a system of training the Jewish people for its mission during its national life in Palestine." Today, however, the moral laws were primary, plus "only such ceremonies as elevate and sanctify our lives." Specifically mentioned as irrelevant to modern sensibilities were regulations regarding eating, dress, and priestly purity. Asserting that Judaism was "no longer a nation," the document rejected any return to Palestine, reinauguration of the Jerusalem Temple, or "restoration of any of the laws concerning the Jewish state." The messianic age, which the platform defined as "the kingdom of truth, justice and peace among all men," was close to realization. In the meantime, Jews were obligated "to participate in the great task of modern times, to solve . . . the problems presented by the contrasts and evils of the present organization of society."[6]

By the end of the century Classical Reform, based on the universalistic, rational, optimistic creed of the Pittsburgh Platform, had crystallized. Since personal religious observances had virtually vanished, Reform practice was limited to the "temple"—Reformers did not like the old-fashioned ghetto connotations of the word "synagogue." The temple service was in English, with organ music. Neither head coverings nor prayer shawls were worn, and men and women sat together. A number of temples replaced Saturday prayer with Sunday services. The Reform movement reacted with outrage to the rise of political Zionism in the 1890s, seeing it as a revival of an atavistic Jewish nationalism that threatened the acceptance of Jews as equal citizens in the nations where they lived.[7]

THE EMERGENCE OF CONSERVATIVE JUDAISM

Although Isaac Mayer Wise's drive to spread Reform in America succeeded brilliantly, his hope that all American Jews would eventually rally behind the Reform banner did not come true. From the outset, there were traditionalist pockets of resistance to Reform initiatives. These were led by Isaac Leeser (1806–1868), a German-born layman who officiated as minister in the Philadelphia Sephardi congregation. A prolific writer who published English translations of the prayer book and the entire Hebrew Bible, and edited *The Occident*, the first successful Jewish periodical in the United States, Leeser tried at first to work together with Wise to create a unified American Jewish community, but the differences between reformer and traditionalist were too great. Leeser organized a rabbinical school in 1867, but his death the next year brought the venture to an end.

The clear drift of American Reform further away from tradition induced its opponents to organize. While the promulgation of the Pittsburgh Platform in

1885 was the last straw, an event two years earlier—the so-called *Trefa Banquet*—had made the break inevitable. At the dinner honoring Hebrew Union College's first graduating class, shellfish (prohibited by the kosher laws) was served, and the traditionalist guests walked out. In 1886, leading traditionalists met in New York City to found the Jewish Theological Seminary of America. This institution carefully distinguished itself from HUC by stressing adherence to Jewish law in addition to study.

Although the Jewish Theological Seminary (JTS) would become the central institution of what would become known as Conservative Judaism, the roots of that movement trace back to Europe.

Reform was not the only religious response to the onset of modernity and the promise of emancipation in Central Europe. A movement known as Positive-Historical Judaism also developed, which agreed with Reform that changes were necessary in Jewish life to meet the new circumstances, but that Jewish ritual law, not only the moral law, retains its binding character. That law, however, could be adapted to changed circumstances through a process of interpretation. It was argued that previous generations of Jews had done exactly this, albeit without the historical self-consciousness of the nineteenth century. Learned European Jews who espoused this approach studied the texts of the Jewish tradition using the tools of modern scientific scholarship on the assumption that an accurate understanding of how the religion changed in the past would provide guidance for legitimate change in the present and future.[8]

It was this ideology, with its emphasis on traditional practice in alliance with objective, high-level scholarship, that came to animate the Jewish Theological Seminary in New York, especially after the accession to the presidency in 1902 of Solomon Schechter (1847–1915), a world-renowned rabbinic scholar. Schechter gathered a distinguished faculty and made the Seminary a world-class center of Jewish scholarship.

But a seminary does not make a movement. In fact, the mass constituency for the nascent Conservative movement—the children of the millions of East European Jews who arrived in America between the 1880s and World War I—had little knowledge of, and even less interest in, the scholarly work done at the Seminary. Eager to escape the immigrant slums they grew up in, to Americanize, and attain to middle-class respectability, relatively few of these Jews identified with the Old-World Judaism of their parents. Yet Reform temples did not draw many of them either, since the lack of Hebrew, the truncated service, the organ music, the austere architecture, the lack of a sense of Jewish peoplehood or appreciation of Jewish folk-culture seemed forbiddingly un-Jewish to those who were but one generation removed from the shtetl. But the steadily growing circle of synagogues served by graduates of the Jewish Theological Seminary—organized in 1913 as the United Synagogue of America—fit their needs.

These synagogues, increasingly called "Conservative" to differentiate them from Reform temples on the one hand, and Old-World-style Orthodox congregations on the other, held on to enough of the Jewish tradition to make second-generation Jews feel at home, but not so much as to interfere with modern American values. The prayer service was basically traditional, in Hebrew, with English responsive readings. Men wore head coverings and prayer shawls, but the rabbi, who was clean-shaven, would preach in English, often on topics of the day. In the great majority of such congregations men and women sat together and the rabbi and cantor used a microphone; organ music was rare but not unknown. The Conservative synagogue became especially popular in new areas of Jewish settlement, which meant, after World War II, the suburbs of large cities. Rabbis and lay leaders were optimistic that this Conservative synthesis of tradition and innovation was not simply the beginning of a new denomination, but would soon become the quintessential American form of traditional Judaism as the immigrant generation that clung to European forms passed from the scene.[9]

Relations between Conservative congregations, their rabbis, and the Seminary faculty were ambiguous and often strained. For one thing, the level of personal observance among Conservative Jews did not resemble the traditional Judaism preached by the rabbis. Only a minority of Conservative Jews lived by the Sabbath laws—still officially espoused by the movement—and many kept kosher only at home. Furthermore, the Seminary scholars, most of them highly traditional in personal behavior, did not sanction the deviations from accepted Jewish practice that developed de facto in the movement. Symbolic of this gap was the maintenance of the traditional separation between men and women in the Seminary synagogue, while mixed seating prevailed in Conservative synagogues around the country. Official Conservative ideology held that objective Jewish scholarship would indicate the parameters of valid religious change, but for years no such guidance was forthcoming from the Seminary. Complicating matters further, the professors there expressed an academic bias verging on contempt not only toward the ordinary, uneducated laymen, but against pulpit rabbis, and this led many graduates to feel both inadequate and resentful.[10]

The transformation of American Jewry from a community of Central European lineage to one predominantly East European in origin also affected Reform. Recognizing that its rather abstract emphasis on theology and its untraditional services attracted neither the new immigrants nor many of their children, and influenced by a new generation of Reform rabbis, many of whom had been brought up in religiously traditional or ethnically Jewish homes, Classical Reform began to adapt to the changing community. In 1937 it adopted the Columbus Platform. While still citing "the doctrine of the One, living God" as the core of Jewish identity, it did acknowledge "the group-loyalty of Jews" who were not religious. And, moving away from its old negative attitude toward ritual practice and ethnic expression, the document spoke affirmatively of "the preservation of the Sabbath, festivals, and Holy Days," and "the cultivation of distinctive forms of religious art and music, the use of Hebrew, together with the vernacular, in our worship and instruction." Noteworthy, too, was a more positive attitude toward Zionism. "Many of our brethren," the platform noted, would "behold the promise of renewed life" in a rehabilitated Palestine, and Jews were therefore obligated "to aid in its upbuilding . . . to make it not only a haven of refuge for the oppressed but also a center of Jewish culture and spiritual life." [11]

But even this reorientation was not enough to win the loyalty of the younger generation. By the 1930s, Reform had been replaced by Conservatism as the most popular form of American Judaism—a situation that would continue till the 1960s.

ORTHODOXY AMERICANIZES

Just as Classical Reform had been wrong in assuming that it was the wave of the future, so Conservatism erred in assuming that it was the only form of traditional Judaism that could survive in America. There were American Jews in the late-nineteenth and early twentieth centuries—mostly from the ranks of the newest immigrants—who felt that the Jewish Theological Seminary, its rabbis, and their congregations had departed too far from age-old Jewish practice and belief.

Orthodox Judaism as an ideology emerged in early nineteenth-century Germany among traditionalist Jews who opposed the changed advocated by Reform. In fact, the term "Orthodox" seems originally to have been coined by Reformers as a pejorative epithet. By mid-century, under the leadership of Samson Raphael Hirsch (1808–1888), there developed what became known as "neo-Orthodoxy" in Germany, which maintained a stance of resistance to religious change while embracing Westernization in dress, language, and culture. There were relatively few German-Orthodox Jews in America in the nineteenth century, and—since there was as yet no clear distinction between "Orthodox" and "Conservative"—they tended to associate with the anti-Reform forces that built the Jewish Theological Seminary. Indeed, the first national organization of Orthodox synagogues, the Union of Orthodox Jewish Congregations of America (founded 1898), was supported by many of the same people who backed the Seminary.

Orthodoxy in Eastern Europe was quite different. Jews there were not yet legally emancipated, and even among those acculturated enough to demand equal rights, relatively few yearned for acceptance as Poles or Russians, and Reform had made no inroads to speak of. In Eastern Europe, Orthodoxy mobilized at the end of the century to fight a different enemy: The secularization of the Jewish community at the hands of socialists, assimilationists, and Zionists. When such Orthodox Jews arrived in America, the cultural modernity of the "traditional" Jewish Theological Seminary looked hardly more acceptable than outright Reform.

There is, in fact, considerable scholarly disagreement over the "Orthodoxy" of the large waves of East European Jews who came to the United States beginning in the 1880s. At the time, their Old-World looks and manners identfed them as Orthodox in the eyes of Jewish and non-Jewish observers. But the

swiftness with which many of the immigrants jettisoned hallowed laws and traditions under the pressure of economic necessity and social pressure—working
on the Sabbath, men cutting off earlocks, married women discarding wigs—and
the haphazard Jewish education most gave to their children have led some
scholars to conclude that their "Orthodoxy" was more social than religious. It
was not, after all, mainly the rabbis and scholars nor the more Jewishly serious
laymen who came; they, heeding the warnings of their spiritual leaders that
ungodly America would undermine their Judaism, tended to stay put. Most of
the Jews who did come were marginal: Those who had the least to lose in terms
of social status and economic class and those least rooted in the old religious
way of life.[12]

To be sure, the congregations that these immigrants founded looked like
transplants from the old home: Small, intimate synagogues, many of them
organized by people who came from the same town or region in Europe. And
large numbers of these Jews tried—despite the economic problems involved—
to keep up the traditional Sabbath and holidays, and to observe the kosher laws.
They even attempted to replicate the system of rabbinic authority they were
used to: A community rabbi who was responsible for all aspects of Jewish religious life in a town, and whose major source of income came from supervising
kosher food suppliers. Slowly, traditionally trained rabbis began to arrive to fill
these posts. (This proved impossible in New York City, the largest community,
where disunity doomed an effort to establish a unified community rabbinate in
the 1880s.) In 1902, these Orthodox rabbis—all of them born and trained in
Europe and all Yiddish-speaking—formed the first Orthodox rabbinical organization in the country, Agudath Harabbonim (Union of Orthodox Rabbis). But
the institution of communal "chief rabbi" in America was only a pale shadow of
its European model, in which the rabbi functioned as both legal authority and
quasi-government official. Once again, the openness and individualism of
American society and the separation of church and state that made religion
purely voluntary altered the shape of Judaism, stripping these learned rabbis of
their old sources of power and prestige and rendering their authority more hon-
orific than real.[13]

With the rise of a second, American-born generation at the beginning of
the twentieth century, the weakness of this nominally "Orthodox" community
became evident, as the increasingly acculturated, public-school-educated
youngsters deserted the "old-fashioned" synagogue in droves. This was the
phenomenon that encouraged the embryonic Conservative movement in its
aspiration to appropriate the banner of traditional Judaism in America. But it
also provided impetus for the Orthodox to make adjustments in order to hold
on to their children.

A significant step in the Americanization of the Orthodox synagogue was the
establishment of the Young Israel movement in 1912. Without in any way altering the basics of the traditional service, Young Israel synagogues (with the help,
ironically, of rabbis associated with the Jewish Theological Seminary) instituted
changes that appealed to the American-born generation: Decorum, congrega-

tional singing, the encouragement of young people to lead services, the elimination of announcing monetary contributions in return for synagogue honors, English-language adult education, and greater participation of women. The original Young Israel on the Lower East Side of New York City was soon joined by others, and the movement became national in scope. And many Orthodox synagogues outside the Young Israel orbit adopted similar innovations.[14]

Around the same time, an Americanizing trend developed in Orthodox education. A small, European-style rabbinical school in New York City, the Rabbi Isaac Elhanan Seminary, instituted a secular high-school program in 1916, largely under pressure from students who felt that, unlike the case in Europe, they could not function in America as rabbis, or indeed as ordinary Orthodox Jews, with only a traditional Jewish education. In 1925, under the leadership of Rabbi Dr. Bernard Revel (1885–1940), this institution opened a college as well. This new Yeshiva College—which, with the later addition of graduate schools, would become Yeshiva University—developed into a training ground for a new type of Orthodox rabbi: Fluent in the English language, conversant with wordly knowledge, dressed in modern garb, and yet committed to Orthodoxy and learned in its sacred books. The hope was that such rabbis could successfully compete with their counterparts in the Conservative movement for the allegiance of American-born traditional Jews.[15] In 1935 the Rabbinical Council of America was organized to represent these modern Orthodox rabbis.

This form of Orthodoxy, originating in the practical need to draw the younger American generation, received its theological legitimacy from Rabbi Joseph B. Soloveitchik (1903–1993), who taught at Yeshiva University from 1941 till 1984. Heir to a leading dynasty of Lithuanian Talmudic scholars, Soloveitchik also had an extensive secular education capped by a doctorate degree in philosophy from the University of Berlin. Since he was acknowledged as a Talmudic genius even by the antimodernist rabbinic circles that disdained all study that was outside the parameters of Jewish tradition, Soloveitchik functioned as a role model for those American Jews who wanted to believe that they could live Orthodox lives while participating in the real world of the twentieth century.

KAPLAN AND RECONSTRUCTIONISM

Reconstructionist Judaism, which still struggles today to establish itself as a "fourth movement" in American Jewry alongside Orthodoxy, Conservatism, and Reform, is the only stream within American Judaism whose roots are totally American and whose principles were the work of one man—Mordechai Kaplan (1881–1983). Brought up as an Orthodox Jew in a rabbinical family on the Lower East Side of New York City, Kaplan was ordained at the Jewish Theological Seminary. He abandoned Orthodoxy as a result of his studies in the social sciences. While serving on the Seminary faculty, Kaplan developed Reconstructionism, a system best described in his 1934 book, *Judaism as a*

Civilization. Kaplan rejected supernaturalism, biblical revelation, messianism, and the doctrine of the chosen people as incompatible with modern thought. Yet he sought to restore the old, premodern, collective Jewish identity that had been shattered by individualism. To do this, he suggested that Jewish peoplehood, not religion, be seen as the core of Jewish identification, thus substituting what we call today ethnicity (though he did not use that term) for faith in a supernatural Being. On that basis, Kaplan tried to reorganize the institutions of American Jewish life—synagogues, schools, Jewish centers—so that American Jewry might function as an organic community.[16]

Kaplan faced rejection and even attack from many sides. The institutions of Reform Judaism, still unenthusiastic about the notion that Jews were a people and not just a religion, could not accept his sociological approach. The Orthodox decried his abandonment of tradition; the Union of Orthodox Rabbis even "excommunicated" Kaplan after he published an innovative prayer book. And his colleagues at the Jewish Theological Seminary, committed as they were to traditional Jewish law, were appalled at his radicalism, and some sought to have him dismissed. In 1954 Kaplan finally gave up hope of capturing the Conservative movement, and his followers launched an independent movement, founding the Reconstructionist Federation of Congregations. A Reconstructionist Rabbinical College was established in Philadelphia in 1968, and a Reconstructionist Rabbinical Association in 1974.

Reconstructionism remained a small but influential movement. Its honest confrontation with twentieth-century thought attracted considerable enthusiasm from Jewish intellectuals, and influenced the thinking of many Reform and Conservative rabbis who admired Kaplan and his vision of Jewish life, but did not officially join the movement.[17]

POSTWAR JUDAISM

The decade of the 1940s marked a watershed in Jewish religious life, though it would take two decades and more before this was fully recognized.

The experience of World War II and the Holocaust, as well as the establishment of the first Jewish state in nearly 2,000 years, would come to have profound theological repercussions for serious Jews. Holocaust commemoration and support for Israel would become integral elements of Jewish religious life. The evidence of the death camps would put an end to secularized messianism, Jewish belief in the inevitable perfectibility of mankind, a notion deeply rooted in Classical Reform and found in the other denominations as well. The Holocaust would also call into question Jewish universalism, the tendency among all sectors of American Jewry except the most insularly Orthodox to minimize Jewish distinctiveness while emphasizing what Jews have in common with other Americans. After all, Hitler had singled out the Jews for death, and the world had stood by. Perhaps the lesson was that Jews were indeed a "people that dwells alone," one that could not rely on the goodwill of others. This conviction was reinforced for many American Jews by what seemed like the miraculous emergence of the State of Israel in 1948. In dramatic counterpart to the helplessness of Hitler's victims, the creators of the Jewish state had taken their fate into their own hands. For the first time since the dawn of the European Enlightenment, the key challenge for Judaism—American Judaism emphatically included—would no longer be finding a way to fit into Western society, but devising means to maintain a clear Jewish distinctiveness while remaining part of that society.[18]

But in the decade of the 1950s these long-range trends were not yet spotted. Indeed, the Jewish urge to Americanize, made easier by economic prosperity and the fall of old anti-Semitic barriers that had limited Jewish participation in important sectors of the economy, was stronger than ever. After all, Judaism—a tiny religion when compared to Protestantism and Catholicism—was now given public recognition as one of America's three great faiths. Jewish movement to the suburbs accelerated, and with it the construction of many new synagogue buildings and a rise in synagogue membership. Neither contemporary observers nor later scholars saw such trends as signs of true religious revival. Rather, Jews were conforming to the broader national association of religious affiliation with Americanism, and their synagogues were used less for prayer and study than for social purposes. Many of the Jewish children raised in these suburbs would come to reject what they considered the hypocritical Judaism of their parents.[19]

Institutionally, both Reform and Conservative Judaism prospered. In 1947, Hebrew Union College, the training school for Reform rabbis located in Cincinnati, merged with the Jewish Institute of Religion (founded by maverick Reform Rabbi Stephen Wise) in New York, and the combined institution maintained both campuses; seven-years later a third branch was opened in Los Angeles. The trauma of the Holocaust tipped the balance within Reform decidedly in the direction of support for a Jewish state. In 1942, Reform Jews uncomfortable with the movement's increasing warmth toward Zionism founded the American Council for Judaism, which continued to argue the Classical Reform position that Judaism has no national dimension. The emergence of the State of Israel as a *fait accompli* in 1948 weakened the Council considerably. For all intents and purposes, Reform Jewry had been Zionized.[20]

Soon after the end of World War II Reform became heavily involved in social-justice issues. In doing so, it saw itself as fulfilling the biblical prophetic mandate to help the weak and provide justice to the oppressed. At a time when anti-Communism was riding high, Reform took a principled stand in favor of civil liberties. The movement opened a Religious Action Center in Washington in 1961 to coordinate social-action programs. The civil-rights movement received strong support from Reform Jews, many of them giving large sums of money to fund civil-rights organizations and participating personally in civil-rights marches. A number of Reform rabbis in the South spoke out bravely against racial segregation. Reform leaders were among the first to challenge the escalation of the war in Vietnam. In taking these stands, Reform Judaism clearly placed itself on the political left.[21]

Meanwhile, Conservative Judaism was growing strongly, continuing the process that had begun before the War. From 1945 to 1960 the number of Conservative synagogues jumped from 350 to 800. The movement started a highly successful network of summer camps called Ramah, and a somewhat less successful network of Solomon Schechter day schools. A branch of the Jewish Theological Seminary was founded in Los Angeles in 1947, called the University of Judaism.

Still targeting the Americanized children of Orthodox parents, Conservative Judaism for the first time—through its Committee on Jewish Law and Standards—started issuing decisions on Jewish law that eased some of the more onerous restrictions and ended some perceived inequities imposed by Orthodox Jewish law. In the 1940s a clause was inserted in the Conservative marriage contract that made it more difficult for a recalcitrant husband to deny his civilly divorced wife a *get,* a Jewish divorce. In 1950 Conservative Jews were allowed to drive to synagogue services on the Sabbath, a Sabbath violation in the eyes of the Orthodox. This move reflected the reality that few suburban Jews lived close enough to the synagogue to be able to walk. A 1954 decision gave women the right be called up to the Torah, and beginning in 1973 women could be counted for the *minyan,* the quorum of ten people needed for communal prayer. Taken together, these steps began to clarify what had previously been a rather vague distinction between modern Orthodox and Conservative practices.[22]

It was Orthodox Judaism that underwent the most surprising change in the postwar period. Unable, despite its acculturated, English-speaking rabbis, to capture the allegiance of many American-born Jews, Orthodoxy found itself on the defensive through the 1940s and 1950s. For example, many Orthodox rabbis had no choice but to make their peace with men and women sitting together in family pews in the synagogue, despite the tradition against it, because they feared that the congregation would switch its affiliation to the Conservative movement if they showed no flexibility. (Yeshiva University, bowing to reality, allowed its rabbinic graduates to take such pulpits if there was a realistic chance of ultimately instituting separate seating.) And while no official Orthodox approbation of driving to the synagogue on the Sabbath was forthcoming, de facto acceptance of the practice was evidenced by filled parking lots. To avoid the opprobrium that was widely felt toward Orthodoxy, some of these synagogues went so far as to call themselves "traditional" rather than Orthodox.

But at the same time, a new wave of immigrants was both reinforcing and transforming American Orthodoxy. These were the rabbis and scholars of Eastern Europe, uprooted by the horrors of the Holocaust, who found their way to America. Among them were leaders of hasidic sects (the rebbes of Lubavitch and Satmar are the best known) as well as prominent heads and promising students of the great Lithuanian yeshivas (Rabbi Aharon Kotler, founder of a yeshiva in Lakewood, New Jersey, and Rabbi Moshe Feinstein preeminent among them). Uninfluenced, indeed repelled, by a modernity they associated with a threatening non-Jewish world, they were unprepared to compromise with it.

At first—in the late 1940s and through the 1950s—these newcomers were viewed as a curiosity and nothing more. By the 1960s, however, they were taken much more seriously as it became evident that they were successfully withstanding the pressures of acculturation. Previously, all religious expressions of Judaism in America, even—albeit reluctantly—the Orthodox, had deemed it essential to accommodate contemporary mores to survive. But for the newcomers, it seemed that their very refusal to compromise with the outside world enabled them to thrive.[23]

The refusal to Americanize took many forms. One was outward appearance: Full beards and long black coats for men, "modest" clothing for women—and covered heads for married women. Another was language: While basic English proficiency was deemed necessary for interaction with the non-Jewish environment, Yiddish was retained for communicating within the family and community. The synagogue life of the newly arrived Orthodox was also distinctive: Prayer was intense and informal, as Western notions of decorum that had been adopted by earlier American Orthodoxy were ignored. But the most important factor was cultural: These Orthodox Jews saw themselves as separate and apart from American society and, in certain respects, from the rest of American Jewry as well. They tended to live in enclaves where their exposure to foreign values could be minimized. Television and the movies were shunned. While countenancing secular education to the extent that it prepared one to earn a living, the ideal male role-model was the Talmudic scholar. Women, given a far less rigorous grounding in Jewish tradition than men, were expected to fulfill themselves as wives and mothers—families of ten or more children were not uncommon.[24]

To be sure, the refusal to modernize was selective, not total. For one thing, unlike such groups as the Amish, Orthodox Jews have no religious objection to new technology. Thus employment in emerging fields like computers helped solidify the economic base of the community. Furthermore, while culturally isolationist, these Orthodox quickly caught on to the intricacies of the American political system and utilized the ballot box to protect their interests. Agudath Israel of America, which had been around since the 1920s as the American branch of a worldwide, antimodernist Orthodox movement, took on a new life in the 1960s as a potent lobbying group in Washington and on the state and local levels for the sectarian Orthodox. Public relations was another modern tool that these Orthodox Jews learned to use with great skill. In 1963, Agudath Israel began publication of the *Jewish Observer,* a glossy and well-written English monthly that conveyed the anti-acculturation message through a contemporary medium.

The primary complaint that the more rigorous Orthodox had about the modern Orthodox was the latter's participation in umbrella organizations of a religious nature together with non-Orthodox denominations, such as local boards of rabbis and the Synagogue Council of America, set up in 1926 to represent the common interests of Orthodox, Conservative, and Reform Judaism. Orthodox participation, the more rigorous Orthodox charged, granted unwarranted legitimacy to heterodox versions of Judaism. In 1956, ten heads of rabbinical semi-naries issued an edict forbidding membership in such bodies. Believing that withdrawal from umbrella organizations amounted to a policy of isolationism that would jeopardize gains that Orthodoxy had made through involvement with the other denominations, the modern Orthodox, under the leadership of Rabbi Soloveitchik, ignored the ban. In the years that followed, separatist Orthodoxy kept up a barrage of criticism against the moderates, even going so far as to charge that failure to distance oneself from non-Orthodox rabbis cast doubt on one's Orthodox credentials.

THE UPHEAVAL OF THE SIXTIES

The Jewish optimism of the 1950s, shallowly based as it was on institution-al growth alone, came under serious question in the 1960s. A number of com-munity-demographic surveys that indicated a rising rate of intermarriage and dis-affiliation was confirmed for American Jewry as a whole by the National Jewish Population Study, carried out by the Council of Jewish Federations in 1971.[25] While in retrospect it is clear that the increased postwar acceptance of Jews in educational institutions and places of employment where they previously had no entree made this virtually inevitable, the Jewish community reacted to the evi-dence of demographic erosion—broadcast by *Look* magazine in 1964 in an arti-cle about "The Vanishing American Jew"—with dismay.

Toward the end of the 1960s and well into the 1970s the involvement of young Jews in radical causes far out-of-proportion to their numbers provided another cause for communal concern. Reflecting the anti-institutional ethos of the time, many of the Jewish activists demonstrating for civil rights and against the Vietnam War were openly contemptuous of mainstream American Judaism and the way they had been brought up as Jews.

Declining numbers and alienated young people were proof that convention-al suburban Judaism could not sustain American Jewry. To replace it, many Jews strove to make Judaism more spiritual, more socially relevant, or both.

Thus the most important Jewish religious phenomenon of this period was the loosely organized *Havurah* ("Fellowship") movement. Abandoning the formal structure of synagogue and rabbi, small groups of well-educated Jews in their twenties and thirties, mostly of Conservative background, would meet together regularly for study, prayer, and social action. (The first of these began in Somerville, Massacusetts, in 1968.) While the individual *havurot* had different emphases, they generally stressed intense spirituality, intellectually sophisticated wrestling with classic Jewish texts, and the application of Judaism to progessive social causes—things the members felt had been lacking in the religion they had been taught. Suspicious of hierarchy, each *havurah* was a society of equals in which everyone would share rabbinic, cantorial, and teaching functions.

Although the movement was criticized for sacrificing Jewish institutional imperatives for the sake of individual religious satisfaction, the *havurot* suc-ceeded in establishing an alternative structure for the expression of Judaism. As a result, a number of non-Orthodox synagogues adapted the *havurah* model to their own situation: Within the larger congregation, small groups would constitute themselves as *havurot,* and thus provide the intimacy of the fellowship within a larger communal context.

The *havurah* movement also had broader ramifications. The immensely popular and influential *Jewish Catalogs* (three were eventually published by the Jewish Publication Society), guides to a practical, politically progressive "do-it-yourself" Judaism, emanated from *havurah* circles and expressed its ethos. Also, the equal participation of women in *havurot,* coming at a time when feminism was beginning to exert a potent influence on American culture, allowed for the first time the articulation of the special religious concerns—practical, liturgical, and theological—of Jewish women.[26]

RESURGENT REFORM

In the aftermath of the 1960s, Reform, the least traditional branch of American Judaism and therefore the most vulnerable to outside cultural influences, has been profoundly influenced by the proliferation of mixed marriages. The movement's rabbis are split over the question of rabbinic officiation, or co-officiation together with non-Jewish clergy. Some believe that Jewish marriage is inappropriate where one party is not Jewish. Others suggest that refusal to officiate is likely to alienate the couple, while officiation increases the likelihood that the bride and groom will maintain a Jewish connection and raise the children as Jews. To complicate matters, among those rabbis who would not themselves participate in a mixed-marriage ceremony, many had no compunction about referring such couples to more liberal rabbinic colleagues. And never far from the surface is the allegation that mixed-marriage performers are in it for the money: The law of supply and demand enables a rabbi to charge far more to officiate at a mixed marriage than at an endogamous one. The matter was brought before the Central Conference of American Rabbis in 1973, and a three-to-two majority passed a resolution stating "opposition to participation by its members in any ceremony which solemnizes a mixed marriage."[27]

But no sanctions were spelled out for those rabbis who did perform intermarriages, and their numbers have grown over the years. To some extent, lay pressure played a role, as members of congregational search-committees, eager to ensure that their own children would have Jewish marriages even should they decide to intermarry, tended to hire rabbis expressing a willingness to officiate at such weddings. The Rabbinic Center for Research and Counseling, founded in 1970 to represent the Reform rabbis who officiate at mixed marriages, conducts periodic surveys of the Reform rabbinate's attitudes on the issue, and they appear to indicate that the official restrictive policy of the movement is fast becoming a dead letter in many parts of the country. Yet, despite considerable debate, that official position has not yet been reversed.

Another Reform response to the proliferation of mixed marriages has been the "outreach" initiative first enunciated in the late 1970s by Rabbi Alexander

Schindler, the president of the Union of American Hebrew Congregations. Ostensibly directed at interesting "unchurched" Americans in joining the Jewish faith, its actual intention was to win over the non-Jewish spouses and children in mixed marriages for Judaism through specially targeted educational and social programs that would ultimately lead to conversion. Some exponents of this strategy have suggested that intermarriage should not be viewed pessimistically as a problem in need of a solution, but rather optimistically, as an opportunity to enhance Jewish numbers. In adopting outreach, of course, Reform Judaism went counter to the traditional Jewish reluctance to seek converts.

While such outreach programs often did result in the conversion of non-Jewish spouses, in other cases the outcome was the Jewish affiliation of mixed-married families in which one parent remained Gentile. This raised the sensitive question of what role these non-Jews should play: Might they be temple members or officers? Might they receive religious honors? If yes, was there any distinction between Jew and non-Jew? If no, was this not a humiliating exclusion? Each Reform congregation devised its own policy, with the great majority permitting at least membership for the spouse.

Despite the problems, the idea of outreach to the intermarried quickly spread beyond Reform, since it gave some hope of arresting demographic erosion. Increasingly, Jewish federations across the country have been funding outreach projects in synagogues, Jewish community centers, and other sites.[28]

Rabbi Schindler then led the Reform movement into a far more controversial policy—patrilineal descent. In traditional Jewish law the religion of the mother determines the religious status of the child: The son or daughter of a Jewish mother is Jewish, irrespective of the father's religion, but the child of a non-Jewish mother is not Jewish, even if the father is, unless that child is converted. Since the great majority of mixed marriages were between Jewish men and non-Jewish women, most offspring of these marriages were non-Jews, unless conversion took place. To ease the barrier to the identification of these children as Jews, the Reform acceptance of patrilineal descent—adopted in 1983 after several years of heated debate—meant that one was a Jew if either parent was Jewish, and the individual took active steps—not specifically defined—to identify him or herself as a Jew. This change was justified historically on the grounds that the matrilineal criterion was postbiblical.

The patrilineal-descent decision has had complex ramifications. Predictably, it aroused criticism in Orthodox and Conservative circles for unilaterally altering the age-old criterion for establishing Jewishness, and thereby creating a population considered Jewish by Reform but not by the more traditional branches. This has raised numerous practical difficulties on the local level: Should patrilineal Jews be accepted into Jewish institutions, such as communally supported schools, Jewish community centers, and old-age homes? What about burial in Jewish cemeteries? To be sure, as Reform leaders were quick to note, the Orthodox had never recognized Reform conversions anyway, so that the decision to eliminate the need for such conversions if the father was Jewish was hardly as revolutionary as it seemed.[29]

But patrilineal descent does seem to have precipitated a drop in conversions to Judaism: Those born of Jewish fathers were now considered Jews with no need to convert, and non-Jewish wives of Jews, knowing that their children would be Jews in any case, no longer felt the need to convert "for the sake of the children." Critics of the patrilineality decision, both within and outside Reform, have argued that the experience of undergoing a formal conversion is likely to leave a more lasting Jewish impression on the family than no conversion or the patrilineal conferral of "automatic" Jewishness, with only a vague requirement of positive Jewish actions.

There are Reform rabbis who deplore the breakdown of a universally recognized standard of Jewishness because it can lead to the human tragedy of a patrilineal Jew not being able to marry a Conservative or Reform Jew, whose denomination does not recognize the patrilineal as Jewish. Feeling an obligation to make sure that all Reform Jews are accepted by the other denominations, these rabbis advise patrilineal Jews in their congregations to undergo the same conversion as their standard converts, which, in the case of these rabbis, comes complete with immersion in a *mikvah* (ritual bath) and certification by a sympathetic, local Orthodox rabbi.

The decision on patrilineality has created tensions between American Reform and its counterparts elsewhere, notably Canada, Europe, and Israel, where Reform (sometimes called "Progressive") Judaism is more traditional than in the United States. In Israel, Reform's campaign for government recognition and funding has been seriously damaged by American Reform's acceptance of patrilineal Jewishness, which appears radical even to secular Israeli Jews.

While there is little chance that Reform will reverse its stand on patrilineality, there have been recent signs that the movement is recognizing that there are limits to outreach. In many mixed-religion families—whether the mother is Jewish and the children are undoubtedly Jews, or whether the father is Jewish and the children are patrilineal Jews—those children are often exposed to two religions. In a historic 1995 decision, the Reform movement declared that no child who is also being educated in another faith may be enrolled in a Reform educational program. Although it remains unclear how strictly this limitation will be implemented, its very promulgation elicited strong protests from those who considered it a betrayal of the openness of the movement.

It is undeniable, however, that Reform outreach, capped by the decision on patrilineality, has had an energizing effect on Reform as a movement. The influx of new Reform Jews—patrilineal, converted, and also unconverted spouses who join Reform temples—played a major role in a Reform resurgence, helping make Reform the leading Jewish denomination. The 1990 National Jewish Population Survey indicated that self-identified Reform Jews (42.4 percent of American Jews), had surpassed self-identified Conservative Jews (37.8 percent of American Jews).[30] The swelling numbers, however, did not necessarily measure depth of commitment. The fact that, even with this Reform surge, a greater percentage of American-synagogue members were Conservative rather than Reform seemed to suggest that, for many, Reform identification was little more than an admission that one was a nominal, non-practicing Jew.

The movement is well aware of this weakness. Reform rabbis have demonstrated serious concern about the low level of Jewish observance among the laity, and have sought ways to disabuse Reform Jews of the widespread assumption that Reform makes no ritual demands on its adherents. But rabbinic attempts to prescribe standards of observance have been consistently frustrated by Reform's historic commitment to individual autonomy.

Nevertheless, the contemporary search for spirituality that affects many Americans of all or no religious affiliation, and which first impacted on Jews through the *havurah* phenomenon, is influencing Reform Jews as well. Periodic surveys taken by the Union of American Hebrew Congregations show a growing interest in Jewish ritual and custom, especially among the young. Use of Hebrew in the services, wearing a prayer shawl and covering the head during prayer, adherence to the laws of kashrut at synagogue functions, reciting the *hamotzi* blessing over bread and the *havadala* service after the Sabbath, are on the rise. Paradoxically, the movement whose outreach program brought a revolutionary new definition of Jewishness has simultaneously traced a path back to tradition, at least for those of its members who opt to take it. And this trend in the movement is likely to intensify. Rabbi Eric Yoffe, who replaced Rabbi Schindler as president of the UAHC in 1996, has made Torah study and "the poetry of faith" his priorities.[31]

At the same time, Reform maintains the enthusiasm for progressive social causes that has animated the movement since the 1950s. Outspokenly feminist, American Reform broke its last religious taboo against women when it ordained its first female rabbi in 1972. It has also championed the freedom of women to choose abortions. In this and on many other social and economic policy issues, Reform's positions still tend to coincide with contemporary liberalism and the left wing of the Democratic party.

A case in point is gay rights. While Jews have traditionally rejected homosexuality on the basis of the biblical ban on it as an "abomination," Jewish gays and their supporters have argued that this should now be considered obsolete, either because it refers only to coerced or idolatrous sexual practices, or because the Bible assumed that sexual preference was a matter of free will, whereas contemporary science (allegedly) shows that it is not. In 1990, after four years of study and debate, the Central Conference of American Rabbis declared that all Jews are equal regardless of sexual orientation, and that gays and lesbians might be ordained as rabbis. Five years later it endorsed civil marriage for homosexuals, but reserved *kiddushin,* the sanctification of a Jewish marriage, for heterosexual couples. Nevertheless, it has become increasingly common for Reform rabbis to perform "commitment ceremonies" for gays and lesbians, and pressure is mounting within the Reform movement for official religious recognition of such unions.[32]

Reform theology, like that of liberal religion generally, is extremely flexible, but a 1994 case showed that it does have boundaries. A "humanistic" congregation that had removed all references to God from its liturgy applied for membership in the UAHC. After considerable discussion about whether denial of God placed a synagogue outside Reform Judaism, the application was denied. While individual Jews who did not believe in God could be Reform Jews, the decision stated, a nontheistic synagogue could not be part of a God-centered religious movement.

In recent years Reform has stepped up its involvement in Israeli affairs. Having long since shed the anti-Zionist odor that clung to Classical Reform, the movement's efforts to develop congregations in Israel that would offer a Jewish alternative to secularism and Orthodoxy have been frustrated both by widespread public apathy and by the political muscle of Israeli Orthodoxy. Calling for the recognition of non-Orthodox rabbis and for government funding of non-Orthodox institutions on the same basis with their Orthodox counterparts in Israel, American Reform organized the Association of Reform Zionists of America (ARZA) to contest for power within the World Zionist Organization (WZO). While ARZA did very well in WZO elections, the quest for formal recognition of Reform in Israel has not yet overcome the intricacies of the Israeli political system, where neither of the two major parties are willing to court the ire of the Orthodox.

CONSERVATISM DEFINES ITSELF

For three decades now the Conservative movement has found itself caught between resilient Orthodoxy and aggressive Reform. Until the 1960s the preferences of second-generation Jews for a traditional yet Americanized Judaism provided Conservative Judaism with enough strength in numbers that it did not have to address the movement's two basic internal problems. One was an ideological fuzziness that made Conservatism seem little more than a compromise between Orthodoxy and Reform. Related to this was a second problem, the apparent contradiction between official adherence to traditional Jewish law, alongside widespread lay ignorance of, and apathy toward, that law.

The emergence of a new generation that grew up, not with memories of old-fashioned Orthodoxy, but with recollections of suburban Conservatism, created a crisis. What their parents saw as a reasonable facsimile of the "authentic" Judaism they knew in their youth adapted to modern America— officially maintaining traditional forms and norms while practicing them on a selective basis—many of the children saw as bourgeois hypocrisy masking the celebration of materialism. The movement stopped growing by the mid-1960s, as many Jews who had been raised in Conservative families chose to affiliate with Reform. According to the National Jewish Population Survey of 1990, fully 26 percent of Jews who said they came from Conservative backgrounds now called themselves Reform. A much smaller number, seeking greater religious consistency, opted for Orthodoxy. In 1990, 5 percent of those raised Conservative considered themselves Orthodox.[33] Clearly, the Conservative movement could not thrive by simply muddling through. It would have to define itself more clearly: Was it a form of progressive Orthodoxy, cautious Reform, or something else?

The battleground on which the future of the movement was fought was the issue of ordaining women. With women already eligible to be called to the Torah and be counted for a *minyan,* the United Synagogue (Conservative Judaism's congregational organization) in 1973 and the Rabbinical Assembly in 1977 called for the admission of women to the Rabbinical School of the Jewish Theological Seminary. Seminary Chancellor Gerson Cohen, who was personally sympathetic, set up a special commission representing all elements of the movement to make recommendations. The majority report of the commission, issued in 1979, declared that Jewish law did not forbid women's ordination and urged the Seminary faculty to approve the change. The more traditionalist scholars at the Seminary fought to stave off women's ordination, but in 1983 the faculty passed it by a vote of 34 to 8. Five senior Talmud scholars, opposed to the proposal, refused even to participate in a vote they considered a violation of Jewish law. Two years later, the school graduated the first female Conservative rabbi, and soon the Cantorial School also began graduating women.[34]

While Chancellor Cohen and other proponents of the initiative viewed it as a classic example of how the movement adheres to Jewish law while adapting it to new circumstances—in this case, the new role of women in modern life—others considered women's ordination a sellout of Jewish tradition to contemporary fashion, a giant step in the direction of Reform. A number of Conservative opponents of the change, rabbis and laypeople, organized the Union for Traditional Conservative Judaism in 1984. Originally intended to be a traditionalist lobby within the Conservative movement, it broke with Conservatism entirely by 1990, setting up its own rabbinical school (its first four rabbis were ordained in 1996) and deleting the word "Conservative" from its name. Unsuccessful so far in establishing a mass movement, the Union for Traditional Judaism sees itself as the continuation of what the Conservative movement was originally intended to be, genuinely loyal to tradition but open to the modern world. In that sense, little distinguishes it from modern Orthodoxy.[35]

Once the issue of women's ordination was resolved, the next bone of contention between the traditional and innovative forces in Conservative Judaism was theological. Hoping to address the criticism that Conservative Judaism was not clearly enough defined, the movement established a commission in 1985 to draw up a statement of beliefs. What emerged in 1988 was *Emet Ve'Emunah.* Unfortunately, the need to accommodate divergent points of view undermined the effectiveness of the document, especially among the laity, who had hoped for clarity rather than theological nuance. On some points the statement is quite untraditional, stating that the Torah is a human document and that Jewish law constitutes human beings' understanding of what God wants. On other matters, *Emet Ve'Emunah* validates a plurality of views—for example, it asserts the centrality of belief in God while recognizing the right to challenge God's existence. The overall effect of this statement of principles was, like women's ordination, to strengthen the hand of the forces of change within the movement.[36]

The leftward drift of the Conservative movement has also manifested itself institutionally. While in earlier years the Conservative movement had rarely challenged Orthodox control over such areas of Jewish ritual as kashrut, circumcision, ritual bath supervision, and religious divorces, in the 1980s and 1990s Conservatism sought to develop its own cadre of experts in these fields so as to make the movement religiously independent of the Orthodox, and thus no longer bound by Orthodox stringencies. Another sign of independence from Orthodoxy was the decision to align with the Reform movement in pursuit of religious pluralism in Israel. While the refusal of the established Israeli Orthodox rabbinate to countenance Conservative Judaism made the alliance with Reform politically understandable, the decision of a movement officially committed to Jewish law to make common cause with Reform in the quest for recognition in Israel gave further indication of the antitraditional drift. If any further indication were needed that Conservative Judaism now considered itself a distinct denomination and not merely a modernized version of traditional Judaism, its organization of synagogues changed its name in 1991 from the inclusive-sounding United Synagogue of America to the denominationally specific United Synagogue of Conservative Judaism.

In confronting the phenomenon of widespread mixed marriages the Conservative movement has not gone nearly so far as Reform. While there are Conservative voices that call for ambitious outreach programs on the Reform model, and even a number of Conservative rabbis who want the movement to at least look into the possibility of enacting patrilineal descent, the predominant view opposes initiatives to mixed marrieds that might send a message that such marriages are condoned. Thus the movement has tended to concentrate on "inreach," meaning programs to strengthen the Jewish identity of young Jews so as to encourage marriage to fellow Jews. Attempts by Conservative synagogues to reach the intermarried, known as "Gateways" programs, which focus primarily on achieving the conversion of the non-Jewish spouse, are controversial within the movement.

The question of the Jewish status of gays and lesbians has embroiled Conservative Judaism in an intense internal struggle that could well prove as divisive as the controversy over the ordination of women. Unable, like the Orthodox, to ignore or dismiss the change in societal attitudes toward homosexuality, or, like Reform, easily to reject or reinterpret biblical strictures against it, the Conservative movement has so far proven unable to develop a consensus on the issue.

In 1990 the Rabbinical Assembly (RA) voted overwhelmingly to welcome gays and lesbians into the synagogue. The next year, the RA's Committee on Law and Standards tried but failed to articulate a unified position on the role of gays in Jewish life. Opinions on the Committee ranged all the way from a reiteration of the traditional characterization of the homosexual act as "abomination," thereby ruling out gay rabbis or gay marriages, to the Reform position that the biblical stance was no longer applicable and that sexual orientation was Jewishly irrelevant. In 1992 both a reassertion of the traditional view and a compromise statement calling for a broad-based study of human sexuality as a whole were passed by the Committee. The Rabbinical Assembly convention in 1993 witnessed a dramatic confrontation between the two wings of the movement over this issue. Speaking for the liberals, Rabbi Harold Schulweis urged that the moral imperative of equality for gays must supersede considerations of Jewish law. But JTS Chancellor Ismar Schorsch countered that there was little lay interest in the rights of homosexuals, and that most Conservative Jews were searching for a tradition-based spirituality rather than innovative social causes.

In 1994 the committee set up to study the broad issue of human sexuality issued its report. In a departure from traditional Jewish teachings, it approved of sex outside of marriage so long as it was part of a loving relationship, in which case it had "a measure of holiness." As for homosexuality, the report advised the movement to continue the status quo pending further study: Gays should not be ordained, their relationships should not be recognized by rabbinic ceremonies, but they should be welcomed in Conservative synagogues.[37] Clearly, the movement was too divided either to accept the biblical ban or to break new ground.

As is the case with Reform, Conservative attempts to temper religious obligations with contemporary values—gender equality, a greater openness to alternative lifestyles—have been accompanied by programs of spiritual renewal, inspired in large measure by the *havurah* movement. Increasingly, Conservative synagogues have substituted informal study sessions for formal sermons in order to give congregants a feeling of greater participation. Many congregations have dispensed with the late-Friday-evening service so that families might spend Sabbath eve together at home, and the Jewish Theological Seminary has introduced more courses stressing spirituality rather than textual knowledge. More than their older colleagues, younger Conservative rabbis tend to speak about the importance of Jewish law. And the expansion of the network of Solomon Schechter day schools has produced more Conservative congregants with the linguistic and ritual skills to live more observant lives.

In 1995 the Conservative movement was beset with an internal crisis that to some extent reflected these crosscurrents. The University of Judaism, the Los Angeles branch of the Jewish Theological Seminary, which had never before offered a rabbinical program, announced—without previous consultation with New York—the establishment of its own, independent Conservative rabbinical seminary. In answer to the outraged complaints from JTS, backers of the Los Angeles initiative argued that West Coast Jews needed a different kind of rabbi, one more "spiritual" than that produced in New York, even if he or she turned out to be less scholarly. The two sides eventually entered into negotiations to ensure some degree of coordination between the programs.[38]

A recent study of affiliated Conservative Jews in North America, sponsored by the movement, yielded ambiguous results.[39] Unlike earlier generations of Conservative Jews, for whom the movement was often a compromise prompted by rejection of the Orthodox and Reform alternatives, today's Conservative

Jews, especially the younger cohorts, identify positively with Conservative principles. And the movement has succeeded in instilling allegiance to the idea of Jewish law: 62 percent of its synagogue members agree that Conservative Jews are obligated to obey the law. But actual practice lags far behind, as only 24 percent say they keep kosher, and 37 percent say they light Sabbath candles (the percentages for self-styled Conservative Jews who do not affiliate with a synagogue are even lower). And despite the nominal allegiance to Jewish law, 76 percent say that a Jew can be religious without observance; a surprising 69 percent accept the patrilineal definition of Jewishness practiced by Reform but resisted by the Conservative leadership; and 28 percent even feel that their rabbis should perform intermarriages—a position that even the Reform movement has never officially condoned.

THE NEW RECONSTRUCTIONISM

Since the 1960s Reconstructionism has radically transformed itself. The naturalistic Judaism of Mordechai Kaplan, based on the scientific and sociological assumptions of the early twentieth century and the philosophy of pragmatism that was so influential at that time, has been largely replaced by an emphasis on individual religious experience and, for some, mysticism. A heavy influx of young Jews from the *havurah* movement brought about the change, a fact recognized in the renaming of the Reconstructionist Federation of Congregations as the Federation of Reconstructionist Congregations and Havurot. (In 1995, however, fearing that the absence of the word "Jewish" might confuse the group with the fundamentalist Christian Reconstructionists and concluding that the acronym FRCH was too difficult to pronounce, the organization changed its name to the Jewish Reconstructionist Federation.)

As a result, Reconstructionism has become the branch of Judaism least tied to the past and most willing to experiment. In line with the informality and democracy of *havurah* life, the Reconstructionist rabbi is viewed as a resource person, not an authority figure. Each Reconstructionist congregation decides policies by consensus or majority vote, so that there is great variation between congregations. There is also considerable lay participation in the liturgy, including leading services and delivering talks, tasks that are generally reserved for cantors and rabbis in Reform and Conservative Judaism.

Nevertheless, the central bodies of Reconstructionist Judaism have developed guidelines for the movement that are widely accepted by Reconstructionists. Some of these positions, when adopted, anticipated those taken later by Reform—ordination of women, patrilineal descent, outreach to intermarried families, and the ordination of gays and lesbians. In fact, the movement went beyond Reform in 1992 when it ended all distinctions based on sexual preference, including the right to a Jewish ceremony—not just a civil one—equivalent to marriage.

Reconstructionism has also innovated in theology. Its interest in mysticism shows the influence of Eastern and New Age motifs, in addition to older Jewish mystical ideas. Feminists have felt most comfortable within the movement, and having achieved religious equality, are seeking to revise the traditional male-centered liturgy to reflect a feminine religious sensibility, even a perception of God as having a feminine identity. Indeed, critics have charged that a reversion to the ancient practice of Goddess worship may be in the offing. Possibly connected to feminism—the Earth as "mother"—environmentalism has also become prominent within Reconstructionism. All of these themes are developed in a series of new prayer books issued by the movement.

To be sure, Kaplan's original rejection of such classic Orthodox doctrines as the chosen people, the personal messiah, and divine revelation of the Torah still guide Reconstructionists, as well as his insistence on the peoplehood of all Jews. Nevertheless, the diminishing number of "classical" Reconstructionists have criticized the movement's direction as a betrayal of Mordechai Kaplan's legacy.[40]

The distinctive features of contemporary Reconstructionism would have a far greater impact on the larger Jewish community if the denomination were larger. Despite the founding of many new Reconstructionist congregations in recent years, the 1990 National Jewish Population Survey showed that only 1.4 percent of American Jews (2 percent of synagogue members) identified themselves as Reconstructionists.[41]

A DYNAMIC ORTHODOXY

The ferment within Orthodoxy that began in the 1960s with the emergence of a sectarian, immigrant-led group resistant to Americanization has accelerated. A new adjective, *haredi*, came to be applied to this group. The word means "fearful," in this context referring to the awe that the Jew is supposed to feel toward God. The rigor and self-assurance of this element—buttressed by parallel developments within Israeli Orthodox society—has had a spill-over effect on American Orthodoxy as a whole, making it both more extreme in religious expression and less willing to accept direction from, or to compromise with, non-Orthodox forms of Judaism.[42]

The increasing dynamism and heightened morale of American Orthodoxy is demographically puzzling. Between 1970 and 1990 the percentage of self-defined Orthodox Jews in the United States, as measured by national surveys, declined from 11.5 to just 6.6 percent. These numbers, of course, must be taken with some skepticism, since it is likely that the surveys undercount the growing *haredi* element, whose insularity makes it suspicious of interviews and questionnaires about religion. Also, much of the decline is due to the heavy concentration of Orthodox in the older, immigrant generation that is rapidly dying off. Even so, it is difficult to fathom why many in the Orthodox community believe that their high fertility rate and the alleged success of the *teshuvah* (Orthodox outreach) movement not only compensate for the defections of many born Orthodox, but also swell their ranks.

Yet even if Orthodoxy is declining in numbers, the remaining pool of Orthodox today are undoubtedly more ideologically committed than any previous generation of American Orthodox Jews. It is this noticeably heightened intensity, not numbers, which may give some credence to Orthodox claims that theirs is the only denomination that is likely to escape the ravages of assimilation and survive as a recognizable Jewish community. Indeed, the qualitatively disproportionate impact of Orthodoxy is reflected in the 1990 survey data: Orthodox Jews make up 16 percent of all synagogue members, close to two-and-a-half times their proportion of all self-identified Jews. And while less than half of Reform and Conservative Jews join a synagogue, 80 percent of the Orthodox are synagogue members.[43]

Ironically, trends in American—"non-Jewish"—society have strengthened the most insular Orthodox elements. The assertion of Black Power ideology in the late 1960s and the subsequent legitimization of racial and ethnic identity chipped away at the homogenized Americanism of the postwar generation, and it became acceptable, indeed laudable, to celebrate one's group identity. Thus wearing a *kippah* (skullcap) in public, sending one's children to a Jewish all-day school, dressing in a long black coat, letting *tzitzit* (ritual fringes) dangle from one's pants, were no longer perverse signs of a refusal to Americanize but rather healthy affirmations of ethnicity.

Determined to rebuild the Orthodox Jewish societies that had gone up in the flames of the Holocaust, the leaders of sectarian Orthodoxy concentrated on education. Prewar Orthodoxy had created a number of day schools and yeshivas in New York and other large Jewish communities, but most parents affiliated with Orthodox synagogues believed that such educational "segregation" would hurt their children's chances to succeed, and so sent them to supplementary Hebrew schools that met after the public-school day. Rejecting this as woefully insufficient, the newly arrived Orthodox created elementary and high-school yeshivas in cities across the country. In most of these institutions the morning and early afternoon hours are devoted to religious studies, and the late afternoon to secular subjects. Largely thanks to *haredi* educational zeal, a Jewish day-school education through high school, for boys and girls, has become virtually de rigueur in the broader Orthodox community as well.

New schools of higher Jewish education proliferated, where young men (Orthodoxy still did not encourage this regimen of study for women) study Talmud and related texts for 12 or more hours daily. Such institutions are not, strictly speaking, rabbinical schools, since they are not intended to prepare students for the profession of the rabbinate. They stress instead the traditional Jewish value of sacred learning for its own sake. Some of the graduates do indeed enter the rabbinate or the field of Jewish education, while others become professionals or businessmen. In the 1950s and 1960s students at almost all of these schools were given several evening hours off to attend college part-time on the understanding that some higher secular education was necessary to make a living. Recently, administrators in many of these higher yeshivas have made it more difficult for students to attend college, and some carefully monitor what courses are taken so as to minimize exposure to the liberal arts, which are considered particularly threatening to religious belief. This change has further sharpened the sense of insularity among the younger sectarian Orthodox.[44]

Standards of synagogue practice and personal religious behavior have tightened in the larger Orthodox community due to the influence of "yeshiva Orthodoxy." Mixed seating of men and women in the synagogue and the use of a microphone on Shabbat, both of which had been quite common in Orthodox synagogues well into the 1960s, came to be seen as beyond the pale. In fact, synagogue partitions between men and women grew higher and thicker.[45] Activities that few Orthodox people in America found objectionable before, like eating fish in a nonkosher restaurant, men and women dancing or going swimming together, men listening to women singing, men going bareheaded in public, are now avoided by many. Foods previously considered kosher are no longer eaten. And more and more married Orthodox women cover their hair.[46]

The infusion of this new strain of Orthodoxy in American life has also transformed the public posture of Orthodox Jewry. Although the Orthodox percentage of American Jewry has not increased, the assertiveness of the sectarian Orthodox has made the Orthodox community as a whole less defensive in its relations with non-Orthodox denominations. Primarily through the Agudath Israel, the Union of Orthodox Jewish Congregations, and the National Council of Young Israel, American Orthodoxy increasingly lets its voice be heard in government circles on issues of concern to it—such as kashrut regulation, legislation to protect Jewish women from unfair demands of recalcitrant husbands in divorce cases, government aid to nonpublic education, and U.S. policy toward Israel—espousing positions that are independent from, and sometimes opposed to, those of non-Orthodox and secular Jewish bodies.

The strides made by the sectarian Orthodox have created several points of tension with the older, modern Orthodox, represented institutionally by Yeshiva University and the Rabbinical Council of America. The original dispute over Orthodox membership in umbrella organizations of a religious nature together with non-Orthodox representatives has never been resolved, although the demise of the Synagogue Council of America in 1995 for financial reasons—hailed by opponents of Orthodox membership as a great victory—removed a major bone of contention. But the basic dispute remains over whether non-Orthodox forms of Judaism should be ignored or respected, and at times it has had serious practical consequences. In the 1980s an unpublicized rabbinic arrangement in Denver, Colorado, to perform conversions acceptable to all the denominations, including the Orthodox, collapsed when the more stringently Orthodox found out and denounced it.[47] In 1989 an Israeli government plan to set up a joint rabbinic body in the United States to deal with conversions for those intending to settle in Israel, a scheme intended to end once and for all the perennial "Who is a Jew?" controversy in Israel, was also torpedoed by *haredi* opposition.[48] And the 1993 Israel Day parade in New York City was almost cancelled when sectarian Orthodox circles exerted pressure on the modern Orthodox—whose young people made up the bulk of the participants—to withdraw on the grounds that a gay synagogue was marching. The parade went forward only after the gay synagogue was barred.[49]

There is still considerable philosophic distance between modern and sectarian Orthodoxy over Judaism's proper relationship to secular culture. Under the leadership of Yeshiva University and the charismatic Rabbi Soloveitchik, generations of Orthodox students were taught that tensions between Jewish and secular outlooks could yield a spiritually fruitful synthesis that would enable one to be a faithful Orthodox Jew and a full participant in the modern intellectual adventure. The new wave of *haredi* Orthodoxy, however, denied this, and cautioned instead that any study outside classical Jewish learning carries serious religious risks. There is a similar split over the objective, scientific study of Judaism, such as is practiced in the religion departments of major universities: At Yeshiva University such pursuits are officially encouraged, while the "yeshiva world" considers them heretical.[50]

The role of women has recently come to the fore as an emotional battleground for the two Orthodox camps. Modern Orthodoxy, having pioneered women's religious education in the United States—now including even study of the Talmud, which *haredi* Orthodoxy resists—has also begun exploring new possibilities within the bounds of Jewish law for enhancing women's religious expression. These have taken the form of women's prayer groups, women reading the *Scroll of Esther* for the congregation on Purim, women as presidents of synagogues, and other innovations. Pressure for doing something about the husband's advantage in Jewish divorce law (a woman can only be divorced if her husband willingly grants her a *get*) also reflects a growing sensitivity within modern Orthodoxy to the status of women. All of this is anathema to the sectarian Orthodox. Quite apart from whatever issues of Jewish law may be involved, this group views attempts to address women's grievances as illegitimate instrusions of secular feminist ideology into Judaism, threatening the traditional role of the Jewish woman as wife and mother. This position, however, is complicated by the reality that economic necessity has forced many women in the sectarian community into the workforce to help support their large families, a situation that itself calls into question the traditional role of women.[51]

The sectarian critique of modern Orthodoxy is increasingly heard within modern Orthodox institutions, a sure sign of its effectiveness. Much of the Talmud faculty at Yeshiva University is hostile to the modernist ideology of the institution. Although they are students of the late Rabbi Soloveitchik, these rabbis minimize the significance of their mentor's interest in secular knowledge and try to reinterpret him to fit into a more sectarian mold. Their students, in turn, are more insular in their interests and concerns than Yeshiva University graduates in the past, and since they will be the rabbis of the next generation, it is hard to see where modern Orthodoxy will get its future leadership. Even Dr. Norman Lamm, Yeshiva's president, a stanch defender of an open, tolerant Orthodoxy, prefers to identify his institution as "centrist" rather than "modern" Orthodox.

Another example of the growing *haredi* influence on mainstream Orthodoxy is the Young Israel movement. Young Israel, as noted above, began in 1912 as a kind of "outreach" initiative to young Orthodox Jews to keep them in the fold, and as late as the early 1960s, its synagogues sponsored coed dances and other such social activities. Today, however, many of the younger rabbis in Young Israel congregations are graduates of sectarian yeshivas, and they—and the Young Israel movement as a whole—tend to turn to their alma maters, not to Yeshiva University, for religious guidance. Seeing itself as a more authentically Orthodox congregational organization than the Union of Orthodox Jewish Congregations (which still has as members a few synagogues without separations between men and women), it has recently announced that it will sponsor its own kashrut-supervision operation, in direct competition with the Orthodox Union.

One major issue in Jewish life cuts across these fault lines within Orthodoxy—Israel. True enough, in terms of ideology, modern Orthodoxy, unlike the sectarians, tends to view the existence of the Jewish state in religiously positive terms, as part of God's redemptive plan. But in practical terms, all sectors of American Orthodoxy have tended to sympathize with the Likud position in Israel, and oppose the return of territories or any other concessions to the Arab world or the Palestinians. This puts American Orthodox Jews at odds with the rest of the American Jewish community: Polls taken since the Oslo agreement show that the Orthodox were the only Jewish subgroup in America opposed to the peace policies of the Rabin–Peres Labor governments.[52] Furthermore, it was within Orthodoxy that the late Meir Kahane had the bulk of his American support; within Orthodoxy that some backing—albeit rare and muffled—was voiced for the actions of Baruch Goldstein, who massacred some 30 Arabs in Hebron in 1994; and within Orthodoxy that the theoretical halakhic basis for killing a *rodef* (someone who threatens one's life) was discussed, before it was acted upon by the Orthodox Israeli student who assassinated Prime Minister Yitzhak Rabin in 1995. The Likud victory in the 1996 Israeli elections has delighted American Orthodoxy and may well encourage an even more confrontational Orthodox posture vis-à-vis the rest of American Jewry on Israel-related issues.

AMERICAN HASIDISM

The various Hasidic groups constitute a significant Orthodox subculture in America. Hasidism began in eighteenth-century Poland as a folk movement that stressed emotional religion as against what it perceived as the dry rationalism of the scholarly leadership of the time. The movement quickly spread through Eastern Europe. American Hasidism is overwhelmingly a post-World War II phenomenon, brought to these shores by refugees from Hitler.

While for purposes of broad classification the Hasidim can be identified as part of American *haredi* Orthodoxy, they have certain characteristics setting them apart. For one thing, while leadership in non-Hasidic circles is primarily determined by superior Talmudic scholarship, Hasidic leadership is charismatic and hereditary. Each group gives allegiance to a *rebbe* who is viewed as the repository of God's will and who, in most cases, descends from a long line of Hasidic masters. Although they have established their own yeshivas in America,

Hasidic Judaism remains much more focused on relationships with the *rebbe* than on study in the yeshiva. Hasidic Jews are generally more isolationist in relation to the outside world than other *haredim,* tending to live in self-contained neighborhoods in close proximity to their *rebbe,* either in urban centers or in suburban villages. Hasidic sects differ greatly from each other: Those of Hungarian origin, for example, are more hostile to modernity than those from Poland. A case in point is the Satmar group, which remains adamantly opposed to the very existence of the State of Israel on the grounds that Jews may not create a state until the messiah comes.[53]

By far the most successful Hasidic sect on the American scene has been Lubavitch, also known as Habad. Under the energetic leadership of Rabbi Menachem Mendel Schneerson (1902–1994), who assumed control in 1951, Lubavitch has made Jewish outreach its priority. Avoiding an all-or-nothing approach, Lubavitch emissaries around the country (and all over the world) have influenced many Jews, if not to join Lubavitch or commit themselves to live by Jewish law, then at least to perform certain rituals, feel positively toward Jewish tradition, and maintain a personal allegiance to the *rebbe.*[54]

The movement is now undergoing a crisis, however. Speculation began in 1991 among Lubavitchers that the elderly and ill Rabbi Schneerson was the messiah, and enthusiasm for the idea escalated steadily within the movement. Even the *rebbe*'s death three years later did not resolve the issue. Many of his followers continue to hold out the hope that he will rise from the dead, and even those Lubavitchers who disagree will not openly condemn the messianists. Meanwhile, no successor has been chosen for the childless *rebbe,* and it remains to be seen whether Lubavitch will be able to continue its outreach activities with the same success as before.

For its part, non-Lubavitch Orthodoxy has been shocked and embarrassed by the messianic fervor, especially since the ascription of redemptive powers to a dead man bears an all-too-close resemblance to early Christianity at the point where it began to diverge from its Jewish origins. In 1996 the Rabbinical Council of America issued a resolution declaring that the doctrine of a messiah who will arise from the dead has no basis in Jewish tradition.[55]

FACING THE TWENTY-FIRST CENTURY

The foregoing discussion, focusing as it does on the historical development of the different forms of American Judaism, tells only one side of the story, that of controversy and division. There has never been a consensus, it would appear, over basic issues of theology, ritual, or policy. Indeed, the course of recent events gives the impression that the fissures within American Jewry are getting wider. Issues such as the appropriate balance between American and Jewish culture, what "Judaism" teaches in regard to current political and social questions, to what degree—if at all—Jewish law remains binding, what is the process whereby that law is interpreted, the role of women in Judaism, the Jewish legitimacy of homosexual relationships, and the very definition of Jewishness in cases of conversion and of mixed-religion families are all matters of dispute. And these divisions are made more acrimonious by a pervading sense of crisis: American Jews increasingly realize that their achievement of acceptance in American society is sapping their numbers and endangering their group survival. True enough, this is the same quandary that modernity, particularly in its American version, has set for Judaism since the eighteenth century. But today there seems to be less confidence than ever before that the community has the strength to surmount it.

However, there is another side to the story. On many matters of deep importance, Jews unite. While the officially recognized and government-backed Jewish-community organization collapsed with the onset of modernity, its spirit survives in the voluntary actions of Jewish individuals and groups. When Jews abroad are endangered—in Ethiopia, in Russia, in South America, or elsewhere—American Jewry mobilizes its diplomatic influence and philanthropic muscle to help. This impulse, deeply rooted in Jewish tradition, has been reinvigorated by a broad-based Jewish "Holocaust consciousness" that will not allow American Jews to stand by while their brothers and sisters across the sea are in danger. Also, despite the controversy among American Jews over the best policies for Israel to pursue, any serious threat to the Jewish State brings a closing of ranks. And for all the Jewish disunity over domestic American-policy issues, the public expression of anti-Semitism, whether from the right or left of the political spectrum, elicits unanimous Jewish condemnation.

Indeed, even the religious controversies that bedevil American Jewish life reflect the common situation of all American Jews. Modernity implies the freedom to choose: Even the most insular Orthodox Jew, like the most secular, can walk away from his or her family and neighborhood, become Conservative, Reform, or Reconstructionist, convert to another religion, or meld into the general American population. Thus all attempts to bring Jews close to Judaism, from whichever denomination they originate, try to make the religion a positive experience, one that will make the Jew want to be more Jewish. Whatever American Judaism will be like in the twenty-first century, it will be the result of the free decisions of individual American Jews.

NOTES

1. The classic study of premodern Jewish society—at least in its Ashkenazic form— and the forces that would ultimately undermine it is Jacob Katz, *Tradition and Crisis: Jewish Society at the End of the Middle Ages* (New York: New York University Press, 1993).

2. The social and economic shifts are analyzed in Jacob Katz, *Out of the Ghetto: The Social Background of Jewish Emancipation, 1770–1870* (Cambridge, MA: Harvard University Press, 1973), while the new intellectual currents are treated in Arthur Hertzberg, *The Enlightenment and the Jews* (New York: Columbia University Press, 1968), and Michael Meyer, *The Origins of the Modern Jew: Jewish Identity and European Culture in Germany, 1749–1824* (Detroit: Wayne State University Press, 1967).

3. The most recent comprehensive survey of American Jewish history is Howard M. Sachar, *A History of the Jews in America* (New York: Alfred A. Knopf, 1992). A treatment of the early period, containing considerable information about religious life, is Eli Faber's *A Time for Planting: The First Migrations, 1654–1820* (Baltimore: Johns Hopkins University Press, 1992), the first volume in the series, *The Jews in America.*

4. Michael A. Meyer, *Reponse to Modernity: A History of the Reform Movement in Judaism* (New York: Oxford University Press, 1988), chapters 1–3.

5. Ibid, chapter 6.

6. Ibid, pp. 387–388.

7. Ibid, chapter 7.

8. Ismar Schorsch, the current chancellor of the Jewish Theological Seminary, delineates the European roots of his movement in *From Text to Context: The Turn to History in Modern Judaism* (Hanover, NH: University Press of New England, 1994), chapters 8–13.

9. The definitive work on the sociology of Conservative Judaism in the first half of the twentieth century—and one of the classic books on American Jewry—is Marshall Sklare, *Conservative Judaism: An American Religious Movement,* new, augmented edition (New York: Schocken, 1972).

10. Charles S. Liebman, "The Training of American Rabbis," *American Jewish Year Book, Vol. 69* (New York: American Jewish Committee and Jewish Publication Society, 1968), pp. 34–53; Abraham J. Karp, "The Conservative Rabbi—'Dissatisfied But Not Unhappy,'" in Jacob Rader Marcus and Abraham J. Peck (Eds.), *The American Rabbinate: A Century of Accommodation and Change, 1883–1983* (Hoboken, NJ: KTAV, 1985), pp. 132–165; Richard L. Rubinstein, *Power Struggle: An Autobiographical Confession* (New York: Charles Scribner's Sons, 1974), pp. 126–129.

11. Meyer, *Response to Modernity,* chapter 8. The text of the Columbus Platform is on pp. 388–391.

12. Charles S. Liebman, "Orthodoxy in American Jewish Life," *American Jewish Year Book, Vol. 66* (New York: American Jewish Committee and Jewish Publication Society, 1965), pp. 27–30.

13. Jeffrey S. Gurock, "Resisters and Accommodators: Varieties of Orthodox Rabbis in America, 1886–1983," in Marcus and Peck, *The American Rabbinate,* pp.10–37 (cited above).

14. Jenna Weissman Joselit, *New York's Jewish Jews: The Orthodox Community in the Interwar Years* (Bloomington: Indiana University Press, 1990), chapter 2.

15. Aaron Rothkoff, *Bernard Revel: Builder of American Jewish Orthodoxy* (Philadephia: Jewish Publication Society, 1972); Jeffrey S. Gurock, *The Men and Women of Yeshiva: Higher Education, Orthodoxy, and American Judaism* (New York: Columbia University Press, 1988), chapters 2–4.

16. Mel Scult, *Judaism Faces the Twentieth Century: A Biography of Mordechai M. Kaplan* (Detroit: Wayne State University Press, 1993).

17. Charles S. Liebman, "Reconstructionism in American Jewish Life," *American Jewish Year Book, Vol. 71* (New York: American Jewish Committee and Jewish Publication Society, 1970), pp. 3–99.

18. A comparison of the Commentary symposium, "The State of Jewish Belief" (August 1966), with the symposium, "What Do American Jews Believe," in the same magazine thirty years later (August 1996) demonstrates how long it took for these changes to register.

19. Samuel C. Heilman, *Portrait of American Jews: The Last Half of the 20th Century* (Seattle: University of Washington Press, 1995), chapter 1.

20. Meyer, *Response to Modernity,* pp. 326–334. (Cited above.)

21. Ibid, pp. 309–313, 364–368.

22. Neil Gillman, *Conservative Judaism: The New Century* (West Orange, NJ: Behrman House, 1993), chapter 6.

23. Among the first to note this was Charles Liebman, who, in "Orthodoxy in American Jewish Life," op cit, devoted considerable attention to what he called the "sectarian Orthodox."

24. The classic—and bitterly satiric—fictional portrayal of the newcomers' effect on the Americanized Jewish community is Philip Roth's story, "Eli the Fanatic," originally published in *Commentary* (April 1959), then included in Roth's *Goodbye Columbus* (Boston: Houghton Mifflin, 1959), and reprinted many times since.

25. Fred Masarik and Alvin Chenkin, "United States National Jewish Population Study: A First Report," *American Jewish Year Book, Vol. 74* (New York: American Jewish Committee and Jewish Publication Society, 1973), pp. 292–296.

26. Heilman, *Portrait of American Jews,* pp. 88–94. (Cited above.)

27. Meyer, *Response to Modernity,* pp. 371–373. (Cited above.)

28. Neither the Reform outreach initiative nor the momentous decision on patrilineal descent discussed in the next few paragraphs have received scholarly treatment, although there is a considerable polemical literature, pro and con. The best place to start is with the organs of the movement itself, *CCAR Journal* and *Reform Judaism,* which published much on these topics in the late 1970s and early 1980s.

29. An entire issue of *Judaism* (Winter 1985) was devoted to a fascinating symposium on the ramifications of patrilineal descent.

30. Walter Ruby, "Reform vs. Conservative: Who's Winning?" *Moment* (April 1996), p. 32.

31. "Rabbi Eric H. Yoffie: Teacher of Living Torah," *Reform Judaism* (Fall 1996), pp. 13–19, 76–78, 80–81.

32. Beth M. Gilbert, "Gays and Lesbians Under the Chupah," *Reform Judaism* (Summer 1996), pp. 17–21, 61.

33. Ruby, "Who's Winning?" pp. 30–39, 67. (Cited above.)

34. Gillman, *Conservative Judaism,* chapter 8. The debate within the Conservative movement over women's ordination unleashed a broader discussion over the historical development of Jewish law, which had implications for the other Jewish movements as well. See Robert Gordis, "A Dynamic Halakhah: Principles and Procedures of Jewish Law," *Judaism* (Summer 1979), and the symposium on Jewish law in the Winter 1980 issue. After the ordination question was decided, *Judaism* ran a symposium on the topic (Winter 1984). The movement marked the tenth anniversary of the decision with a symposium in *Conservative Judaism* (Fall 1995) on its impact.

35. Gillman, *Conservative Judaism,* pp. 145–148. (Cited above.)

36. Ibid, chapter 9.

37. Lawrence Grossman, "Jewish Communal Affairs," *American Jewish Year Book, Vol. 95* (New York: American Jewish Committee, 1995), pp. 171–172; *Vol. 96* (1996), pp. 161–162.

38. The dissatisfaction that led to the establishment of a West Coast seminary was articulated earlier by Daniel H. Gordis, who would be appointed its first head, in "Positive–Historical Judaism Exhausted: Reflections on a Movement's Future," *Conservative Judaism* (Fall 1994), pp. 3–18.

39. *Conservative Synagogues and Their Members: Highlights of the North American Survey of 1995–96* (New York: Jewish Theological Seminary of America, 1996).

40. All of these issues can be followed in the movement's magazines, *The Reconstructionist* and *Reconstructionism Today.*

41. Ruby, "Who's Winning?," pp. 32–33. (Cited above.)

42. Haym Soloveitchik brilliantly dissects the reasons for this in "Rupture and Reconstruction: The Transformation of Contemporary Orthodoxy," *Tradition* (Summer 1994), pp. 64–130. A perceptive journalistic treatment is Eli D. Clark, "Orthodoxy Lurches to the Right," *Moment* (June 1996), pp. 28–35, 58–59.

43. Ruby, "Who's Winning?," pp. 32–33. (Cited above.) For detailed treatments of Orthodox trends see Samuel C. Heilman and Steven M. Cohen, *Cosmopolitans and Parochials: Modern Orthodox Jews in America* (Chicago: University of Chicago Press, 1989), and M. Herbert Danzger, *Returning to Tradition: A Study of the Contemporary Revival in Orthodox Judaism* (New Haven: Yale University Press, 1989).

44. William B. Helmreich, *The World of the Yeshiva: An Intimate Portrait of Orthodox Jewry* (New York: Free Press, 1982).

45. Lawrence H. Schiffman, "When Women and Men Sat Together in American Orthodox Synagogues," *Moment* (December 1989), pp. 40–49.

46. While there has been no scholarly treatment of this, the radical shift in what it meant to be "Orthodox" is eloquently captured in many of the oral histories that Jenna Weissman Joselit quotes in *New York's Jewish Jews* (cited above).

47. Special section in the *Intermountain Jewish News,* December 2, 1983.

48. Lawrence Grossman, "Jewish Communal Affairs," *American Jewish Year Book, Vol. 91* (New York: American Jewish Committee and Jewish Publication Society, 1991), p. 201.

49. Ibid, "Jewish Communal Affairs," *Vol. 95,* pp. 172–173.

50. Norman Lamm, president of Yeshiva University, explores this controversy in *Torah Umadda: The Encounter of Religious Learning and Wordly Knowledge in the Jewish Tradition* (Northvale, NJ: Jason Aronson, 1990).

51. There is considerable information about Orthodox developments in Sylvia Barack Fishman, *A Breathe of Life: Feminism in the American Jewish Community* (New York: Free Press, 1993). There is also a lively polemical literature on the topic. See, for example, "Symposium on Women and Jewish Education," *Tradition* (Spring 1994), and Blu Greenberg, "Ultra-Orthodox Women Confront Feminism," *Moment* (June 1996), pp. 36–37, 63.

52. *American Jewish Attitudes Toward Israel and the Peace Process: A Public Opinion Survey* (New York: The American Jewish Committee, 1995); *In the Aftermath of the Rabin Assassination: A Survey of American Jewish Opinion About Israel and the Peace Process* (New York: The American Jewish Committee, 1996).

53. Allan Nadler, *The Hasidim in America* (New York: The American Jewish Committee, 1994).

54. There is a large and growing literature on Lubavitch. Two excellent recent theological and sociological treatments are Aviezer Ravitzky, "The Contemporary Lubavitch Hasidic Movement: Between Conservatism and Messianism," and Menachem Friedman, "Habad as Messianic Fundamentalism: From Local Particularism to Universal Jewish Mission," both in Martin E. Mary and Scott Appleby (Eds.), *Accounting For Fundamentalisms: The Dynamic Character of Movements* (Chicago: University of Chicago Press, 1994), pp. 303–327, 328–357. A skillful journalistic account is Lis Harris, *Holy Days: The World of a Hasidic Family* (New York: Macmillan, 1986).

55. David Berger, "The New Messianism: Passing Phenomenon or Turning Point in

the History of Judaism?," *Jewish Action* (Fall 1995), pp. 34–44, 88, and the correspondence in the Winter 1995 issue, pp. 59–68.

SUGGESTED READINGS

The History of American Judaism

Glazer, N. (1988). *American Judaism* (2nd ed.). Chicago: University of Chicago Press.

Jick, L. A. (1976). *The Americanization of the synagogue, 1820–1870.* Hanover, NH: University Press of New England.

Marcus, J. R., & Peck, A. J. (Eds.). (1985). *The American rabbinate: A century of continuity and change, 1883–1983.* Hoboken, NJ: KTAV.

Raphael, M. L. (1984). *Profiles in American Judaism: The reform, conservative, orthodox, and reconstructionist traditions in historical perspective.* New York: Harper & Row.

Sarna, J. D. (1995). *The evolution of the American synagogue.* In R. M. Seltzer, & N. J. Cohen (Eds.), *The Americanization of the Jews.* New York: New York University Press.

Wertheimer, J. (ed.). (1995). *The American synagogue: A sanctuary transformed.* Hanover, NH: University Press of New England.

Reform Judaism

Borowitz, E. B. (1978). *Reform Judaism today* (3 vols.). New York: Behrman House.

Meyer, M. A. (1988). *Response to modernity: A history of the reform movement in Judaism.* New York: Oxford University Press.

Temkin, S. D. (1973). A century of reform Judaism in America. In *American Jewish Year Book.* New York: American Jewish Committee and Jewish Publication Society.

Conservative Judaism

Gillman, N. (1993). *Conservative Judaism: The new century.* New York: Behrman House.

Karp, A. J. (1986). A century of Conservative Judaism in the United States. In *American Jewish Year Book.* New York: Behrman House.

Sklare, M. (1972). *Conservative Judaism: An American Religious Movement* (new, augmented ed.). New York: Schocken.

Reconstructionist Judaism

Liebman, C. S. (1970). Reconstructionism in American Jewish life. In *American Jewish Year Book,* reprinted in Liebman's *Aspects of the religious behavior of American Jews.* Hoboken, NJ: KTAV, 1974.

Scult, M. (1993). *Judaism faces the twentieth century: A biography of Mordechai M. Kaplan.* Detroit: Wayne State University Press.

Orthodox Judaism

Helmreich, W. B. (1982). *The world of the Yeshiva: An intimate portrait of orthodox Jewry.* New York: Free Press.

Joselit, J. W. (1990). *New York's Jewish Jews: The orthodox community in the interwar years.* Bloomington: Indiana University Press.

Liebman, C. S. (1965). Orthodoxy in American Jewish life. In *American Jewish Year Book,* reprinted in Liebman's *Aspects of the religious behavior of American Jews.* Hoboken, NJ: KTAV, 1974.

American Judaism Today

Fishman, S. B. (1993). *A breath of life: Feminism in the American Jewish community.* New York: Free Press.

Grossman, L. (1988–1996). Jewish communal affairs. In *American Jewish Year Book.* New York: Free Press.

Heilman, S. C. (1995). *Portrait of American Jews: The last half of the 20th century.* Seattle: University of Washington Press.

Kosmin, B. et al. (1991). *Highlights of the CJF 1990 national Jewish population survey.* New York: Council of Jewish Federations.

Wertheimer, J. (1993). *A people divided: Judaism in contemporary America.* New York: Basic Books.

7

The Way We Are: Planning Policy To Serve the Contemporary Jewish Family

SYLVIA BARACK FISHMAN

American Jewish households have often been portrayed as the epitome of traditional, middle-class family values. Whether satirized by novelists and screenwriters for seemingly obsessively nurturing, close-knit, and sober family groupings, or extolled by clergymen for the same attributes, Jewish families have often been portrayed as the ne plus ultra of normative middle-class virtues.

The picture of Jews as unusually oriented to marriage and the family had a genuine basis in reality in most historical, traditional Jewish communities and in the recent past as well, especially in the post-World War II period in the United States. In the 1950s the traditional Jewish religious and cultural emphasis on family life was in almost perfect confluence with the national ethos. As Americans yearned for normalcy after the trauma of the war years, movies, magazines, radio, and television glorified family life. Religious traditions such as Judaism that supported normative family constellations seemed very much in harmony with American mores. Americans married young and had their babies young. Women were strongly encouraged to devote their energies to homemaking and communal volunteerism.

This national cultural emphasis on marriage and the family reinforced Jewish values that had been in place for hundreds of years. Within traditional Jewish culture, marriage was seen as the only salutary and productive state for adult human beings. Within Jewish life there was simply no comfortable cultural niche for an adult without spouse and children; there was no celibate clergy, no tradition of a son or daughter remaining unmarried to care for a widowed father or mother. On the contrary, rabbinical literature warned Jewish congregations to avoid hiring an unmarried rabbi or religious teacher, and a child who remained unmarried was often regarded by parents as a source of shame. Similarly, it was unheard of for a Jewish couple to remain deliberately childless;

infertility was the source of anguish when it occurred, and couples often took whatever heroic efforts were available to them in an effort to have children.

Contemporary American Jewish households, however, are dramatically altered. The extent of change is remarkable when one realizes how recent it is. Twenty years ago, American Jewish households were still, in terms of family formation, fairly traditional. A National Jewish Population Study in 1970 showed that at that time 78 percent of American Jewish households consisted of a married couple who had or planned to have children.[1] Only 6 percent of American Jewish adults in 1970 had never been married. In comparison, the 1970 U.S. Census showed that 16 percent of all Americans were single, and 72 percent were married. The nature of Jewish families in 1970 was distinctive as well. For many years the Jewish divorce rate was low. In addition, popular perceptions have held that Jewish families in the past were far less likely than most to be afflicted by such pathologies as alcoholism, wife battering, and child abuse.

To a large extent popular stereotypes about the nature of the American Jewish family remain intact. Woody Allen's Jewish mother's disembodied, nagging head still floats over movie screens in the 1988 film, "New York Stories," advising her middle-aged son to dress properly, to get married, and to eat right. Allen, ultimately listening to Mama, finds serenity and ecstatic happiness in the arms of a Jewish woman who knows how to boil chicken just like his mother.

In real life, however, Jewish family life has been profoundly transformed—as has family life for American households in general. American Jewish households today simply do not look or behave as they did in the post-World War II period. Survey research such as the 1990 National Jewish Population Survey (NJPS) dramatically demonstrates that in terms of their family formation, American Jews today resemble other middle- and upper-middle-class white Americans much more than they resemble the American Jews preceding them in the decades after World War II.[2]

SINGLES

The most striking difference in the adult population of American Jews now and 25 years ago is that many more are unmarried. The large proportion of unmarried American Jews—about one-third of the population—is due primarily to delayed marriage, and secondarily to rising rates of divorce. Today, one-third of American Jewish women ages 25 to 34 are not married. In comparison, in the 1950s half of American Jewish women were married by age 22, and three-quarters were married by age 25. The decline in the proportion of married Jews is due not only to acculturation but, perhaps even more importantly, to changes in American culture. American Jews do not live in a vacuum. They have always been extremely responsive to middle- and upper-middle-class American culture. When American Jews married early and had their children early in the 1950s they were following American patterns and Jewish patterns, which at the time had considerable overlap. When they marry late today they are following American patterns only. Later marriage is part of the middle- and upper-middle-class white American behaviors.

American Jews today are overwhelmingly likely to work towards graduate or professional training and to begin establishing their careers before they make a permanent romantic commitment. While Jewish young men and women were more likely than the general public to acquire a college education in the 1950s, 60s, and 70s—and consequently to marry slightly later than average—their eventual rates of marriage were almost universal. Today, not only do a substantial number marry late, but it is not even clear that they will ever marry.

The policy implications that flow out of these statistics are based on the now-unavoidable fact that more American Jews today are unmarried. Some of them want to be unmarried, and some do not. Jewish institutions require refocusing to meet the very diverse needs of singles of various ages—a never-married 25-year-old clearly has different needs than a 60-year-old divorcee—and with varying marital aspirations.

For much of American Jewish history, synagogues and Jewish institutions made few efforts to attract singles, assuming that when Jews married and started their families they would naturally be attracted to synagogue affiliation. This approach worked reasonably well as long as Jews were likely to get married, and sooner rather than later. Today, however, when marriage may be postponed or simply not in the cards for younger adults, synagogues and Jewish institutions must consider the specific needs of this constituency if they hope to attract them to participation and membership. Beyond this utilitarian reason for serving the singles population, one might cite a religious and moral reason to reach out to them and serve them: Singles are Jews with legitimate spiritual needs and with valuable talents to contribute to the community, regardless of their marital status.

First, the most obvious implications of this statement are financial and social. Since singles are, by definition, living on a single salary and may have lower household income than married couples, they are most comfortably served by synagogues with sliding-dues scales. Synagogues are sometimes resistant to providing such financial aid because the popular stereotype of singles regards them as having few demands on their salaries. However, sliding scales for singles have important and psychological rationales: a) singles may perceive themselves as having limited income, even when objectively they may have more discretionary income than married couples with children; b) they may perceive themselves as having fewer consumer needs in relationship to the synagogue than a household with persons of many ages, and may balk at the idea of paying full membership for a limited menu of services; and c) the same factors which contribute to the singlehood of the individual may make them more resistant to affiliation; therefore, whatever can be done to mitigate this resistance should be employed. A sliding scale is to be preferred over "scholarships," since the process of applying for such a scholarship and appealing one's case before board members is often profoundly unappealing, and may drive the less-committed away.

Second, efforts should be made to educate synagogue and Jewish institutional activists to be welcoming to new or potential members. Persons who are deeply entrenched in boards, committees, sisterhoods, brotherhoods, etc., often treat these organizations as their own private social clubs and can leave the impression that newcomers are unwanted. This is, of course, a problem that exists in other areas of Jewish life as well; it is not unique to synagogues. However, social exclusiveness is of particular concern in synagogues because the synagogue world is the largest window of opportunity available to the Jewish community, in terms of Jewish-identity concerns. City studies and 1990 NJPS data indicate that while only a little over a third of American Jews belong to synagogues at any one time, four out of every five adults who call themselves Jewish by religion will belong to a synagogue at some point in their life cycle. If they are engaged by some aspect of synagogue life they may retain their membership. Otherwise, membership seems to be entered into on a service-and-needs basis.

Third, human beings prefer seeing someone like themselves in leadership positions in order to feel that they truly belong. When only married couples attain leadership positions in Jewish institutional and synagogue settings, singles can receive a message that these are institutions geared primarily to one's marital status. In fact, for much of Jewish history, this would have been a correct assumption. Marriage was encouraged both by overt encouragement and by applying social sanctions to the nonmarried state. However, making today's singles feel that they are not legitimated in synagogue and Jewish institutional settings will not make them want to get married faster; it will simply make them avoid synagogue settings. In keeping with the voluntary nature of American Jewish life, grooming singles for leadership positions within the synagogue structure is a practical step toward giving singles an emotional niche in the worship and social worlds of the synagogue.

Fourth, every synagogue and Jewish organization should have some type of ongoing market research, which can be as simple as intake and exit questionnaires or interviews. Knowing why people chose to enter an environment is extremely useful in determining their perceived needs and expectations. Such information makes it much more likely that new members' needs will be met, enhancing the possibility that they will be drawn into active membership rather than being alienated by disappointments.

Jewish organizations and agencies as well as synagogues have cooperated in some communities to create a special Friday-night service for singles, which has been widely successful despite initial skepticism. Late Friday-evening services followed by an Oneg Shabbat have proved to be a popular program in at least two very different settings: More than 1500 individuals attended such services in one year in Washington, D.C., and 4000 asked to be put on the mailing list of a rotating, suburban, Friday-evening program in New Jersey (Silverstein & Rubin, 1985).

Jewish organizations can be useful as well in creating Jewish dating services, both commercial and not-for-profit, to serve the needs of their singles-client population. These modern versions of the traditional *shadchen* utilize computer-matching of eligible men and women as well as the skills of human interviewers to combine likely prospects for introductions. While private dating services can be very costly, some communities provide subsidized services aimed at clients ranging from college students through middle-aged singles.[3]

Some strategies seem to work especially well in attracting singles to the Jewish organizational environment. Purely social programs involving food—Bagels Plus—are reportedly perennial winners. Social-action programs are very attractive to large numbers of American Jews, including those who are unsure about their religious orientation; programs to benefit the community at large have proved to be a very effective means of bringing marginal Jews into a Jewish sphere of operations. Political programs can attract persons—including singles—who are not interested in the more standard offerings of Jewish organizational life. Cultural programming—Jewish music, films, drama, graphic art exhibitions—also comprise an important vehicle for attracting singles and other young or unaffiliated Jewish adults. All of these kinds of programs have the additional advantage that they allow singles to network without feeling that they have been placed on the shopping block of a singles' meat-market. Singles are brought together with a purpose beyond themselves, creating a far more natural environment than many dances and bars.

Significantly, singles themselves have indicated a strong interest in Jewish sponsorship of singles programs in many communities. The strength of these preferences varies from community to community. In general, the more "untraditional" the community, the less the preference on the part of singles for Jewish sponsorship of services; the more traditional the community, the greater the preference. In addition, the more intensely Jewish the attitudes and Jewish communal-involvement of the singles involved, the more likely they are to prefer Jewish sponsorship of singles programs.

Much evidence exists that a contributing factor to extended singlehood in the Jewish community is the negative image of Jewish men and women that prevails in literature, the media, and popular culture. These negative images produce precarious relationships among Jewish singles and work to undermine feelings of erotic attraction between Jews. Many professionals believe that it is most important for Jewish organizations and institutions to combat these negative images on both a formal and informal basis.[4]

A word of caution is in order in dealing with singles: The assumption should not be made that every single wants to marry, although many of them reportedly do. For those singles who do not wish to marry because of sexual orientation or for other personal reasons, a constant stress on marriage may feel oppressive or alienating. Jewish communal institutions have a delicate but critical task in creating an environment that enhances family formation, but makes room for those for whom the formation of a normative family is not an option. Failure to respond to the needs of singles may work to dissipate such levels of involvement as currently exist. Therefore for reasons arising out of organizational self-interest as well as altruism, Jewish communal institutions and agencies may do well to address themselves wholeheartedly to the Jewish singles population.

DIMINISHED FERTILITY

A second major change in American Jewish families, linked to later marriage, is that American Jews today have smaller completed families than in traditional Jewish communities or in American communities of the recent past. In the 1950s and 1960s, when non-Jews had 3.5 children per family, Jewish couples had almost three (2.8) children per family; today, as the size of white, non-Jewish families has diminished to slightly fewer than two children per family, Jewish women have slightly fewer children on average than non-Jews. Working with 1990 NJPS data, sociologists Moshe Hartman and Harriet Hartman found that professional Jewish women have 1.4 children; those employed in technical jobs have 1.5; and those working in other capacities have between 1.8 and 1.9 (Hartman & Hartman, 1996). Demographer Sidney Goldstein found that Jewish women ages 40 to 44 averaged 1.6 children, compared to 2.1 children among all U.S. white women (Goldstein, 1992, p. 169; Mott & Abma, 1992).

Some Jewish communal leaders find this decline in family size disturbing for its own sake; later marriage and smaller families mean fewer Jews in an already-shrinking American Jewish population. From a woman-centered standpoint, this figure would be less disturbing if it were an accurate reflection of expected and desired family size. However, Jewish women say they want the same number of children as they did three decades ago. Indeed, American Jewish women who acquire higher degrees say they want more children than American Jewish women who do not finish college. This desire is unique to Jewish women—in other ethnic and religious groups, more education brings with it a tendency to want no children, or only one child (Goldscheider & Goldscheider, 1989).

Despite these stated family goals, the same women who say they want two or three children are often postponing marriage and starting families until they finish their graduate and professional training and establish their careers. The end result is that Jewish women with master's degrees have the lowest actual rate of childbirth of any cohort in their age group. Thus today's smaller Jewish-family size seems to indicate unwanted infertility (Mott & Abma, 1992). As maternal populations age, infertility problems increase, and expertise in using contraceptive devices ceases to be a good indicator of whether couples will complete their families with the number of children they hoped to have (Maranto, 1995). Looking both at medical literature and at the proportion of Jewish couples who have no children and pursue adoption procedures, it is estimated that 15 percent of Jewish couples who want children find it difficult or impossible to physically give birth to them.

The size of American Jewish households has shrunk partially through family planning. This is not a new phenomenon among American Jews. Like high levels of secular education, the widespread commitment to family planning is a long-standing and well-established phenomenon in the American Jewish community—indeed, it is probably one of the first and most profound aspects of the merging of distinctively Jewish and American ideals. Activists on behalf of birth control, such as Emma Goldman and immigrant women who read about contraceptive techniques in the Yiddish translation of Margaret Sanger's *What Every Girl Should Know,* probably felt that they were rebelling against Jewish culture (Gordon, 1977; Lederhendler, 1992). However, for their daughters and granddaughters, birth control and reproductive choice are officially espoused by such mainstream Jewish organizations as Hadassah, and are axioms of American Jewish culture.

Contemporary American Jews are vigorously in favor of family planning, both on a personal and communal level. Too few of today's potential parents realize that family planning implies not only preventing conception when a child is unwanted, but enhancing possibilities for conception when a child is wanted as well. No woman should ever give birth to a child she does not want, but many Jewish women are not having the children whom they do want.

Despite insistence by some feminists that the specter of infertility has been exaggerated as part of an antiwoman "backlash," fertility is not an even playing field bounded on one side by menarche and on the other by menopause. As maternal populations age, infertility problems increase. For reasons still not clearly understood by the medical community, some women who easily conceive and carry pregnancies to term in their mid- to late twenties have problems with conception and gestation in their thirties and forties. Even among those couples who have conditions that would cause infertility at any age, beginning the process of trying to conceive earlier gives them and infertility specialists more time to work with and more chance of a desired outcome. Without adequate knowledge about the ramifications of their family-planning decisions, women sometimes make decisions that they later regret.

In addition, the revolution in lifestyles inflicted by an infant upon a relatively older, career-oriented couple may be experienced as more disruptive than in a younger, more flexible household. Couples who have established patterns for many years of devoting themselves to their careers, of enjoying adult social lives and entertainments and vacations, may have difficulty adjusting to the restrictions of a household with children. Even those who thoroughly enjoy their new responsibilities may find that their energy levels flag. Under such circumstances, couples who started out expecting to have two children may decide they are better off with one.

While many in the Jewish community have lamented the later and smaller families of American Jews, little has been done to address related issues in terms of policy. One of the reasons that so little has been said by Jewish communal agencies and institutions is that speaking up on behalf of childbearing is "politically incorrect" in our society. However, avoiding this issue ignores those Jewish women who want to have children and discover, amidst heartache and regret, that time is no longer on their side. In a nonsectarian, downtown, infertility support group for career women in Chicago, Illinois, for example, all but four women enrolled are Jewish; the remaining four are non-Jewish women married to Jewish men.

This disdain for aspiring mothers is of course not unique to the Jewish community. A nurse who works in infertility clinics reports in a medical journal that some feminists condemn women who avail themselves of treatments as pawns in a male-controlled technology, asserting that women would not want children so much if they were not brainwashed by male-dominated society (Sandelowski, 1990). Even "early" marriage at age 23, reports a bride in *Newsweek* magazine, brings scornful reactions from co-workers and friends (Davis, 1995). Many observers who define themselves as "familists" feel that American society is not friendly to stable relationships, to families, and to children. Without in any way relinquishing American Jewish commitments to reproductive freedom and access to family planning, it seems appropriate for Jewish communal leaders and institutions to advocate on behalf of childbearing for women who want to have children.

Some practical suggestions as to how the Jewish community might advocate on behalf of wanted Jewish children and their mothers include: 1) Premarital and early marital family-planning counseling should be available under Jewish auspices. Such counseling should include information about conception as well as contraception. 2) Women-centered information, including that available in scientific and general interest publications, should be made available through Jewish institutions. 3) Infertility hotlines and support groups should be offered under Jewish auspices. Counseling is critical to help women deal with grief, acceptance, and possible adoption. 4) Adoption aid is an important new need in the Jewish community, and is more widely available than people realize. Multifaceted adoption aid should be a staple offering on the Jewish communal menu.

DUAL-CAREER FAMILIES

A third major change in the American Jewish family has to do with dramatically transformed patterns of labor-force participation among American Jewish mothers. For a good part of the twentieth century, American Jewish women were distinguished by how readily they dropped out of the labor force and stopped working outside the home for pay as soon as they married or started a family. According to Goldscheider, in the 1970s Jewish women were far more likely than other American women to cease working outside the home as soon as they became pregnant with their first child (Goldscheider, 1986). They returned to the labor market only after all their children were well into their adolescent years. Economist Barry Chiswick has suggested that this pattern of Jewish women acquiring higher education and then remaining at home to raise their children prior to 1970 probably resulted in the even higher educational level and resourcefulness of Jewish children, since Jewish women devoted comparatively more time to "educational care" activities such as playing, reading, and talking with their children than did women in the general population (Chiswick, 1985).

But this readiness to terminate labor-force participation was in itself an accommodation to non-Jewish behavior patterns. Eastern European Jewish women routinely worked outside the home for pay, and such marketplace activism was viewed positively by many traditional Jewish communities because it facilitated male devotion to the study of scholarly texts. When Eastern European women emigrated to the United States, such working outside the home for pay among married women was severely discouraged by the German-Jewish Americans who had already become doubly adapted to women being full-time homemakers: First, as German Jews assimilated to the bourgeois German pattern (Kaplan, 1991), and second, when German Jews adapted to the United States. Eastern European Jewish women also quickly adopted the Americanized pattern of looking down on outside employment for married women; indeed, when financial necessity forced them to work, they often reinterpreted reality so that they could reply that they were not working outside the home for pay (Glenn, 1990). In contrast, today, dual-career Jewish households have become the new normative Jewish family; well over half of American Jewish women with children under six years old are employed outside the home.

Jewish women stayed home and took care of their families not because this was originally a Jewish value, but because it was originally an outside cultural value. After a time, they came to believe that they did it because it was a Jewish value—indeed, when they left their homes to go to work, many felt that they were disobeying Jewish norms. Today, only a small minority of Jewish households consists of a mother at home, who divides her time between raising her several children and volunteering for philanthropic communal causes, and a father who functions as the family's sole breadwinner. Contemporary Jewish women have been at the forefront of feminist striving, almost universally acquiring higher education and pursuing career goals. Recent studies of Jewish populations in cities across the United States and the National Jewish Population Survey both reveal that at the present time the majority of American Jewish mothers with children under six years old work outside the home for pay.

Partially as a result of this feminist revolution, American Jewish fathers have become more involved with the day-to-day raising of their young children. While this behavior is perceived as gender neutral, sensitive, etc., it actually is more in keeping with the traditional role of the Jewish father as moral educator of his family, which was abandoned by many American Jewish immigrants and second-generation males in their entrepreneurial, economic strivings earlier in the century.

The Jewish community in certain ways has had the bad habit of taking its normative families for granted. Families with working parents have their own set of needs, often passionately articulated. Even though the dual-career family is the new normative-family unit, Jewish schools and institutions often behave as though they are living in the 1950s. When schools continue with such practices as insisting on daytime volunteers, or arranging for mid-day dismissals in the case of snow without first calling parents, they make the assumption that every household has a parent on duty at home, while the fact is that few Jewish households today have such arrangements. Then, to add insult to injury, many parents report that schools and institutions often refer to the household without an at-home parent as deficient, adding a "guilt-trip" to the logistical difficulties. No one will ever know to what an extent such punitive attitudes serve as unwitting spurs to smaller families; and, likewise, it will never be known to what extent a more working-family-friendly attitude might encourage dual-career couples to have more children.

Perhaps the most outstanding opportunity created by the prevalence of dual-career households is connected to expanded modes of Jewish education. Dual-career families can and do pay for child care from infancy onward; their preferred setting for child-care arrangements is in a Jewish one. Nevertheless, only a small proportion of Jewish parents actually enroll their children in Jewish-sponsored child care (Berger & Sternberg, 1988). Optimally, Jewish child care should run the gamut from babies through high-school-age children, with specialized programming for each.

JEWISH EDUCATION AS A FULL-SERVICE OPPORTUNITY

Jewish-content, early childhood education can provide the infant and young child with both formal and informal Jewish educational experiences, which echo in many ways the types of Jewish enculturation that are typical of traditional Jewish homes, such as learning Jewish prayers and songs as part of the daily routine. Jewish parents want "only the best" for their young children, and high-quality programs soon pay for themselves after start-up time. The demand for such programs still far exceeds the availability in most communities.

For school-age children, an important opportunity exists for Jewish communal institutions and synagogues to work together to create after-school, cross-institutional, comprehensive programs. Such programs can provide children with diverse activities, including religious education, sports, supervised homework time, and social interactions with other Jewish children. In those communities where pilot initiatives have created programs that transport children from school to Jewish community centers to synagogue religious education and back, response has been positive, but to date such programming has been available only in a few, pioneering locales.

Perhaps the most critical—and underserved—age group is American Jewish teenagers. A series of studies based on the 1990 NJPS indicate that full engagement in the many opportunities offered by America's open society does not necessarily erode Jewish involvements—as long as children are provided with an intensive and extensive Jewish education. The most effective programs are comprised of a multiday education that spans the early childhood, school age, and teenage years, supported by a Jewishly active homelife and complemented by Jewish youth groups, camping experiences, and trips to Israel.

Research based on the 1990 National Jewish Population Survey and the city studies shows that the most powerful positive impact comes from a day-school education that spans the early childhood, school age, and teenage years. Inmarriages are found among 80 percent of Jews who receive six years of day school, and 91 percent of those who receive nine or more years of day school. Some reports indicate that 95 percent of those who attend for the full 12 years and graduate day school are married to born Jews. Other forms of multiday Jewish education (more than one day a week) have an impact as well. Inmarriages are found among over half of Jews who received at least six years of multiday Jewish education. Recent reports by researchers such as Mordechai Rimor and Elihu Katz (Rimor & Katz, 1993), Seymour Martin Lipset (Lipset, 1990), and Alice Goldstein and Sylvia Barack Fishman (Fishman & Goldstein, 1993; Goldstein & Fishman, 1993) repeatedly indicate the powerful cumulative effect of Jewish education, and especially of day-school education. These studies based on the 1990 NJPS are further supported by independent studies of the impact of Jewish day schools, such as the recent survey by Alvin Schiff and Mareleyn Schneider (Schiff & Schneider, 1994).

Moreover, the impact of day school and of Jewish education crosses denominational lines. For example, among Jews raised in Conservative homes, over 70 percent of those who received six or more years of day school are married to born Jews. While there are certainly differences from denomination to denomination, those households that have strong ties to Judaism are not exclusively Orthodox. Highly involved Jews continue to thrive in every wing of Judaism within households that follow certain critical patterns. About one-third of the Jewish community falls into a group that several social scientists have suggested calling "activist" Jews (Cohen, 1988). "Activist" Jews demonstrate or "act out" their Judaism in a wide variety of ways. Activist households are found among the Conservative, Reform, and Reconstructionist populations. Within each wing of Judaism extensive Jewish education makes a powerful, positive difference for activism in every measurable behavior: marrying a Jew, joining and attending a synagogue, contributing to and volunteering time for Jewish causes, and regarding Israel as a central aspect of existence.

Conversely, rather marginally involved households are found even among Jews who call themselves Orthodox. Simply affiliating with Orthodoxy does not guarantee generational continuity, unless other patterns, such as extensive Jewish education, are followed as well. Even among Orthodox households, the home cannot do everything. The mixed-marriage rate of 20 percent among Jews who identify their parental home as Orthodox demonstrates that the cultural pull of secularized Protestant America and the high level of secular educational sophistication of most American Jews demand a high level of Jewish educational sophistication for the optimum enhancement of Jewish identity. Optimum levels of Jewish connectedness are obtained when Jews are raised in highly identified and practicing homes and receive substantial levels of Jewish education.

Activist Jews almost always identify with one or another branch of Judaism. Especially among younger American Jews (ages 25–44), they almost never call themselves "just Jews" or "secular Jews." This religious identification of activist Jews seems to have been less striking in the past, when American Jews often "specialized" in one or another aspect of Jewish behaviors. A Jew might consider himself to be a secular or cultural Jew and might demonstrate his Jewishness by working for a Jewish federation or the Anti-Defamation League; or he might consider himself to be an ethnic Jew and demonstrate his Jewishness by having many Jewish friends.

Today, however, there is an overwhelming tendency toward overlap of Jewish activities. The younger American Jew, ages 25 to 44, who works for so-called secular Jewish organizations such as federations, the Anti-Defamation League, the American Jewish Congress, the American Jewish Committee, etc., is very unlikely to think of himself or herself as a secular Jew. Instead, the data indicate that younger Jews who work for "secular" Jewish organizations almost always identify as Jewish by religion. Younger workers for "secular" Jewish organizations are also likely to be married to Jews, to belong to synagogues and to be among the more frequent attenders, to perform a higher-than-average number of Jewish rituals, and to have significant involvement with Israel. Among younger American Jews, only those who say that they are Jewish by religion are likely to have primarily Jewish-friendship circles; ethnicity per se is losing its grip. Activist Jews are created Jews now, more than ever in the past, and one of the most powerful shaping forces in their lives is Jewish education.

Israel programs are often touted as a panacea, an alternative to classical educational settings, but research indicates that the Israel experience is best viewed as a complement to, rather than a substitute for, Jewish schools. Steven M. Cohen's research, based on a 1993 national sample of over 1400 Jewish parents and their 615 teenaged children, who were accessed as a subsample of a Market Facts, Inc., Washington-based Consumer Mail Panel, shows: "Youth groups and adolescent Israel travel are associated with increments in Jewish involvement, even after controlling for parents' Jewish involvement, Jewish schooling, and youth groups and other factors. . . . The Israel visit of one's youth seems to bring with it a 15 percent increment in the chances of scoring high on Jewish involvement" (Cohen, 1995).

It is important for us to remember that Cohen's research shows that Israel programs boost sustained support for Israel—but have very little lasting impact on other types of Jewish involvements. In studies generated by the 1990 NJPS and in Cohen's data, the cumulative impact of Jewish education from generation to generation is quite clear. When both parents have received six or more years of Jewish education, virtually all of their children receive Jewish education. Indeed, by the time they have reached 16 to 18 years old, the children of parents who received six years of Jewish education have received more than nine years of Jewish education.

And yet, despite the proven effectiveness of longer years and longer hours of Jewish education, fewer than one-quarter of American teenagers ages 16 to 18 are involved in Jewish educational programs. Of those who are involved, 44 percent are attending all-day schools, 29 percent are attending afterschool programs that meet more than once a week, and 27 percent are attending one-day-a-week programs. In many communities, day-school high-school programs are only available under Orthodox auspices. In fact, in many communities there is no Hebrew high-school program available either. Thus during the all-important teen years many communities have a dearth of appropriate programming on any level.

When one thinks of teenagers, especially those who come from dual-career families in which parental supervision may be lacking during the afterschool hours, Jewish community centers (JCCs) are an obvious target-locale in which to serve this population. In a Brandeis University report by Amy Sales and Gary Tobin on revitalizing Jewish community center youth services, JCC personnel were asked to what extent their institutions engaged in using evaluation, needs assessment, feasibility studies, and marketing studies to guide them as they created programming for teenagers. They found that most JCCs do not engage in systematic planning nor implementation of youth services. Thus although teenagers have very definite ideas about what kinds of programming and what locales might be attractive to them, little is being done systematically to access their ideas and put them into play. The authors come to the conclusion that "teens are often a lower priority in JCCs than are seniors, preschoolers, and other groups. Their low status is reflected in the youth departments' budgets, in the low level of stafftime allocated to teens, in the limited availability of Center resources for teen services, and in the lack of available and/or appropriate space for teen activities." They comment wryly, "JCC leadership may claim that youth are a priority for the Center, but their actions frequently belie this assertion" (Sales & Tobin, 1995).

The Brandeis report on JCC teen services highlights what all of us know to be one of the primary stumbling blocks in creating effective programs for Jewish teenagers—money. The revitalizing effect of money can be seen in hopeful, new directions in Hillel programming, which addresses the next age group up, late teens and early twenties. According to a recent article by Yossi Abramowitz in *Moment* magazine, a generous infusion of money is already changing the direction and impact of Hillel programs (Abramowitz, 1995).

The data indicate strong support for family education. They highlight the fact that Jewish education for parents and children is linked. Certainly, no one can turn back the clock and provide contemporary adults with the extensive Jewish educational experiences they missed in their childhoods. However, households in which parents are currently receiving some type of formal or informal Jewish education also have very high measures of Jewish education for children. No doubt, the influence goes both ways.

When Jewish children are urged to take piano and ballet and karate lessons, when they are chauffeured to and from team-sports events, when they are pushed to be at the top of their classes and get into prestigious schools—when parents are actively involved in every aspect of their development but their Jewish development, they learn that Jewish development is not a priority. If we want a broad change in the lives of Jewish teenagers today, we have to educate their families as well. We must work for an increased accessibility of the potential "late saves"—a successful Israel trip, a vibrant youth group, a transformative Jewish camp, a charismatic Jewish-studies teacher. But we must also be aware of the paradox that background is important in the likelihood that teenagers will involve themselves in these activities. Our chances for broad-based change in the lives of Jewish teenagers are immeasurably enhanced by broad-based change in the Jewish texture of family life.

DIVORCED INDIVIDUALS AND FAMILY UNITS

The American Jewish family is not only formed later than in the recent past, but is also often less durable as well. Rates of divorce, once far lower in the Jewish community than among non-Jews, are climbing and, while still lower, are close to the national average. Increased divorce has produced increased numbers of Jewish single-parent families as well. The number of Jewish single-parent families, like the number of divorces, seems deceptively small at first glance, but because of the generally low Jewish birthrate, it is a significant factor in the number of households with children, comprising about 10 percent of all Jewish households with children. Divorce is twice as likely to terminate a mixed-married relationship as an inmarried Jewish household; conversely, once a Jewish–Jewish couple has divorced, the ex-spouses are twice as likely to marry non-Jews the second-time around than they were when entering into a first marriage.

In single-parent households—usually headed by women—annual income is in general severely diminished, when compared with the income of both divorced men and married couples. In Boston, for example, twice as many divorced women as divorced men reported annual incomes of under $15,000 a year in 1985 (Israel, 1985). Thus single Jewish mothers and their children comprise the new poor in American Jewish society, rivaled only by certain segments of the elderly and the newest immigrants.

Almost one-third of American Jewish children live in homes that have been affected by divorce. Blended families, even more than single-parent families, have been proliferating in the Jewish community, with about one-fifth of Jewish children living in such households. For both parents and children in single-parent and blended families, Jewish life-cycle events can present stressful situations (Friedman, 1993). Planning for celebrations can pull children in two directions. They often have difficulty dealing with the Jewish emphasis on family, especially around Sabbaths, holiday times, and life-cycle events. Rates of divorce are far lower among Jews who call themselves Orthodox or who have a high rate of ritual observance, which is twice as high as the average among Jews married to non-Jews. Nevertheless, when divorce does take place in Orthodox households, it brings its own set of problems.

Many of the emotional problems generated by synagogues, Jewish schools, and Jewish community centers can be minimized if Jewish educators adopt the attitude that Jewish customs and ceremonies are not pegged to gender divisions and to stereotypical images of the normative family, but are the birthright of all Jews. For example, references to Sabbath and holiday celebrations should make it clear that rituals such as candle lighting and kiddush over wine emphatically are not the "property" of the two-parent family, but can and should appropriately be part of the repertoire of the single or single-parent household as well. Jewish singles and children should be empowered to participate in their spiritual birthright as Jews, insofar as they desire to do so.

One of the most distinctively "Jewish" problems associated with divorce is that of the *agunah*—the woman whose husband has obtained a civil divorce but who will not cooperate in providing her with a religious divorce; under the terms of Jewish law such a husband is free to remarry, while his wife is not. Some religious movements and communities have attempted to deal with the problems of women caught in such situations, either on a systematic or a case-by-case basis. Still, thousands of women are trapped in situations in which husbands and lawyers use the obtaining of a Jewish divorce as a tool for unfair bargaining or wreaking vengeance. A clear, forceful, Jewish communal response to this issue would benefit countless women and their children (Friedman, 1994).

Communal responses to the large number of divorced Jews and children living in households affected by divorce should also certainly include sensitivity training for all professionals who come into contact with a diverse population. Language is important: Many divorced persons have voiced their dislike of the use of terms such as "intact" and the common assumption that Judaism is the property of two-parent families. When dealing with divorce, as when dealing with singleness, communal workers face the challenge of supporting normative-family units and also behaving in a supportive mode with other types of family units.

ABUSIVE HOUSEHOLDS

One of the sadder developments of contemporary Jewish life, even among highly Orthodox populations, is that substance abuse, wife abuse, and child abuse are now recognized phenomena in Jewish households.[5] No doubt there was always some incidence of these problems in traditional Jewish societies and in the United States decades ago, even when communal leaders were unable to recognize them and unwilling to deal with them. Today all segments of the Jewish community have begun to work with incidences of problem families and to try to deal with them. One of their most difficult tasks is raising communal awareness.

There is no doubt that contemporary American Jews now consume alcohol in more American patterns, and that alcoholism is a larger problem than it used to be. The perceived rise in spousal abuse may also be linked to increased alcohol consumption. Many communities have established kosher facilities for battered women and their children, and it seems appropriate that such facilities should be available in every major metropolitan area. Other necessary programming for problem households would include efforts to locate Jewish homeless individuals and families, and to meet their needs in kosher, Jewishly aware facilities.

The Jewish community is much more aware now than it was decades ago about the sweeping nature of abuse situations. Nevertheless, it is important to keep communal consciousness raised about these important issues and to continue dealing with their ramifications. Not least, it is important for the Jewish community to provide therapeutic settings, such as counseling and psychiatric help, which do not deride religious commitments. Persons who do not wish to jettison their religious behaviors, but still need help in dealing with psychological problems, need to be able to access the kind of help that is sympathetic to the complexities of their lives.

MEETING THE NEEDS OF THE ELDERLY

Elderly Jews have also been sharply affected by new trends in American Jewish family life. Today's Jewish families are geographically mobile with very specialized patterns, resulting in polarization by age: families with children at home seek-out suburban or exurban areas; childless careerists occupy revitalized urban areas; and the elderly either move to communities specifically designed for their needs or are left behind in less desirable urban areas largely devoid of Jewish youth. Like other elderly urban dwellers, isolated older Jews often suffer from the common problems of poverty and violence. Thus although traditional Jewish law emphasizes the irrevocable debt that biological children owe to their parents, and urges middle-aged children to personally look after their aging parents' physical and emotional needs, American Jews have been extraordinarily mobile, pursuing vocational and personal advantage even at great distances from other family members. Mobility—including the chronological segmentation of families—has become an American Jewish characteristic.

It should also be said that the elderly themselves often opt for this arrangement, and many of them seem to prefer to live in same-age villages in the Sunbelt, even when these arrangements take them far from children and grandchildren. In making these choices, they also are responding to values that may in fact be alien to Jewish tradition, although they are perceived as being characteristically Jewish. One thinks of the fiercely traditional mother in Harvey Fierstein's *Torch Song Trilogy,* who declares, after her husband dies: "I'll go to Florida. I want to die. But first I'll go to Florida. That's what we do," implying that Jewish widows traditionally find a place for themselves among their own in Florida.

Since older American Jews come in a variety of sizes, physical conditions, and basic needs, the community needs to plan comprehensive programming: The most pressing needs of the elderly will probably always be physical, especially as the proportion of 75-year olds and over and the frail elderly grows (Rosenwaike, 1990, 1992). However, even physically able older Jews often have unmet needs. Psychological-support services and friendly visitor-volunteer programs are critical for persons who are emotionally isolated—a condition that can afflict older people regardless of economic status. Logistical support, such as providing transportation to doctors and shopping, can make the difference between continued independence and institutionalization. Some communities have done very well with programs that bring the elderly to college and communal activities that are already taking place, mainstreaming otherwise isolated elderly persons into multigenerational settings. In addition, communities should look increasingly to creating semi-independent settings where older people can partake of opportunities for assisted living.

FAMILIES WITH NON-JEWISH SPOUSES

Not least, the American Jewish home has been changed by high levels of outmarriage. The percentage of Jewish marriages that involves a non-Jew has escalated from the relatively low rates in the 1950s to about half of first marriages conducted in the 1980s. Rates of outmarriage for second marriages are considerably higher. While scholars have argued as to whether the outmarriage percentage of first marriages conducted in the last decade is closer to 40 or 50 percent, the pattern is clear (Medding et al., 1992). American Jews today are likely to fall in love with and marry partners whom they meet at school or work without giving much thought to their religious background. Highly educated Americans are not more likely to marry non-Jews than those who are modestly educated; indeed, in contrast to patterns observed in the 1950s, Jews who have a more impressive secular education are more likely to marry within the faith. Outmarriage is not a route to socioeconomic upward mobility for Jews as it was earlier in the century; nevertheless, rates of outmarriage are far higher than they were when marrying a non-Jew positively benefitted one's chances in life.

High rates of outmarriage themselves are testimony to the Americanization of the Jewish population; in a culture that emphasizes the autonomy of the individual, the epitome of individualism is romantic choice. From childhood onward, American children are indoctrinated with motifs of romantic individualism. One has only to think of recent Disney creations such as *The Little Mermaid,* who gives up her own voice and the glorious diversity of her father's kingdom "under the sea" to be "part of his world"—part of the human world of her conventionally handsome prince charming. From Bambi and Thumper and the forest creatures on up, the American birthright is the right to make romantic life-choices freely. The person who would interfere with that right is viewed as the "Grinch Who Stole Christmas." Only extensive, formal Jewish education has a positive link with the propensity to marry a Jewish mate, to establish a Jewish household, and to raise Jewish children.

Statistics from the 1990 NJPS tell us why outmarriage is a problem: only half of the households with one Jewish parent and one non-Jewish say they are raising their children as Jews. Only 40 percent of those children will receive any type of formal Jewish education. The vast majority of these households will have little or no connection to the Jewish community. Children raised in these households will be likely to feel that they are Jewish and something else; they will have a dual-psychological identity. Most of them will end up having no religion, or perceiving their Jewish ethnicity as an incidental aspect of their lives. By contrast, in households where a conversion into Judaism has taken place, the household's Jewish behaviors very closely approximate those of inmarried households.

Responses to the rising rates of outmarriage need to take place on both a before-and-after basis. Clearly, educating children and teenagers so that they internalize the desire to create Jewish homes of their own is the most effective response. Discouraging interdating, while not "politically correct," is probably a useful strategy. After mixed marriages have taken place, outreach, including conversion advocacy, can be useful in many cases.

BEYOND "VALUE FREE" SOCIAL WORK—ADVOCATING FOR JEWISH VALUES

For some American Jews, assimilation is the family tradition, sanctified by generations. It is their American Jewish heritage to live in an area where there are some Jews—but not too many, to affiliate with organizations that are Jewish—but not too Jewish, and to have friends of many types, although perhaps very secretly preferring the company of Jews.

The incorporation of the values of individualism into American Jewish life has often proceeded in an unself-conscious mode. Living in a culture that privileges individual choice over family or community, American Jews quickly absorbed the individualistic ethos but frequently did not perceive it as being in ideological conflict with their Jewish ties. They were much more likely to perceive it in personal terms: America gave them the right to break free of familial ties, to pursue their own education and occupational dreams, to postpone marriage, to choose romantic partners according to their own preferences and orientation. American individualism, as my qualitative research shows me, has been thoroughly coalesced into the value systems of many American Jews, especially in the liberal religious persuasions. Free choice, that hallmark of individualism, is not perceived as being in conflict with Judaism. On the contrary, it is often perceived as being an intrinsic axiom of Judaism itself.

This means that when we think about policy responses to families in the American Jewish community, we are responding not only to changed facts, but to transformations in underlying attitudes. When we subscribe to the notion of "value-free" social work, we need to realize that values are there anyway—but they are not necessarily the values we might wish to advocate. In the absence of Jewish values, we operate in a climate of secularized, Protestant, "American" values.

With the dawning of the 1990s, however, it became clear throughout the American Jewish community that few if any personal decisions are made on the basis of communal exhortations. For the foreseeable future, American Jews, like their middle-class coreligionists throughout contemporary society, seem likely to continue getting married later, having children later, and working throughout their children's preschool years. More of them will be divorced than their grand-parents. It is possible that more of them may have special problems, such as alcoholism or familial dysfunctions. As we provide them with therapies and services we should try to draw on Jewish values as a guide.

Research has shown that contemporary American Jews want communal support for their families. While many contemporary American Jews feel that Judaism as a religion and as a culture is extremely helpful to them as they juggle their complex responsibilities, they also feel that the Jewish communal response in providing adequate family-support programs has been pallid: Needed are more high-quality infant and toddler day-care and afterschool programs, support groups, and communal sensitivity to help individuals and families deal with stressful life-cycle events. Single-parent mothers, often the least-affluent segment of the Jewish community, want the same type of comprehensive communal concern that is often extended to immigrants. The physical and emotional isolation of pockets of Jewish elderly has created the need for intergenerational programming addressed specifically to those issues.

American Jewish families today can be seen as a microcosm of the challenges besetting middle-class America. Once perhaps the most predictably normative of American family-types, contemporary American Jewish families now seem to be the epitome of change. The manifold transformations implicit in American Jewish households, and the responses they are demanding from their communal institutions, are illustrative of the responses demanded throughout American society for a comprehensive family-support policy that can meet the needs of actual families in their current constellations. The carrot-and-stick techniques of communal approval and disapproval that were effective for centuries do not work in an open society. Ironically, if we wish to strengthen American family-life today, we must deal with it not as some might wish it to be, but the way it is.

NOTES

1. Nationwide figures for the American Jewish population in 1979 are derived from the 1970 National Jewish Population Survey.

2. National statistics on the contemporary Jewish community are drawn from the dataset produced by the 1990 National Jewish Population Survey (NJPS), conducted under the auspices of the Council of Jewish Federations. The first national study of American Jews undertaken since 1970, the 1990 NJPS studied some 6500 individuals in 2440 households, which were found after extensive screening through random-digit-dialing techniques. These households represent Jews across the country living in communities of diverse sizes and composition. A summary of the findings is provided by Barry Kosmin et al. in *Highlights of the CJF National Jewish Population Survey* (New York: Council of Jewish Federations, 1991).

3. Evidence of the wide variety of dating aids used by American Jews is found in every general and Jewish newspaper. Beyond the personals columns, with their ubiquitous SJMs, see, for example: B. Drummond Ayres, Jr., "For Jews Only, a Computer Dating

Service," *The New York Times,* 27 June 1974; Judith L. Kuper, "2000 Singles enrolled in Dating Service," *The Jewish Post and Opinion,* 16 July 1976; Yitta Halberstam, "Today's Shadhan: Popular and Expensive," *Jewish Week,* 31 July 1977.

4. See Susan Weidman Schneider, "Detoxifying Our Relationships: An Interview with Esther Perel," *Lilith Magazine 17* (Fall 1987), pp. 15–19.

5. Many articles have been written about the rising rates of Jewish problem households, even among very traditional populations. See, for example: Rabbi Dr. Abraham J. Twersky, "Denial," *The Jewish Homemaker* (December 1989), pp. 20–21; Faith Solela, "Family violence: Silence Isn't Golden Any More," *Response xiv 4* (Spring 1985), pp. 101–106; Barbara Trainin, "Facing up to the problem of Jewish wife abuse," *Jewish Week,* 18 January 1985; Nadine Brozan, "Wife Abuse in Jewish Families," *The New York Times,* 26 December 1982.

REFERENCES

Abramowitz, Y. I. (1995). The denerdification of Hillel: Can Richard Joel and Edgar Bronfman keep our college kids Jewish? *Moment, 20,* 36–43.

Berger, G., & Sternberg, L. (1988). *Jewish child care: A challenge and an opportunity* (Report No. 3). Waltham, MA: Brandeis University Cohen Center for Modern Jewish Studies Research.

Chiswick, B. R. (1985). The labor market status of American Jews: Patterns and determinants. In David Singer (Ed.), *American Jewish Year Book* (pp. 131–153). New York: American Jewish Committee.

Cohen, S. M. (1988). *American assimilation or Jewish revival?* Bloomington: Indiana University Press.

―――. (1995). The impact of varieties of Jewish education upon Jewish identity. *Contemporary Jewry, 16,* 68–96.

Davis, K. (1995). I'm not sick, I'm just in love. *Newsweek, 12.*

Fishman, S. B., & Goldstein, A. (1993). *When they are grown they will not depart: Jewish education and the Jewish behavior of American adults.* Waltham, MA: Brandeis University Cohen Center for Modern Jewish Studies.

Friedman, N. (1993). *Remarriage and step-parenting in the Jewish community.* New York: The American Jewish Committee.

―――. (1994). Divorced parents and the Jewish community. In S. Bayme & G. Rosen (Eds.), *The Jewish Family and Jewish Continuity* (pp. 53–102). Hoboken, NJ: KTAV.

―――, & Gertel, E. (1994). Jewish views on divorce. In S. Bayme & G. Rosen (Eds.), *The Jewish Family and Jewish Continuity.* Hoboken, NJ: KTAV.

Glenn, S. A. (1990). *Daughters of the shtetl: Life and labor in the immigrant generation.* Ithaca, NY, & London: Cornell University Press.

Goldscheider, C. (1986). *Jewish continuity and change: Emerging patterns in America.* Bloomington: Indiana University Press, 125–134.

―――, & Goldscheider, F. K. (1989). *The transition to Jewish adulthood: Education, marriage and fertility.* Paper for the 10th World Congress of Jewish Studies, Jerusalem.

Goldstein, A., & Fishman, S. B. (1993). *Teach your children when they are young: Contemporary Jewish education in the United States.* Waltham, MA: Brandeis University Cohen Center for Modern Jewish Studies.

Goldstein, S. (1992). Profile of American Jewry. In David Singer (Ed.), *American Jewish Year Book* (pp. 77–173). New York: American Jewish Committee.

Gordon, L. (1977). *Woman's body, woman's right: A social history of birth control in America.* New York: Penguin Books, pp. 231, 263.

Hartman, M., & Hartman, H. (1996). *Gender equality and American Jews: Are we one?* Albany, NY: SUNY Press, pp. 4–61.

Israel, S. (1985). *Boston's Jewish community: The 1985 CJP demographic study.* Boston: Combined Jewish Philanthropies of Greater Boston.

Kaplan, M. (1991). *The making of the Jewish middle-class: Women, family, and identity in Imperial Germany.* New York: Oxford University Press.

Lederhendler, E. (1992, October). Guides for the perplexed: Sex, manners, and mores for the Yiddish reader in America. *Modern Judaism II, 3,* 321–341.

Lipset, S. M. (1990). *The educational background of American Jews.* Report prepared for the Mandel Institute in Jerusalem through a grant to the Wilstein Institute.

Maranto, G. (1995, June). Delayed childbearing. *The Atlantic Monthly,* 55–66.

Medding, P. Y., Tobin, G. A., Fishman, S. B., & Rimor, M. (1992). *Jewish identity in conversionary and mixed marriages.* New York: American Jewish Committee.

Mott, F., & Abma, J. (1992). Contemporary Jewish fertility: Does religion make a difference? *Contemporary Jewry, 13,* 74–94.

Rimor, M., & Katz, E. (1993). *Jewish involvement of the baby boom generation: Interrogating the 1990 National Jewish Population Survey* (Publication No. MR/-1185B/E). Jerusalem: Louis Guttman Israel Institute of Applied Research.

Rosenwaike, I. (1990). Mortality patterns among elderly American Jews. *Journal of Aging and Judaism 4*(4), 298–303.

———. (1992). Estimates of the Jewish old-old population in the United States. *Research on Aging, 14*(1), 92–109.

Sales, A. L., & Tobin, G. A. (1995). *Moving toward the future: Action steps for revitalizing JCC youth services.* Waltham, MA: Brandeis University Cohen Center for Modern Jewish Studies, p. 23.

Sandelowski, M. (1990). Fault lines: Infertility and imperiled sisterhood. *Feminist Studies, 16*(1), 33–51.

Schiff, A. I., & Schneider, M. (1994). *The Jewishness quotient of Jewish day-school graduates: Studying the effect of Jewish education on adult Jewish behavior.* New York: Yeshiva University.

Silverstein, A., & Rubin, B. (1985). Serving Jewish singles in suburbia. *Conservative Judaism, 48*(1), 71–75.

SUGGESTED READING

Schmelz, U. O., & DellaPergola, S. (1983). The demographic consequences of U.S. population trends. In David Singer (Ed.), *American Jewish Year Book.* New York & Philadelphia: American Jewish Committee and the Jewish Publication Society of America.

8

Intermarriage: Three Views

STEVEN BAYME, DRU GREENWOOD,
AND JOEL A. BLOCK

RESPONDING TO MIXED MARRIAGE

At a recent General Assembly of the Council of Jewish Federations, several Jewish volunteer and professional leaders discussed the virtues of outreach programs to mixed married couples. After over an hour of discussion, a college senior arose to express her deep appreciation for the session. "All my life, I've been told the importance of marrying someone Jewish," she said. "For the first time, today, I'm hearing that intermarriage is all right. Thank you."

This incident crystallizes the dilemmas confronting the Jewish community in trying to grapple with mixed marriage. Well-intentioned efforts at inclusivity can easily be misunderstood as neutrality towards mixed marriage as a phenomenon. Jewish leaders who encourage inmarriage find themselves dismissed as politically incorrect, and the language of intermarriage prevention becomes unacceptable. Already, within Reform Judaism, one finds leaders and educators who claim to be "nonjudgmental" regarding mixed marriage, and rabbis who continue to articulate a language of endogamy find that outreach efforts, where successful, can make it "difficult if not impossible to discourage interfaith marriage."[1] Suggesting that outreach to mixed marrieds serves as primary communal response risks overwhelming the core values undergirding the Jewish family itself. The late Rabbi Joseph Glaser, past executive vice president of the Central Conference of American Rabbis, in fact warned his colleagues that outreach programs to mixed marrieds had already created lobbies within Reform synagogues preventing any serious discussion, let alone exhortation, about the risks intermarriage poses to Jewish continuity.

How, then, ought the community respond? First, it is necessary to acknowledge some of the real, albeit painful truths regarding mixed marriage. Perhaps one of the most remarkable aspects of American society has been the unprecedented willingness of Americans to embrace Jews as marital partners. Much as Jews find it necessary to condemn anti-Semitism in this country, the overriding reality of America has been the collapse of Gentile resistance to prospective marriages with Jews. In the early 1980s, well before the widespread attention devoted to interfaith marriage, almost 80 percent of Americans already viewed the prospect of interfaith unions with Jews benignly.[2] That percentage surely has only increased since then. In short, if Jews are going to discourage interfaith marriage, they must recognize that they stand alone in doing so.[3] From the perspective of American values, intermarriage in many ways celebrates American pluralism. In the context of Jewish continuity and preserving Jewish distinctiveness, however, intermarriage has been little short of a disaster.

Some observers have sought to soften this language by declaring intermarriage to be only the symptom of a problem rather than its cause. For these observers, the core problems are assimilation and decreasing Jewish commitments. Intermarriage is only the result and the most vivid expression of these underlying problems. The language of symptom and expression provides some solace to parents of mixed marrieds, but it understates how mixed marriage raises its own set of issues, in turn resulting in even greater mixed marriage.

First, according to the National Jewish Population Study (NJPS), over 90 percent of the children of mixed marrieds themselves marry Gentiles. Once the parents have married out, all constraints against mixed marriage vanish, and marital patterns approximate and reflect the tiny percentage of Jews within American society generally. Therefore mixed marriage is causative in bringing further mixed marriage. Secondly, and perhaps more importantly, the pervasiveness of mixed marriage as a phenomenon creates a climate of opinion within both American society and the Jewish community that mixed marriage is only to be expected. As a result, the Jewish communal will to resist mixed marriage and encourage children to marry other Jews becomes even further weakened.

Lastly, despite herculean efforts, researchers have not been able to discover much in the way of good news regarding mixed marriage. Conversion has plummeted as mixed marriages have become more acceptable, and the patrilineal-descent decision in 1983 of the liberal Jewish movements upholding the Jewishness of a child with one Jewish parent of either gender in effect removed a major stimulus towards conversion. Indeed, although many Reform rabbis had been practicing patrilineality since World War II, the public attention focused on the 1983 decision coincided in time with a significant decline in the conversion rate from 20 percent of mixed marriages to as few as 5 percent of marriages contracted between 1985 and 1990. The dangers of the Reform position on patrilineality became quickly evident to many of its proponents, who discovered that in the public mind patrilineality meant conferral of Jewish status to children who possess one Jewish parent of either gender. Forgotten were the explicit criteria of both parents committing themselves to the exclusive raising of that child within the Jewish faith.

In the absence of conversion to Judaism, mixed marrieds are approximately only half as likely to participate in Jewish communal activities as inmarrieds, and little more than a quarter of mixed marrieds even claim that they are raising their children as Jews. Whether that quarter of children of mixed marrieds will identify as Jews as adults remains to be tested over time, but thus far the evidence seems compelling that mixed marrieds themselves identify only minimally as Jews, their children even less so, and their grand-children not at all. Attempts to interpret mixed marriage as a significant oppor-tunity to enlarge the Jewish people amount to wishful thinking at best and demographic nonsense at worst.[4]

Therefore some losses due to mixed marriage are virtually inevitable. If at most a quarter of mixed marrieds raise their children as Jews, we can expect siz-able losses, at the very least, among the remaining three-quarters. However, obstructing serious policy discussion is that very often lay leaders within the community, who have given generously of their resources and talents to the wel-fare of the Jewish people, find their very own children marrying out of the faith. These lay leaders ask that the community launch initiatives to preserve the Jewishness of their children and grandchildren. The desire, of course, is laudable. It remains a poor basis on which to construct communal policy.

Consider, for example, the recent experience of a large Jewish federation. Lay leaders on the federation board wished for an outreach program for their own children who had married out and therefore allocated a sizable grant for such a program. A year later the federation board had to acknowledge that, despite all the best intentions, not a single child of a board member had partic-ipated. In effect, a costly program had failed to attract precisely the people for whom it was designed.

This, unfortunately, represents one of the painful realities of mixed mar-riage. Two-thirds of mixed marrieds express no interest in any form of Jewish communal outreach. At most, a third of them are at all receptive to any commu-nal overtures. Serious erosion due to mixed marriage appears virtually inevitable.

What then can the community do? Suggestions that the community abandon a language of prevention will accomplish little save to create a climate even more encouraging to mixed marriage. In other words, if single Jews will not hear a lan-guage of endogamy from the Jewish community, they will be sure not to hear it elsewhere in American society. Conversely, it is very clear that classical respons-es of disowning children who marry out will mean very little in a Jewish com-munity that is so well integrated into American society. Therefore vehicles must be found for preserving dialogue with mixed marrieds, while mounting efforts to secure the conversion to Judaism of the non-Jewish spouse.

I have argued for an intermarriage policy along three diverse tracks: Prevention, conversion, and outreach. Prevention efforts might favor two dis-tinctive policies: Encouraging young people to seek out Jewishly dense environ-ments, for example, college campuses with large Jewish concentrations and stu-dent bodies, and an ideological strategy that maximizes the joys of leading a Jewish life to the degree that one regards Judaism as so precious that one will seek out marital partners who can partake fully in those joys. This latter strategy suggests maximizing intensive Jewish experiences—e.g., day-school education, summer camps, and trips to Israel—that seek to reach the participant ideologically and intensify commitments towards leading a Jewish life.

The case for Jewish density responds to the current sociological argument that intermarriage results primarily from propinquity to Gentiles rather than from disaffection from Judaism. For example, New York City, despite large percentages of unaffiliated and under-affiliated Jews, contains an intermarriage rate only half that of the rest of the United States.[5] Larger numbers of Jews simply increase the odds of finding a Jewish mate. To be sure, some oppose a public strategy of exhorting Jews to choose colleges containing a critical mass of Jewish students, for inevitably some students will not do so and may become alienated by a language that places a premium upon choosing a Jewishly dense environment. Ironically, it is that very unwillingness to give discomfort to some that may, in fact, be harmful to all.

Intensive Jewish experiences are designed to maximize communal commitment and involvement. A serious, well-educated, and literate Jew will be far less likely to marry out of the faith than an illiterate and uncommitted Jew. The solutions therefore must lie in intensive Jewish education. Day-school students are far less likely to intermarry than supplementary school students. And those who attend day schools during the pivotal high-school years are least likely to intermarry.[6] To be sure, the more committed the population, the less likelihood of mixed marriage to begin with, and day schools, therefore, may only be reflecting their clientele. Yet the opportunity to influence the family values and aspirations of teenagers ought not be missed. For example, the youth arm of the Conservative movement—United Synagogue Youth—has required its officers to refrain from interdating. By contrast, the National Federation of Temple Youth, the Reform movement's youth arm, chose to emphasize outreach as progressive thinking rather than underscore the importance of marriage to other Jews.[7]

To be sure, these strategies are by no means foolproof. Intermarriage is sufficiently pervasive in American society that it occurs within all types of Jewish homes. Nevertheless, the relatively rare occurrence of mixed marriage within intensively Jewish homes must be noted. When intermarriage does occur, for example, within Orthodox homes, it remains a major scandal. By contrast, the danger for the Reform movement is for mixed marriage to become normative—a development only facilitated by the willingness of a sizable minority of Reform rabbis to officiate at interfaith weddings. In short, Jewish density and ideological commitment cannot guarantee that mixed marriage will not occur, but it can "stack the decks" in favor of inmarriage.

The decline in conversion to Judaism most likely results from the pervasiveness of mixed marriage. As long as mixed marriage remained rare, conversion was relatively common in an effort to rectify the unusual phenomenon of a dual-faith household. Once intermarriage became more acceptable, the desire to extricate oneself from that situation declined, especially if one now learned that in any case children could remain Jewish.

Yet the community has a vested interest in maintaining and enhancing efforts designed to secure greater conversion. Reform Judaism deserves great credit for restoring conversion to the Jewish communal agenda. In ancient times Judaism had clearly been a proselytizing faith, despite considerable risk in doing so. Historians estimate that as much as 10 percent of the citizens of the Roman Empire may have been Jews, and Jews were expelled twice from the city of Rome for seeking converts. By the modern period Jews claimed to leave the seeking of converts to other faiths, stressing that Judaism offered salvation regardless of organized religion. The Reform movement correctly challenged this notion in the 1970s by claiming that one cannot be sure of the treasures of one's own faith unless one is prepared to share them with others.[8]

What then can be done to enhance conversion? Research has demonstrated the centrality of the Jewish spouse to the possible conversion of the non-Jewish partner. Jewish spouses who are committed Jewishly are far more likely to encourage conversion, while those who are indifferent or alienated are least likely to do so. The implication becomes targeting those mixed marrieds who are most interested in leading a Jewish life and whose spouses therefore are the most likely candidates for conversion, rather than outreach on a wholesale basis to whoever is mixed married, regardless of the relative degree of commitment.

Lastly, these observations suggest criteria for effective outreach to mixed marrieds for whom conversion is not an immediate possibility, but for whom it may become so in future years. First, outreach must be targeted to those mixed marrieds truly interested in pursuing a Jewish life. Regrettably, the overwhelming majority of mixed marrieds do not meet this criteria, and it is wasteful of communal resources to chase those who have no desire to be chased. Indeed, the very price of living in an open society connotes the freedom to opt out of the Jewish community. Those are choices that must be respected and that bear consequences—however painful personally.

Second, outreach must be designed so as to preserve rather than undermine Jewish communal values of inmarriage and formation of a Jewish home. The price of outreach for mixed marrieds cannot be communal neutrality towards mixed marriage itself. To accomplish this goal, the community should design outreach so as to mainstream mixed marrieds within Jewish communal activities and programs generally. Maintaining the mixed marrieds as a special group within the institution and focusing upon their own unique problems will create precisely the internal lobby that will, in all probability, demand that the community refrain from articulating values that mixed marrieds, corporately, do not practice. Conversely, mainstreaming mixed marrieds within general communal activities carries little price either culturally or economically, for the community may continue to advocate its core message of greater engagement of Jews generally.

Third, outreach must sharply and unequivocally repudiate all forms of religious syncretism. The Reform movement, in particular, has been struggling with the question of involving non-Jews in the life-cycle events of Jewish family members—including the spectre of calling Gentiles to the Torah. To its credit, the Reform movement has recently acted to bar Jewish education to children being raised even partially within another faith—much to the consternation of more than one prominent lay leader within the movement. Yet outreach remains a slippery slope: From the welcome inclusion of mixed marrieds; to ideological neutrality towards mixed marriage; to rabbinic co-officiation at interfaith weddings with Gentile clergy; to "how-to" books endorsed by prominent Jewish leaders and intellectuals advising parents on raising children within two faiths.[9]

Lastly, outreach poses painful human dilemmas of relationships with loved ones. The criteria outlined above, however, suggest distinguishing between respect for personal choice and maintaining communal norms. As individuals, mixed marrieds should not be written out of the Jewish faith unless they themselves choose to do so. Yet inclusion of mixed marrieds within communal institutions risks diluting the core values of what it means to have a Jewish family.

Take, for example, the somewhat trivial issue of greeting cards printed for both Hannukah and Christmas. As a vehicle of personal outreach to loved-ones, the greeting cards seemingly respect both traditions. For the Jewish community, however, such cards suggest the theological possibility of being both Jewish and Christian and thus so denude Hannukah of any particularly Jewish content as to be a pale imitation of Christmas, which represents the majority faith. Well-intentioned personal outreach, in short, may often be at odds with communal norms and messages.

What, then, ought we conclude? In addressing intermarriage, the Jewish community must confront realistically its considerable and painful toll and the limits of Jewish communal policy. The Jewish community must remain honest about its values and maintain ideological clarity concerning the risk rather than opportunity mixed marriage poses. Within these parameters, the Jewish community must seek ways for an outreach limited to those mixed marrieds truly interested in enjoying a Jewish life and encouraging their conversion while, at the same time, launching efforts to intensify the quality of Jewish life generally that, over time, may in fact decrease the rate of mixed marriage.

The community, in short, must retain its distinctiveness to survive. Yet intermarriage rates signal how profoundly the Jews have become like everyone else. Failure to articulate a distinctive language of norms, values, and commitments connotes a Jewish identity so bland and meaningless as to be devoid of content.

Television, perhaps unwittingly, has given us a vision of the world to come. The popular science fiction series *Star Trek* depicts a multicultural federation preserving diverse cultures and traditions. Absent, however, are any Jewish characters. A Jewish spirit of optimism and faith in humanity pervades the scripts, yet the federation itself harbors no Jews. The series' creators seemingly have declared that increased Jewish assimilation at the close of the twentieth century meant broadening accessibility to Jewish memories and teachings but ending the corporate aspirations and expectations of the Jews as a people.

This scenario, to be sure, is by no means inevitable. Intensive Jewish living and commitment to Jewish renewal may well mean a future vision of Jews more intensively committed and involved in Jewish communal life. Yet we err profoundly if we believe that intermarriage is irrelevant to the future quality of Jewish life. For that reason, efforts ought to be geared first to preserving the Jewish core and strengthening Jewish marriages. Second, we should encourage the conversion of the non-Jewish spouse in cases of mixed marriage. Lastly, we should keep the door open to conversion through dialogue with those mixed marrieds for whom conversion is currently not a prospect, but who remain interested in leading a Jewish life.

NOTES

1. Fuchs, Stephen. (1991, March 8). Reach out—but also bring in. *Sh'ma,* 69–70.

2. Smith, Tom W. (1994). *Anti-Semitism in Contemporary America.* New York: American Jewish Committee, 12.

3. Sarna, Jonathan. (1992). Interreligious marriage in America. In *The Intermarriage Crisis: Jewish Communal Perspectives and Responses.* New York: American Jewish Committee, 2–3.

4. See, for example, David W. Belin, "Confronting the Intermarriage Crisis With Realism and Effective Action," in *The Intermarriage Crisis: Jewish Communal Perspectives and Responses* (New York: American Jewish Committee, 1992), 39. Egon Mayer attempted to argue for the continued Jewishness of the third generation of mixed marrieds; see his "Will the Grandchildren of Intermarrieds Be Jewish? The Chances Are Greater Than You Think," *Moment* (April 1994): 50–53. See also the somewhat testy exchange between Mayer and his critics (including myself) in *Moment* (August 1994): 11–14, and Ellen Jaffe McClain, *Embracing the Stranger: Intermarriage and the Future of the American Jewish Community* (New York: Basic Books, 1995), 126–127, 263–264. Despite Mayer's efforts to underscore the Jewishness of grandchildren of mixed marrieds, never once does he acknowledge that his own research suggested just the opposite. See Egon Mayer, *Children of Intermarriage* (New York: American Jewish Committee, 1983). Subsequent research has only corroborated the tendency towards "terminal" Jewish identity in the third generation. See Peter Medding, et al., "Jewish Identity in Conversionary and Mixed Marriages" in *American Jewish Yearbook,* David Singer (Ed.) (New York: American Jewish Yearbook, 1992), 39–41.

5. Horowitz, Bethamie. (1993). *The 1991 New York Jewish Population Study.* New York: UJA-Federation of Jewish Philanthropies, 96–97.

6. Seymour Martin Lipset, *The Power of Jewish Education* (Los Angeles: Wilstein Institute of Jewish Policy Studies, 1994), 20. See also Sylvia Fishman and Alice Goldstein, *When They Are Grown They Will Not Depart: Jewish Education and Jewish Behavior of American Adults* (Waltham, MA: Cohen Center for Modern Jewish Studies, Brandeis University, Council of Jewish Federations, and Jewish Education Service of North America, 1993), 10–11. Alvin Schiff's survey showed an intermarriage rate of 4.5 percent for day-school graduates. See Alvin Schiff and Mareleyn Schneider, *The Jewishness Quotient of Jewish Day School Graduates* (New York: Yeshiva University, 1994), 12. A survey of Ramaz graduates, an Orthodox day school with a significantly large non-Orthodox clientele, revealed an intermarriage rate of only 3 percent. See Nathalie Friedman, "The Graduates of Ramaz: Fifty Years of Day School Education," in *Ramaz School: Community, Scholarship and Orthodoxy,* Jeffrey Gurock (Ed.). (Hoboken, NJ: KTAV, 1989), 102.

7. Vorspan, Albert, & Saperstein, David. (1992). *Tough Choices: Jewish Perspectives on Social Justice.* New York: UAHC Press, 198–199.

8. Berger, Peter. (1979, May). Converting the Gentiles? *Commentary,* 38.

9. The most outspoken example of this genre is Lee Gruzen, *Raising Your Jewish-*

Christian Child (New York: Dodd, Mead & Co., 1987). The jacket cover contains an endorsement by Egon Mayer, a leading sociologist of American Jewry, and the paperback edition contains a foreword by Rabbi Lavey Derby, a Conservative rabbi. Other works of this genre include Rabbi Steven Carr Reuben, *But How Will You Raise the Children?* (New York: Pocket Books, 1987), and a uniquely interreligious composition by Rabbi Roy A. Rosenberg, Father Peter Meehan, and Rev. John Wade Payne, *Happily Intermarried: Authoritative Advice For A Joyous Jewish-Christian Marriage* (New York: Macmillan, 1988).

STEVEN BAYME

INTERMARRIAGE AND REFORM JEWISH OUTREACH: A PORTRAIT OF AMERICAN JEWRY

A short biographical note is important for the reader in putting the following comments in context for this book. I am a Jew firmly rooted in Reform Judaism. Although I am not an academician, I have studied and thought about issues of intermarriage, conversion, and outreach for many years. I am both a recipient of the gentle gifts of Jewish outreach and a long-time practitioner of outreach in the field with individuals, families, small groups, and congregations. What my background prepares me to do is to discuss outreach as realized in the Reform movement both from a theoretical perspective, although I find that it is not a topic that anywhere lends itself to passionless explication, and from the perspective on the ground, where the real work is done.

WHY OUTREACH?

From its beginnings Reform Judaism has always sought to bring together the wisdom of Jewish tradition with the exigencies of contemporary life, not simply from a sense of convenience, but from a deep commitment to the evolving nature of a living covenant. The Reform response to the challenge of intermarriage in late-twentieth-century America grows out of an understanding of this dynamic interaction between things as they are and things as they might be. And so the impetus for Reform Jewish Outreach—a major programmatic initiative of the Reform movement that welcomes the stranger and invites Jewish choices—is two-fold: Demographics and religious vision.

It is probably safe to say that there is no one with any Jewish communal connection at all who is not aware of the current high intermarriage rate among Jews.[1] The problem of Jewish "continuity" in light of the demographics is one that consumes much time and energy among communal planners in the late 1990s, and was certainly a major factor in the establishment of Reform Jewish

Outreach in 1978. At that time, in a seminal speech to the Union of American Hebrew Congregations (UAHC) Board of Trustees, then-president Rabbi Alexander Schindler started with "the recognition of a reality: The tide of intermarriage is running against us. However much we deplore it, however much we struggle against it, these are the facts."[2] In the absence of the fact of intermarriage that has touched virtually every Jewish family, it is doubtful that Reform Jewish Outreach would have developed as it did.

What the shapers of Reform Jewish Outreach did in response to the demographic trends, however, was both revolutionary and rooted firmly in a religious vision, a sense of *mitzvah* (religious imperative) that gives outreach integrity and enables it to succeed. Rabbi Schindler's speech continued: "Now facing reality does not import its complacent, fatalistic acceptance. It does not mean that we must prepare to sit *shiva* for the American Jewish community. Quite the contrary! Facing reality means confronting it, coming to grips with it, determining to reshape it."[3]

He then called for the establishment of a three-pronged outreach program, every aspect of which was controversial at the time. The proposal to actively welcome and involve the non-Jewish partner in an intermarriage, the specific topic of this chapter, was set in a much wider context of *keruv* (outreach, or drawing near those who are far). The first proposal, sensitive assistance to new Jews-by-choice to welcome them as fully equal members of the synagogue family, essentially took conversion out of the closet and acknowledged it as an authentic path to Jewish life. The second proposal addressed intermarried couples:

I believe that our Reform congregations must do everything possible to draw into Jewish life the non-Jewish spouse of a mixed marriage. . . . If non-Jewish partners can be brought *more actively* into Jewish communal life, perhaps they themselves will initiate the process of conversion or at the very least we will assure that the children issuing from these marriages will, in fact, be reared as Jews. We can begin by removing those "not wanted" signs from our hearts. . . . We reject intermarriage—not the intermarried.[4]

Much more controversially, his third proposal urged outreach

aimed at all Americans who are unchurched and who are seeking roots in religion. Unabashedly and urgently, I call on our members to resume their time-honored vocation and to become champions for Judaism. Champions for Judaism—these words imply not just passive acceptance but affirmative action. The notion that Judaism is not a propagating faith is wide of the truth. . . . Abraham was a convert and our tradition lauds his missionary zeal. Isaiah enjoined us to be a "light unto the nations" and insisted that God's house be a "house of prayer for *all* peoples." Ruth of Moab, a heathen by birth, became the ancestress of King David. Zechariah foresaw the time when men of every tongue will grasp a Jew by the corner of his garment and say: "Let us go with you, for we have heard that God is with you."[5]

Rabbi Schindler's effort to reclaim the *mitzvah* of *keruv*[6] forms the basic foundation of outreach. Eighteen years later Mark Washofsky, Associate

Professor of Rabbinics at Hebrew Union College–Jewish Institute of Religion (HUC–JIR) in Cincinnati and chair of the Reform Responsa Committee of the Central Conference of American Rabbis (CCAR), wrote:

Is it a *mitzvah* for Jews to seek converts? . . . when a person comes to us out of sincere religious motivations, we are indeed commanded to welcome that individual into our midst. As the Talmud declares (Yebamot 47b): "once the prospective convert has accepted the Torah and the commandments we convert him immediately, `for we do not delay the fulfillment of a mitzvah.' "

Conversion, in this view, is not simply an act whereby an individual changes the course of his or her life, adopts a new Jewish religious identity, and renounces any and all allegiance to other faiths. It is also a communal *mitzvah*. Like all other *mitzvot*, it is an opportunity for us as a people to realize our Jewish destiny.[7]

It is a truism to say that human motivations are complex and most often multifaceted. Conversion is no exception. Throughout Jewish literature from Talmudic times on, many references are made to possible "ulterior motives," including marriage to a Jew, of converts to Judaism. The tradition holds as an ideal that Judaism should be embraced for its own sake. In the same way, outreach has the greatest integrity when those who engage in it do so for the sake of the *mitzvah*, out of a sense of religious conviction, and not for the "ulterior motive," however well-intentioned, of increasing Jewish numbers. Placing outreach to non-Jewish partners in interfaith marriages in the wider context of *keruv*, a context that welcomes *all* who would explore Judaism as a way of life for themselves, is the firm foundation on which Reform Jewish Outreach is built.

The impetus for outreach arises out of the conviction that Judaism is a deeply meaningful and unique way of life; that it is possible and not at all surprising for those not born as Jews to join themselves fully to the covenant-people Israel and to live out their lives as Jews; and that it is a *mitzvah* for Jews to love the stranger, welcoming him or her with dignity and offering the rich sustenance of Torah and warmth of community, and thereby inviting him or her into the community of Israel and God's sheltering presence. Those who engage in outreach do not fear the stranger nor strive to exclude him or her nor rely on stereotypes to judge a priori the worthiness of the person or classification of the group approaching. (After all, Jews know the heart of the stranger, having been there ourselves.) Rather, outreach depends on the compelling strength of Judaism to attract the stranger; it looks to the unutterable beauty and holiness of Jewish life and the obligation of Jews to invite others to share it.[8]

So why do I insist at such length on the broader context in which the Reform response to interfaith couples and their children sits? It is only through an understanding of Reform's commitment to *keruv*—drawing near those who are far and inviting Jewish choices—that the goals and methodology of Reform Jewish Outreach, including the approach to some of the challenges resulting from outreach, can be understood.

THE PRACTICE OF OUTREACH

Outreach is not simply a theoretical construct. In the years since its inception, Reform Jewish Outreach has been implemented through programs integrated systemically throughout the Reform movement. The Commission on Reform Jewish Outreach, charged with setting policy and developing programmatic responses, is itself a joint body of the Union of American Hebrew Congregations (UAHC, the umbrella for 850 Reform congregations) and the CCAR. It includes representatives from HUC–JIR (the Reform seminary), National Association of Temple Educators (NATE), the American Cantors Association (ACC), and auxilliary organizations as well. Professional outreach staff in every regional office of the UAHC consults with congregations to establish synagogue-outreach committees and coordinate outreach programming and training regionally. Classes in the issues of conversion, intermarriage, and outreach and programmatic responses to them are available to students at HUC–JIR, and workshops and training sessions are held regularly at CCAR conventions.

The broad objectives of Reform Jewish Outreach (inviting Jewish choices) have been answered by a wide variety of programs and resources[9] planned and implemented on every level—congregational, regional, national. They include a number of core programs: Academic/experiential "Introduction to Judaism" classes open to all who seek to investigate Judaism; interfaith-couple discussion programs offered from a Jewish perspective that explore the meaning of religious identity, holiday, and family issues, and the desirability of choosing a single religious identity for children; and "Stepping Stones to a Jewish Me" and other, similar programs that enable children whose interfaith parents have not made a decision about their religious identity to learn and experience Judaism, often involving parents as well. The most recent (1994) addition to the list of primary outreach programs is "A Taste of Judaism: Are You Curious?,"[10] a three-session, free class that engages beginners, Jewish or not, in study of Jewish spirituality, ethics, and community through Jewish texts. Advertised in the secular press, this program has attracted over 4000 people from a range of backgrounds in its first two years. Graduates, including interfaith couples, adult children of intermarriage, and unaffiliated Jews, as well as non-Jews, have gone on to all of the programs mentioned above, as well as to synagogue affiliation.

These core programs are supplemented by others that also encourage positive Jewish choices. Among them are a wide range of programs to assist young people in strengthening their Jewish identity and examining the implications of interdating and intermarriage for themselves; to help teachers address the needs of sometimes confused or ambivalent children from interfaith families in the context of the religious school classroom; and to provide support and counsel for Jewish parents whose children are intermarrying. In addition to these programs that may be sponsored on a regional or congregational level, congregational-outreach committees plan a variety of activities to educate the congregation about *keruv* and to welcome, educate, and integrate those approaching Judaism for the first time. They often sponsor educational series, such as a learner's *minyan,* bulletin articles on Jewish holidays or life-cycle events, and outreach *shabbatot* that educate, model, and encourage Jewish choices.[11] Many Reform congregations now offer those converting to Judaism the option of a public-conversion ceremony during Shabbat services. Like an *aufruf* or a baby naming, such a public affirmation marks a new Jewish beginning and heightens the experience for the new Jew. Equally important, it models a valued choice for others, including non-Jewish partners, who are considering conversion, and acts once again as a powerful and inspiring reminder to the congregation of the *mitzvah* of *keruv* that it is responsible for upholding.

The results of such a comprehensive and integrated approach to outreach have been many. In 1991, 40 percent of Reform congregations reported[12] that between 6 and 15 percent of their membership units were interfaith families, while 15 percent of congregations reported that more than a quarter of their membership units were interfaith families. Sixty percent of congregations reported that more than a quarter of students enrolled in kindergarten were children of interfaith couples. Clearly, many interfaith couples have responded to the welcome extended to them and are taking part in various ways.[13] In addition, although no comprehensive demographic study has been conducted, Reform rabbis report increasing numbers of conversions among non-Jewish spouses who have been raising Jewish children and taking part in synagogue life for a number of years. Inclusion in Jewish life has led to a strong assimilation-in effect, resulting in significant numbers of unanticipated conversions. Such Jews-by-choice are active at every level of synagogue and Jewish organizational life, as congregants and lay leaders, as rabbis, cantors, educators, and other Jewish professionals.

Here I'd like to comment briefly on two policies of the Reform movement enacted by the CCAR in 1973 and 1983, respectively, that bear on conversion, and in fact are sometimes blamed for a decrease in the rate of conversion overall. The first has to do with rabbinic officiation at interfaith weddings. The resolution approved by the CCAR in 1973 remains operative today. It states "that mixed marriage is contrary to the Jewish tradition and should be discouraged" and "declares its opposition to participation by its members in any ceremony which solemnizes a mixed marriage." It goes on to "recognize that historically its members have held and continue to hold divergent interpretations of Jewish tradition."[14] The question of rabbinic officiation is a complex and often painful one within the Reform rabbinate, but the fact is that a significant percentage of Reform rabbis[15] *do* hold divergent views and *do* officiate at interfaith weddings with conditions that vary in stringency. It can be argued (and has) that rabbinic officiation at interfaith weddings reduces the taboo against intermarriage and thereby encourages it. Conversely, it can be argued (and has) that rabbinic officiation works with a fait accompli and strengthens the possibility of a Jewish home resulting from the intermarriage. It may be that both are true. When it comes to conversion, however, the fact that a couple can marry, whether with a rabbi or not, diminishes or eliminates the weight of an impending marriage on a conversion decision.

A similar effect on the conversion decision of a non-Jewish mother occurs with the CCAR's 1983 resolution on patrilineal descent. Because it is often misconstrued, I quote the entire resolution here:

The Jewish status of the offspring of any mixed marriage is established through appropriate and timely public and formal acts of identification with the Jewish faith and people. The performance of these *mitzvot* serves to commit those who participate in them, both parent and child, to Jewish life.

Depending on circumstances, *mitzvot* leading toward a positive and exclusive Jewish identity will include entry into the covenant, acquisition of a Hebrew name, Torah study, bar/bat mitzvah and *Kabbalat Torah* (Confirmation). For those beyond childhood claiming Jewish identity, other public acts or declarations may be added or substituted after consultation with their rabbi.[16]

This resolution is rooted in the Reform movement's commitment to equality between men and women and thus affirms the presumptive Jewishness of a child of an intermarriage, whether the father or the mother is a Jew. (*Halachah,* traditional rabbinic law, holds that Jewish status is conferred by birth to a Jewish *mother* or by conversion.) It is important to note that here, Jewish status is dependent not only on birth, but also on Jewish intent and behavior, a more stringent measure than that required by *halachah.* Again, whatever the wider ramifications of this decision, the result is to weaken the salience in her conversion decision of the desire of a non-Jewish woman to raise Jewish children. She can do so in any case, and many do.

It is possible that the combined effect of these two resolutions may have been a decrease in the total number of conversions that otherwise would have occurred in the Reform movement. But outreach does not look for enforced conversion. Those who do choose to convert under Reform auspices (still the highest percentage of all the movements) neither feel themselves forced nor carry the cloud of possible "ulterior motive" over them in the eyes of the community. Rather, in their own time and with rich Jewish experiences behind them, they come wholeheartedly to embrace Judaism and are able to see their community welcoming them for their own sake, not only for the sake of their offspring. The positive impact on children who witness a parent's conversion can be profound as well.

One of the most remarkable results of Reform Jewish Outreach has been its effect on "inreach," defined here as strengthening the Jewish literacy, practice, and connection of those who are already Jews. Outreach draws on all the commitment and knowledge a Jew owns and demands the ability to articulate it, to effectively invite someone else to join. Harold Schulweis spoke powerfully on this point at a 10-year-anniversary outreach colloquium:

Outreach to the proselyte affects our self-understanding of Judaism. In the conversion of the *ger,* the native-born is forced to confront himself. The *ger* of adoption places greater weight on choice, will, faith, ideology. The contemporary calls for greater Jewish "spirituality," the growing emphasis on theological clarification within the religious movements, the disenchantment with mere belonging, all reflect the shifting of the pendulum from destiny to decision, from being chosen by an external fate to freely choosing by inner conviction.[17]

Being forced to confront oneself is not without pain, but it often leads to unexpected growth. On a personal level, the response from Jews who have enrolled in "Introduction to Judaism" with a non-Jewish partner is, more often than not, "thank you for bringing me back to my Judaism." It is a well-known irony of outreach that interfaith couples who begin a relationship with little sense of the importance of their respective religious identities often spend disproportionate amounts of time discussing religion, and family members who travel the road with the Jew-by-choice are many times transformed by the experience as well.

Similarly, the task of integrating large numbers of interfaith couples has challenged Reform congregations to confront their own questions of identity: What does it mean to be a congregation; to be a synagogue member; to hold a leadership position; to lead the congregation in worship? Although the percentage of interfaith families in a Reform congregation varies widely, with the highest percentages in small congregations, most congregations (88 percent in 1991) do provide for membership of an interfaith family, including the non-Jewish partner.[18] In many congregations questions arise because of specific situations that develop or when similar situations are not handled consistently. Larger numbers mean that situations can no longer be handled on an ad hoc basis. So throughout the 1990s congregations have embarked on study and decision on the role of the non-Jew in the synagogue from membership and voting privileges to holding office or participating on the *bimah* at a child's *bar mitzvah*.[19] The goal of the Commission on Reform Jewish Outreach in providing resources and workshops for congregations for study and decision-making was not to dictate specific policy. Reform congregations are autonomous in that regard.[20] The goals were to encourage congregations to set policy by addressing the above questions

- to help non-Jews and their Jewish partners understand the concerns of the Temple for its boundaries, and

- to help Jews understand the perspective of non-Jews who may choose to deepen their involvement in the life of the temple, but who, for whatever reason, do not currently choose to convert.

Without a strong sense of identity and mission, no institution can function effectively in relation to those it serves. While vague policies may seem to offend no one, they neither serve the reality of the present-day synagogue nor ensure its future.[21]

The resulting policies took many shapes along the continuum from restrictive to inclusive, with the majority taking a middle ground. Virtually every one, however, struck a balance, with even the most restrictive acknowledging the presence of non-Jewish spouses and welcoming them in some way (93 percent of Reform congregations find a way to involve the non-Jewish parent of a bar/bat mitzvah), and even the most inclusive finding some way to make a distinction between Jews and non-Jews, either in the area of governance or the area of ritual participation. In this way both the commitment to inclusion as the way to outreach and respect for the integrity of Judaism have been upheld.

Just as there are different viewpoints in the area of rabbinic officiation at interfaith weddings, even more so are there different viewpoints as rabbis and synagogue lay leaders interpret Jewish tradition to make decisions in light of present-day realities in synagogue life. Even though it may be painful at times, such grappling with the interaction of text and life is a great strength of Reform Judaism. To return to the beginning premise of this section, the intense dialogue and resulting creative resolutions[22] are the traces of Reform Judaism's present engagement in living out the covenant.

NOTES

1. Fifty-two percent of Jews who married each year between 1985 and 1990 married a non-Jew according to Kosmin et al. in *Highlights of the CJF 1990 National Jewish Population Survey* (New York: Council of Jewish Federations, 1991), p. 14.

2. Rabbi Alexander Schindler, "Speech to UAHC Board of Trustees, December 2, 1978, Dallas, TX," reprinted in *Reform Jewish Outreach: A Program Guide,* Lydia Kukoff (Ed.) (New York: UAHC, 1981), p. 2.

3. Ibid, p. 3.

4. Ibid, p. 5.

5. Ibid, pp. 7–8.

6. Since the inception of Outreach, others outside the Reform movement have adopted the language of *mitzvah* and *keruv* as well. Lawrence Epstein, a professor of English and a Conservative Jew who has written extensively on issues of conversion and outreach, argues "that the Jewish community should offer Judaism and welcome converts because such a welcoming attitude is grounded in traditional Jewish religious thought and was practiced at crucial times in Jewish history." He further suggests "that the term 'Jewish universalism' be used to designate a religious interpretation of Judaism in which welcoming converts is central to the Jewish enterprise in history." See Lawrence Epstein, *The Theory and Practice of Welcoming Converts to Judaism* (Lewiston, NY: Edwin Mellen Press, 1992), p. vii.

The Conservative movement's Committee on Jewish Law and Standards published a series of papers in 1982 on the subject of "the *mitzvah* of *keruv*" that drew on Hillel's principle stated in *Pirke Avot* 1:12, "Be of the disciples of Aaron, a lover of peace and a pursuer of peace, a lover of people and one who brings them near to Torah," and examined parameters for including interfaith couples and their children. (See *Conservative Judaism,* Summer 1982, pp. 33–62, especially the first article, "The Mitzvah of Keruv" by Jacob B. Agus.)

7. From a paper entitled "Conversion to Judaism: The Question of Motivation" by Mark Washofsky, published in a revised edition of *Introduction to Judaism: A Course Outline: Instructor's Guide,* Kukoff and Einstein (Eds.), New York: UAHC Press, 1996.

8. Those who engage in Outreach—certainly including many clergy and lay people

throughout the Reform movement—are challenged to be bearers of that message. (This is where Outreach and what has come to be called "Inreach"—strengthening the core—intersect.)

9. The Commission on Reform Jewish Outreach has developed a whole panoply of program guides, pamphlets, and book and video resources to support the programming outlined here. All are available through the Outreach Department or UAHC Press at 838 Fifth Avenue, New York, NY 10021.

10. For a full program description, see *A Taste of Judaism: Are You Curious? Program Guide* (New York: UAHC Press, 1995).

11. An especially beautiful example of a liturgy created for an outreach Shabbat can be found in *Reform Jewish Outreach: The New Idea Book* (New York: UAHC Press, 1995, pp. 113–129).

12. Dru Greenwood, *UAHC Outreach Census 1991: A Report,* UAHC-CCAR Commission on Reform Jewish Outreach, New York, 1991, p. vii.

13. Long-term outcome from Outreach efforts in terms of Jewish practice in succeeding generations of interfaith families will not be measurable for some time, since serious programming for interfaith couples did not begin until the mid-1980s. Statistics from the National Jewish Population Survey that suggest a diminution of Jewish identity are hardly surprising given the attitude such couples have traditionally encountered within the Jewish community. The fact that 28 percent have chosen to raise their children as Jews, the highest percentage for any single religious tradition, is testimony to the strength of Judaism and Jewish connections. By providing a warm welcome, Outreach seeks to build on that strength by involving a higher percentage of interfaith couples with children. The successes that we know about anectodally in congregations are growing and providing models for future successes.

14. *Central Conference of American Rabbis Yearbook, Vol. LXXXIII* (New York: CCAR, 1974, p. 87).

15. Citing statistics from the Rabbinic Center for Research and Counseling, *Moment* reports that 48 percent of Reform rabbis officiate at intermarriages *(Moment,* June 1996, p. 23).

16. Elliot Stevens (Ed.), *Central Conference of American Rabbis Yearbook, Vol. XCIII* (New York: CCAR, 1984, p. 160).

17. Harold Schulweis, "The Stranger in Our Mirror," in *Outreach and the Changing Reform Jewish Community: Creating an Agenda for Our Future* (New York: UAHC Press, 1989, p. 97).

18. *UAHC Outreach Census 1991: A Report,* p. 15. (Cited above.)

19. The experiences of congregations and the depth of study engaged in through the process of making policy decisions are reflected in two publications of the UAHC-CCAR Commission on Reform Jewish Outreach: *Defining the Role of the Non-Jew in the Synagogue: A Resource for Congregations,* published in 1990, and *A Supplemental Process Guide for Congregations: Defining the Role of the Non-Jew in the Synagogue,* published in 1993.

20. A "Suggested Constitution," revised in 1995 and provided by the UAHC to its member congregations, defines a member as "any person of the Jewish faith eighteen years of age or older" and states that "the membership unit shall be either the individual or the family." It makes provision for the continued membership of a non-Jewish partner in the case of death or divorce of the Jewish member. It offers a menu of choices vis-à-vis voting, suggesting "each membership unit," "each adult member," or "each Jewish adult in a membership unit" shall have one vote. It further states that "any synagogue member

in good standing of the Jewish faith may serve as an officer and/or a trustee of the congregation." Ritual matters are not considered appropriate for inclusion in a constitution.

21. *Defining the Role of the Non-Jew in the Synagogue: A Resource for Congregations* (New York: UAHC Press, 1990, p. 6).

22. For an example of a new prayer appropriate for a non-Jewish parent to read from the *bimah* at a son's or daughter's *bar/bat mitzvah,* see Jeffrey Salkin, *Putting God On the Guest List: How to Reclaim the Spiritual Meaning of Your Child's Bar or Bat Mitzvah* (Woodstock, NY: Jewish Lights Publishing, 1993, p. 116).

DRU GREENWOOD

SERVING INTERFAITH FAMILIES IN THE JEWISH COMMUNITY CENTER

The purpose of this section is to give a brief overview of interfaith programs taking place at the Suffolk Y Jewish Community Center in Commack, New York. While each Jewish community center (JCC) differs in its program offerings, the issues presented are similar to those in Jewish community centers around the United States. The Suffolk Y JCC, the second-largest Jewish community center in the United States, began its program for interfaith families in 1992 as part of a special grant from The Covenant Foundation. The rationale for the program and the historical context in which it developed will be addressed.

In 1984 the Jewish Community Centers Association (then JWB) published a report on *Maximizing Jewish Educational Effectiveness of Jewish Community Centers*. This publication was a response to years of discussion regarding the role of Jewish education, both formal and informal, in the Jewish community centers. Its arrival on the JCC scene initiated a more intensive role for Jewish community centers as a gateway for Jews to connect with their Jewish identity. JCCs expanded their existing "Jewish" offerings to include classes in Jewish history and culture. An early outgrowth of this added thrust in Jewish education was the success of programs like the Melton School, which offered a two-year weekly institute geared toward serious Jewish study. At the same time, UJA-Federation of New York, through its Jewish education committee, was discussing additional avenues for enhancing the Jewish component of the JCCs. A primary focus was on reaching the unaffiliated who were categorized as "not connected with any formal Jewish institution." This outreach to the unaffiliated was viewed as an achievable goal for the JCC because of its unique position as a Jewish cultural, rather than religious, institution. Many JCCs began Jewish programs geared toward "welcoming" unaffiliated Jews by providing them with basic knowledge about Jewish holidays and Jewish life-cycle events, enabling them to interact more comfortably in "Jewish society." These programs continued to grow throughout the late 1980s. Many JCCs hired full-time Jewish education directors to facilitate programs and serve as catalysts and Judaic scholars for Jewish educational dialogue in the community.

In 1991 UJA-Federation of New York published the *New York Jewish Population Study,* which followed the *National Jewish Population Study* commissioned by the Council of Jewish Federations. These studies indicated that the Jewish community was faced with a crisis. According to the National Study, more than half of all Jews entering marriage since 1985 had married someone who was not born or raised Jewish. For every Jew who married a Jew, another Jew married a non-Jew. This figure contrasted sharply with the 11 percent who chose non-Jewish partners prior to 1965. The New York Study further suggested that Suffolk County had the highest intermarriage rate in the New York Metropolitan area. Suffolk County's 95,000 Jews in this regard were similar to the wider American-Jewish population observed in the National Study. The statistics revealed that Suffolk County was home to the youngest Jewish community in the New York Metropolitan area, a population preparing to make decisions about marriage. Even without the *New York Jewish Population Study,* the Suffolk Y JCC was cognizant of the growing number of interfaith couples. Suffolk Y JCC staff estimated that 20 percent of parents bringing children to the JCC's early childhood program were interfaith families.

Confronted by the results of the national and New York studies, Jewish organizations began interfaith programs, driven by a growing fear that Jews were fast becoming a demographically endangered species. Several followed the lead of the Reform movement, which launched a national campaign in 1978 that welcomed interfaith couples into Jewish life. These outreach programs encouraged the non-Jewish spouse to convert and offered educational opportunities to ensure that the children of interfaith couples were raised as Jews. Synagogues, Jewish community centers, Jewish family services, and national Jewish service organizations used the outreach model to institute programs to cope with the large-scale entry of non-Jews into the Jewish family. While some programs had conversion of the non-Jewish spouse as a main goal, studies indicated that only a third of interfaith marriages resulted in conversion to Judaism. There remained a great need to help the interfaith family, particularly the non-Jewish spouse and children, feel more "at home" in the Jewish community, even if they did not convert. As was previously mentioned regarding the unaffiliated Jewish community, the JCC was seen as uniquely qualified to offer programs to the interfaith community, since it did not represent any religious movement within Jewry. The JCC's role as a cultural rather than religious institution provided a nonthreatening environment to interfaith families.

The principal goal of the Suffolk Y JCC's interfaith program was: To enhance the Jewish life of interfaith families by providing unique opportunities for them to become integrated participants in Jewish communal life; to participate with other families in programs offering personal/cultural enrichment; and to enhance knowledge of Jewish tradition and familiarization with the various organizations in the local Jewish community. The secondary goal of the program was to increase the sensitivity of other local Jewish institutions to the needs of interfaith families and enhance their capacity to serve them. In essence, the JCC's primary objective was to help the interfaith family become more comfortable in relating to the general Jewish community. This would be accomplished by providing family members, particularly the non-Jewish spouse and their children, the opportunity to acquire the "tools" needed to interact in Jewish society. These "tools" included knowledge of Jewish tradition and holidays as well as opportunities to experience programs and workshops with other interfaith couples.

Conversion of the non-Jewish spouse was not a goal of the interfaith program for a variety of reasons. Foremost, the JCC as a social-group work agency supports the value of self-determination as it pertains to an individual's choice of religious expression. The JCC provides educational opportunities for study of Jewish history and culture as well as exposure to a variety of views of Jewish tradition. The center's role, however, is not to impose a particular view on its members and participants. The Suffolk Y JCC's mission statement emphasizes individual growth through meaningful experiences—growth, in this case, meaning increased comfort and knowledge, which does not require that participants alter their religious belief. Further, because the JCC is not a religious institution, the idea of its participation in conversion, by definition a religious act, is inappropriate and, for practical purposes, impossible.

There was a great deal of discussion regarding a second portion of the JCC's mission statement and its application to the interfaith program. The mission statement refers to "strengthening Jewish cultural identity and the Jewish family unit." In light of the program's goal of increased comfort of the interfaith family, in particular the non-Jewish spouse, the JCC had to consider whether this comfort would support or diminish the strength of the Jewish family in the context of the overall Jewish community. By supporting the interfaith couple, was the program encouraging interfaith marriage by blurring the distinction between "intermarried and inmarried?" These questions cut to the core of the outreach effort and reflected a debate taking place on the national Jewish scene. The lingering issue became whether outreach programs were sending the message that intermarriage was acceptable within the Jewish religion. The fear expressed by some Jewish organizations was that increased acceptance of the interfaith family without a commitment toward Jewish practice by the non-Jewish spouse could lead to Jewish extinction by matrimony into a benignly accepting majority.

The Suffolk Y JCC determined that "strength of the Jewish family unit," as it pertained to interfaith families, reflected an ability to respect and understand their Jewish heritage and to allow for continuity of Jewish practice by family members who wished to do so. In order for this continuity to occur, it was of paramount importance that the non-Jewish spouse not feel threatened or alienated by the Jewish spouse's practice or the institutions necessary for Jewish communal participation. The mechanism for Jewish family strength became the willingness of the non-Jewish spouse to accept the Jewish spouse's communal need.

It was the JCC's mission to assist the family unit in creating an environment that promoted this acceptance. This supportive environment would also benefit the non-Jewish spouse, who would now feel more familiar with traditions and customs that might be practiced in the home.

The interfaith programs offered by the Suffolk Y JCC included county-wide forums, cultural events, author-meets-public dialogue, and workshops for couples of various ages and their children that dealt with the social and emotional issues of interfaith family life. Promotional materials were designed to attract interfaith families to the program and express the essence of the outreach effort. Approximately 600 interfaith families participating in the JCC were contacted as part of a planning effort to determine what would draw families closer to interfaith programs, and what would keep them at arm's length. At the outset, the JCC discovered that its position as a "nonthreatening environment" was a magnet for many couples who otherwise would not have attended programs in a "religious" setting. The JCC also realized that a "nonthreatening environment" is not synonymous with a "neutral environment."

At the first forum conducted by the JCC, several participants voiced their concerns about the Jewishness of the program. One member felt that the emphasis of interfaith programs on "not losing Jews" was alienating the non-Jewish spouse. Others objected to the use of the term "problem" in referring to the National Population Study's conclusions on intermarriage. It was clear even from the terminology used by the guest speaker in addressing the "non-Jewish spouse" rather than the "Christian spouse" that there was a definite Jewish cultural agenda. Interfaith couples were obviously aware that the JCC was a Jewish facility. The JCC, in fact, had spent the previous five years strengthening its "Jewish position" in the community, resulting in an influx of Jewish programs and a visible Jewish ambience. To some degree this meant that couples attracted to the JCC interfaith program were predisposed towards increasing their Jewish identification. Some had already made the choice to practice Jewish traditions in their home. This did not negate the focus of the program; however, it did limit the prospective population from which the agency hoped to draw.

By the end of the first year the participants felt more comfortable engaging in conversation regarding Jewish holidays and practices and felt less like "outsiders" at Jewish communal events. Participants attended workshops on topics such as "Raising Young Children in an Interfaith Home," "Life in the Synagogue: Is There a Role for Interfaith Families?," and "Jewish Information for Interfaith Families (JIFF)." Interfaith couples attending the programs expressed the hope that the Jewish community would accept them and their relationships. Many couples shared their concern about the tendency in the Jewish community to encourage conversion in interfaith families without respecting the decisions the couples had made concerning faith issues. The JCC's position on conversion helped the participants feel more at ease. The bonding that occurred among the interfaith couples invited discussion of common concerns and experiences.

As the workshops and support groups became more cohesive, a new issue emerged. The participants requested that during the Hanukkah/ Christmas season, the JCC invite both a rabbi and a priest to address the unique issues related to the family's holiday celebration. As a social group-work agency, the request had merit, since the objective of social and emotional support of the family included both the Jewish spouse and non-Jewish spouse. However, this directly conflicted with the agency's Jewish cultural mission. Members did make the argument that if the Jewish spouse were more knowledgeable of the non-Jewish spouse's holidays, a goal of mutual understanding could be more easily achieved. To some degree this issue brought to the surface the difference between a "non-threatening" and "neutral" environment, as well as the balance between the social-group work goals and the Jewish mission of the agency.

The JCC determined it could not be neutral on this issue because "strengthening Jewish cultural identity and the Jewish family unit" by definition did not include educational opportunities for non-Jewish practice. In addition, the JCC served as a Jewish address for the county, and for some members it provided the only Jewish environment available for Jewish social-interaction. As a Jewish agency with an open membership policy, this situation was similar to a Catholic hospital being asked to place Jewish stars on its walls in order to equally support its Jewish patients. Individuals choosing a Catholic hospital understand its mission and recognize that the ambience must reflect the institution's history. Exclusion of Jewish symbols is not a value judgment but rather a reflection of the mission of the institution. The discussion of Hanukkah in the group and the decision not to provide Christian education were also reflections of the JCC's mission. The group accepted the decision because they understood the agency's role and respected the caring environment the group leader had helped to create. Cowan (1990, 14) said, "Interfaith married couples don't care as much about the theology or ideology of the sponsoring movement as they do about a knowledgeable, sensitive, nonjudgmental teacher. When sympathetic people open doors to Jewish learning, interfaith married couples and families will walk in."

As the interfaith programs continued to grow at the JCC, new components were added to meet the needs of the couples. Programs included shared holiday experiences, group visits to local Jewish institutions, and support groups for parents of interfaith couples. The interfaith Tu B'Shevat celebration, Purim workshop for interfaith couples, and a Passover Seder for interfaith families allowed the participants to share traditional Jewish holidays with fellow group members. A support group for parents of interfaith couples proved to be highly successful. It had a roll-over effect for the interfaith couples as their parents discovered their "unique" situation was not limited to their family, but was occurring in great numbers throughout the county. Mills (1959) declared that if millions of people are unemployed, that is no longer merely each family's problem—that is a social issue. This realization reduced some of the pressures on the parents, which in turn enabled the interfaith couples to focus on their situation with less concern about the effect of their relationship on their parents.

In the early years of the interfaith program at the JCC success was measured in the number of interfaith families who connected up to the JCC, becoming users of the preschool and adult programs. The level of comfort and warmth provided by the JCC enabled them to become fully integrated into the facility and to view themselves as members of the Jewish community at large. As these couples became more comfortable with their role at the JCC they participated less in the interfaith programs, feeling that the group was more for "point-of-entry" interfaith couples. The group had become a transitional stage for interfaith couples in their journey toward connection with the Jewish community.

The criteria for success and failure depended on the goals of the particular program as well as the expectations of the Jewish community at large. For some Jewish institutions the only acceptable program outcome was conversion of the non-Jewish spouse and reversing the trend toward interfaith marriage. With regard to reversing the trend toward interfaith marriage, the Jewish community had over the last forty years created an environment that encouraged, albeit inadvertently, interfaith dating and intermarriage. With social barriers being broken and the need for acceptance guiding the Jewish relationship with the non-Jewish world, the Jewish community had reached a point where dating and marriage between Jews and non-Jews was no longer taboo, and had in fact become a benchmark for integration into the American "melting pot." This trend would not and could not be reversed by the interfaith programs offered to interfaith couples by the JCC. The hope was that continued Jewish education would stress the importance of shared Jewish heritage in a relationship, and dispel the notion that issues related to blending of faiths could easily be overcome by the love in the marriage.

With regard to conversion the question became more complex. As was previously stated, the goal of the JCC program was not conversion and therefore success was measured by the level of comfort and the feeling of belonging the interfaith couple had toward the Jewish community after participation in the program. The premise for this success rested in the notion that an interfaith couple with strong ties to the Jewish community and without the label of an "outsider" would be able to make clear choices regarding family practice. The JCC hoped that the family's choice would include participation in the Jewish community and affiliation with its heritage, history, and cultural offerings. This did not require conversion, but rather commitment to the Jewish continuity of the Jewish spouse. It was noted that a committed Jewish family could certainly be interfaith and that an uncommitted Jewish family could just as easily be composed of two Jewish parents. Egon Mayer, author of *Love and Tradition: Marriage Between Jews and Christians,* concluded that Jewish levels of observance and identity where a spouse converts are nearly equal to couples where both partners are Jewish. In the final analysis it was recognized that the presence of two Jewish adults in a relationship, whether they were Jews from birth or by conversion, lent itself to fewer obstacles in potential Jewish practice.

CONCLUSIONS

One sidenote pertains to the role of the JCC director in development of interfaith programs. As an Orthodox Jewish JCC professional, I have been asked by colleagues how I reconcile my religious observance with the JCC interfaith initiative. The assumption is that my personal religious practice could hinder the JCC's participation in a program at variance with Orthodox Jewish doctrine. In actuality, the religious practice of the JCC director should not be a factor in the center's ideology and programs. This is clear as one examines the role of the JCC director in the Jewish community. The JCC director is often compared to a religious leader as being the role model for Jewish professional practice. The comparison is inaccurate. The role of the JCC director can be more accurately compared to a civic leader rather than a religious leader. The analogy in this case would depict the JCC director, not as a congregational rabbi, but rather as a mayor of a predominantly Jewish city. Its inhabitants are Jews representing the full gamut of religious practice, as well as non-Jews.

The role of the JCC director is to create a Jewish ambience where each individual feels comfortable and is willing to interact with other members of the community to foster opportunities for Jewish growth. For non-Jewish participants, the aim is to promote community understanding by exposure to Jewish culture. Growth and understanding can only occur in an environment where parity is fostered among the full spectrum of the Jewish community. This parity precludes the imposition of personal religious practice by the JCC director.

The JCC had a secondary goal of increasing sensitivity of other local Jewish institutions to the needs of interfaith families and enhancing their capacity to serve them. For some synagogues, the JCC program was seen as a first step for couples to further their religious participation, and even possibly convert. Several synagogues formed partnerships with the JCC, recognizing that maximizing the number of welcoming hands would improve the interfaith couples' connection to the county's Jewish institutions. To a large degree the attitudes of each of the county's Jewish institutions changed as the organizations they represented dealt with the interfaith issue on a national level. The question for most of these institutions was no longer whether or not programs should exist, but rather, how to implement them within their own mission statements. In the end, regardless of whether Jewish institutions chose outreach or inreach, Jewish education or supportive embracing, conversion or Jewish commitment, intermarriage was a part of American Jewish life. The JCC's ability to play a lead role in this new Jewish phenomenon demanded that it be in the forefront of programs offered to the interfaith community, and that it continue to do so in the years ahead.

ACKNOWLEDGMENTS

The author wishes to acknowledge the assistance of Egon Mayer, Mitchell Jaffee, Jodi Deitch, and Tina Hurwitz.

REFERENCES

Cowan, R. (1990, December). *Moment.*
Mills, C. W. (1959). *The Sociological Imagination.* New York: Oxford University Press.

SUGGESTED READING

Mayer, E. (1990). *Love and Tradition: Marriage Between Jews and Christians.*

JOEL A. BLOCK

9

Israel–Diaspora Relations After the Assassination: Can We Remain One People?

Menachem Kellner

It is a sad fact that human beings rarely learn anything new from their experiences. Most of us are quite adept at assimilating new facts into accepted structures of thought. Rarely are those structures called into question, and even more rarely modified or rejected because of "inconvenient" evidence. The assassination of Yizhak Rabin, however, while it seems not to have impacted seriously on Israeli political realities, does seem to have shaken many Jews to the roots of their souls. We Israelis, at the very least, seem more open to reexamining some of our favorite prejudices (such as our image as "super-men and -women" in areas of security) than at any other point in our history. There is a new openness to learning from our American cousins on how to live successfully in a pluralist society. If peace should actually "break out," as it threatens to do now, we shall certainly need lessons in living in an open society, one not soldered together artificially by the threat of outside annihilation. There is certainly a need to learn how to transmit Jewish identity and values in a noncoercive way.

In this last respect we have failed abysmally. Observant Jews in Israel are less and less interested in real relations (respectful or otherwise) with nonobservant Jews, have little to say to them, and certainly think on the whole that they have nothing to learn from them. Nonobservant Jews, on the other hand, are by and large equally uninterested in real contact with observant Jews and in addition, are quite happy to abandon religion to the religious.[1] If earlier generations of secularists ate *hametz* on Pesach, their children ate bread on Pesach, and their children's children see Pesach as primarily a school holiday long enough for a family jaunt to Turkey.

Many American Jews are worried over whether or not their children will marry Jews and whether or not their grandchildren will be Jewish at all. Israeli Jews often feel superior about this, but without any good reason. Were it not for the Arab–Israeli conflict, intermarriage would be a growing problem here as well. Israeli secularists ought not to feel proud that their children do not marry Gentiles—there are simply not enough Gentiles here currently to go around. Once again, if peace "breaks out" that situation will surely change, and more and more Israelis are suddenly aware of this. But even without peace with our neighbors, the problem is growing at alarming rates. According to many estimates, close to 150,000 non-Arab Israelis fail to satisfy halakhic criteria of Jewishness. These individuals, most of them immigrants from the former Soviet Union, are part of the Jewish population of Israel in every way but halakhically. As they learn Hebrew, assimilate into Israeli society, serve in the army, etc., they will represent a new and unprecedented challenge to the once simple equation, non-Arab Israeli = Jew. The question of intermarriage is thus going to be more and more on the agenda of Israeli public life.[2]

There is a further reason for worry. Chief Rabbi of Great Britain Jonathan Sacks once raised the question of what Herzl meant by the phrase "der Judenstaat": a Jewish state, or a state of Jews? To many secularist Israelis the former option smacks of religious coercion, "medievalism," "obscurantism," etc. They want to be "Jewish" without knowing too much (or often caring too much) about what that has meant in the past and what it means in the present. In consequence, they find the second option, Israel as a state of the Jews, more attractive. The problem here is that once you strip the Jewish state of its cultural, historical, and religious components, and define its Jewishness in terms of the fact that its citizens are Jewish, you are basically using a racist criterion to determine its nature and future.

It is hardly surprising that many Israelis find this unacceptable. There is a movement afoot to turn Israel into a "state of all its citizens." This "post-Zionism" (as it is often called) sounds very attractive to many liberal democrats, especially those raised on the values and ideals of American democracy. If Israel is to be a state of all its citizens (equally), then the Arab minority is subject to horrible discrimination: Israel's public calender derives from the Jewish religion and includes ceremonial days devoted to recalling galling Arab-military defeats; the national anthem dwells upon the dreams and memories of the Jews to the exclusion of all other citizens; higher education is restricted to those who know Hebrew well; most Arab citizens are excluded from the privilege and duty of serving in the army, with all its attendant benefits. The post-Zionist option (which recalls the "Canaanite" movement of the 1950s) in effect is forced to call for the destruction of Israel as a *Jewish* state.

There is a further element of paradox here that would really be interesting were it not so painful: Israelis and Americans are converging at an amazing rate, but that very convergence makes it more and more difficult for them to find common ground as Jews. Let us look at the Israeli side first: the country is simply being overrun by signs (literally, in English) of Americanization; we have been "malled" from north to south and from east to west; we have just been subjected to the most "American" political campaign in our history (our new prime minister often appears more of an American with some Israeli roots than as a real Israeli—it is even reliably reported that he reads English more comfortably than Hebrew!); our president railed against the three "m's" (Madonna, Michael Jackson, McDonalds) worshiped by Israeli youth, etc. This "Americanization" is both caused by and causes a further erosion of contact with Jewish history, culture, religion. The wide world is beckoning and most Israelis are happy to answer its siren call. If Israel is becoming ever more Americanized, it is largely at the expense of its Jewish character (however that may be defined).

On the American side we find a similar phenomenon. In a recent and very perceptive article, Adam Garfinkle pointed out that most American Jews have two religions: Judaism and Americanism.[3] By every possible indicator the latter is winning out over the former.

Israeli and American Jews are thus converging and becoming ever more alike. Should that not be a cause for optimism concerning the future relations between the two communities? Not at all, since the point of convergence is the "American" common denominator, not the Jewish common denominator. In both cases, the convergence is purchased at the expense of Judaism and Jewishness. As American Jews become ever more attached to their American religion, they have less and less in common with Jews in Israel, for whom Jewish culture, history, and religion remain important elements in their makeup. As Israeli Jews become ever more Americanized, they become less and less distinguishable from Americanized Germans, Italians, etc., sharing no special common-ground with heavily "Americanized" American Jews.

With respect to the transmission of Judaism to succeeding generations the American Jewish community is already in a state of crisis, and the Israeli Jewish community may very well be facing a similar crisis in the not-too-distant future. It is against this background that we raise the question of whether or not Israeli and American Jews are now or will be in the future one people. It is in connection with this question that it is useful to address the issue of what it means to be a Jew.

THE MEANING OF BEING A JEW

That the Jews are distinct from the Gentiles is an axiom of Jewish faith and a lesson of Jewish history. But what is the basis of that distinction? Jacob Katz has pointed out that the distinction has been explained in two very different ways. One approach grounds it in theological terms and sees it as "a mere divergence in articles of creed."[4] Katz contrasts this to what we may call an "essentialist view," one which traces "religious and historical differences to the dissimilar character of Jew and non-Jew, respectively." On this view, "a qualitative difference was involved for which the individual was not responsible and which he [or she] could not change." There was, in other words, an essential difference between Jew and Gentile. Katz finds the origin of this view in Midrash, sees its development in Halevi, and explains its wide-spread acceptance among late-medieval Jews to the impact of the *Zohar.*

There is no doubt that the essentialist interpretation of Jewish identity—what, not who, is a Jew—finds expression in Midrash and *Zohar* and that it is a central motif in the philosophy of Judah Halevi (and later of the Maharal of Prague); it is heavily emphasized in Kabbalah and hasidism. Since all of contemporary Orthodoxy is permeated by Kabbalah, this essentialist view is usually thought of as the standard view of the tradition.[5]

The debate between essentialist and nonessentialist interpretations of the nature of Judaism is paralleled by (and may even have been conditioned by) a debate between Plato and Aristotle that informs the entire subsequent history of Western culture, at least so far as the question of human nature is concerned. In a very real sense, European idealists such as Descartes, Spinoza, and Leibnitz followed Plato (who held the soul to be fully formed at birth), while Locke, Berkeley, and Hume, the British empiricists, followed Aristotle (who held the soul to be a potential for learning that we have at birth but that must be developed in order to properly function). In our own century, the claim that "nature" is more important that "nurture" in determining our characters is Platonic in orientation, while the opposite claim follows Aristotle. In this sense, President Lyndon Johnson, who was convinced that disadvantaged children could be given a "head start" and in effect remade, was an "Aristotelian" (although he was probably not aware of it), holding "nurture" to be more decisive than "nature" in fashioning us.[6]

There are many passages in rabbinic literature that reflect a position similar to that of Plato's.[7] There are even parallels to his doctrine of recollection. Every Jewish schoolchild knows the aggadah to the effect that before we are born we are taught the entire Torah; at the moment of birth an angel slaps us on the face and causes us to forget all that we knew.[8]

Turning to parallel developments in Jewish thought, we find that Sa'adia Gaon rejected the Aristotelian approach and adopted a modified version of the Platonic theory. Where for Plato the soul pre-exists the body, for Sa'adia it is created by God "simultaneously with the completion of the bodily form of the human being."[9] But for both Plato and Sa'adia the normal human being starts life with a fully formed soul.[10]

Judah Halevi presents no clear view on the nature of the human soul. He twice cites what appears to be the Avicennian reading of Aristotle in the Kuzari, but it is difficult to judge whether he cites the view and adopts it, or simply cites it as the prevailing philosophic view.[11] What is clear beyond all possible doubt is that Halevi adopts an essentialist interpretation of the nature of the Jewish people, insisting that they are distinct from and superior to all other peoples, and that this distinction is caused by a special characteristic, unique to the Jews, literally passed on from generation to generation.[12]

The *Zohar* is an important expression of the view that human beings are born with fully formed souls. Gershom Scholem summarizes the outlook of the *Zohar* in the following terms: "Like all Kabbalists he [the author of the *Zohar*] teaches the pre-existence of all souls since the beginning of creation. Indeed, he goes so far as to assert that the pre-existent souls were already preformed in their full individuality while they were still hidden in the womb of eternity." [13]

We have adduced evidence to the effect that rabbinic texts, Sa'adia Gaon, and the *Zohar* share in common a view that found its classic philosophic expression in Plato and according to which human beings come "factory equipped" with fully formed souls. What is the importance of this? The Platonic view[14] *allows* one to adopt the essentialist understanding of the nature of the Jewish people. Since God creates souls, He can choose to create them in different ways. This is precisely the express position of the *Zohar.* Jews are differentiated from Gentiles by the fact that Jewish souls are different from (and superior to) Gentile souls.[15] Halevi, without expressly adopting a Platonic view of the nature of the human soul, emphatically adopts an essentialist understanding of the nature of the Jewish people.

If the Aristotelian position commits one to a measure of universalism, with its emphasis on the common starting point of all humans, then this Platonic position commits one to a measure of particularism. Jews are distinct from Gentiles, and that distinction is based on a metaphysical difference between them. There is nothing that can be done to overcome that difference. Such a position immediately runs into problems over the issues of conversion to Judaism and prophetic visions of the time when "My house shall be called a house of prayer for all nations" (Isaiah 56:7). If Jews are essentially distinct from Gentiles, and if that distinction is grounded in an ineradicable difference in the very nature of Jewish as opposed to Gentile souls or in some special characteristic that inheres only in Jews, how could one possibly convert to Judaism? No matter how profound one's religious experience, no matter how sincere one's attachment to Torah and the Jewish people, the hard fact remains that one possesses a Gentile and not a Jewish soul. Similarly, no matter how many swords are beaten into plowshares in the days of the Messiah, the Jews will still have Jewish souls, and the Gentiles, Gentile (and thus inferior) souls.

Halevi meets the problem of conversion by arguing that converts are indeed not the equals of native Jews and that only after many generations, so it would seem, can their descendants be fully amalgamated into the Jewish people.[16] To adopt a brilliant and amusing metaphor of Daniel J. Lasker's, just as IBM PC clones may run the same software as original IBM hardware but are still not the "real thing," so too converts may believe what native Jews believe and act as they do (software), but they are still not the same as native Jews (hardware).[17]

The *Zohar* meets the problem of conversion in two ways. One is to affirm that the proselyte never becomes the equal of the Jew.[18] Alternatively, souls of true converts are souls of Jewish origin and were at Sinai with all other Jewish souls.[19] That these souls ended up in the bodies of Gentiles is, apparently, the result of some sort of cosmic snafu. It is, then, their intrinsically and essentially Jewish nature that brings these individuals to convert to Judaism.[20]

The problem posed by the universalist picture of the messianic era is easier to solve. Jewish particularists from some rabbis quoted in the Midrash through

Sa'adia, Nahmanides, *Zohar,* etc., have found no problem in reading the prophets in a particularist, parochial fashion. As Maimonides commented (in another connection), "the gates of figurative interpretation are not closed."

In another context I examined the position of Maimonides with respect to the cluster of issues here introduced.[21] Maimonides is shown there to have adopted an Aristotelian as opposed to Platonic conception of the nature of the human soul. This philosophical position commits him to a variety of unpopular Jewish positions: he plays down the special character of the Jewish people, and affirms that the difference between Jew and Gentile is theological and not essential (i.e., the difference resides in the "software," not in the "hardware," and is thus in principle subject to "conversion"); he denies that Jews alone benefit from special divine providence, prophesy, or reach ultimate human perfection; he extends an unusually welcoming hand to proselytes; he literally defines "who is a Jew" in terms first and foremost of intellectual commitment as opposed to national or racial affiliation; and he affirms that in the end of days the distinction between Jew and Gentile will disappear.[22]

It is important to understand precisely what Halevi and Maimonides are saying. For the former, the Jews received the Torah because they were already the Jews, the only people in the cosmos capable of receiving the Torah. For Maimonides it is the receipt of the Torah that makes the Jews, Jews. He quite clearly sees *ma'mad har Sinai*—the stance at Sinai—as an act of conversion. For Maimonides as well as for Halevi the Jews are special, unique, particularly beloved of God. It is their acceptance of the Torah, however, that makes them such. (It is for this reason that Maimonides excludes from the Jewish people— and from the world to come—all those born of Jewish mothers who do not properly accept the basic teachings of the Torah as expressed in the "Thirteen Principles." In the eyes of Maimonides such individuals are in an important sense no longer Jews.) Being Jewish is thus for Halevi something handed to you; for Maimonides, something demanded of you.[23]

This point can be made clearer with some concrete examples. For Judah Halevi, the first criterion which must be satisfied by someone who wishes to be a prophet is being Jewish; for Maimonides, the Jewish or non-Jewish character of the prospective prophet is irrelevant and never even mentioned in any of his discussions of prophecy. Most Jews are convinced that being Jewish guarantees a measure of divine providence simply consequent upon one's being Jewish; for Maimonides God's providence is a consequence of other factors altogether— one's religion or national origin not being among them.[24] For Halevi (and most other figures in our tradition) the key to achieving a share in the world to come is fulfillment of the commandments (something open only to Jews); for Maimonides, again, the world to come is open equally to all who have achieved a certain kind of human perfection.[25]

I am urging that the Maimonidean position can and should serve as a model for our understanding of the nature of the Jewish people, and that adopting this model can make a significant contribution towards enriching and deepening Israel–Diaspora relations.

Before turning to that, fairness demands that the opposite "Platonic" view, that the Jews are unique and inherently distinctive and that in consequence conversion to Judaism is not really possible and that all true converts were truly Jews all along, is a position that finds great psychological validity in the personal experience of many converts to Judaism. Many such people testify to the fact that they never felt "at home" in their original religions, and that conversion to Judaism was like "coming home" to where they felt they always belonged.[26] This position can be psychologically valid without being theologically or metaphysically true, and so it appears to be.

The essentialist understanding of the nature of the Jewish people, in all of its historical permutations, has never just maintained that the Jews are essentially or inherently distinct from all other peoples. Agreeing with the U.S. Supreme Court's 1954 decision, *Brown vs. Board of Education,* essentialists have never sought to claim that Jews are "separate but equal." Rather, the claim has always been made that on some level, be it moral, intellectual, or mystical, Jews as such are superior to non-Jews as such. This position is much more widely held than is ordinarily thought and is not restricted to followers of Judah Halevi and the Maharal, to Kabbalists, or to Habad Hasidim.[27] Most Jews today—Orthodox, Conservative, Reform, Reconstructionist, or secular—when "scratched" deeply enough, give evidence of holding this position. It is rarely phrased baldly or clearly, but when pushed hard enough most Jews will admit that they believe that Jews by their nature are more given to intellectual pursuits than Gentiles, are less prone to violence, or are more easily moved by appeals to morality, etc.[28]

This view is not supported by any objective facts and is dangerous, especially with respect to the prospects for a united Jewish people. The opposite Maimonidean view that in effect Jews are made, not born, and that at its deepest level being Jewish is a matter of accomplishing goals and meeting challenges, is certainly irrefutable (if also unprovable) and encourages the kind of activities that can only bring Jews together, as opposed to allowing them to continue growing apart.[29]

According to the essentialist view, one's Jewishness is handed to one upon a silver platter. Once you are Jewish much is demanded of you of course, but in order to be Jewish all you have to do is have a Jewish mother. The Maimonidean view holds, on the other hand, that your Jewishness (indeed, your very humanity) is not a given; you must work to achieve it.[30] According to the essentialist view Jews are defined as such by some inborn characteristic antecedent to anything they do with their lives and in consequence are in some way or another innately superior to non-Jews. The Maimonidean view holds that all human beings are prepared from the same recipe, and what makes Jews distinctive is what they do with their lives.

One can take on faith that Jews are in some sense superior to non-Jews, but there is no way in the world of proving it, and neither is there much objective evidence to support the claim. In dry, cold, hard-factual terms, the thesis that Jews are distinct from non-Jews (and superior to them) suffers from the deficiency of being apparently false. Every so-called "Jewish" characteristic can be explained simply in straightforward sociological or historical terms. Jews as such are not in any measurable way superior to or even distinct from non-Jews.[31] Jews whose lives and characters have been shaped by Torah (or by "Jewish values" if one prefers a less traditional way of expressing it) are, or at least ought to be, better than other people (Jews or non-Jews) whose lives have not been conditioned by those values.

There are further advantages to the Maimonidean view, over and above the fact that it does not demand that we accept as true a claim that on the face of it seems to be false. One is that for Jews in the Diaspora it allows respectful and constructive relationships with their non-Jewish fellow citizens. Non-Jews need not be perceived as in some significant and insurmountable sense essentially different from (and inferior to) us. What we share in common with them (our joint humanity) can be perceived as important as what distinguishes us from them (our adherence to Torah). For Jews in Israel it allows us to see our enemies as enemies, motivated as we Israeli Jews are by love of land and nation, by fear of those who seek to take them away from us, by hate for those who have hurt us, etc. Holders of the essentialist view of Judaism often depict our enemies as demonic creatures so bent on destroying us as to make any hope of an accommodation between them and us a chimera. Not only is there no objective basis for these claims, but beyond this, they certainly make it foolish to seek peace. Peace, however, is one of the highest of Torah values, and we are not allowed not to seek it.

From the perspective of Israel–Diaspora relations, the Maimonidean as opposed to essentialist view is also superior. American Jews and Israeli Jews are clearly moving apart from each other. The less each community is tied to the tradition, the further they grow from their once-shared roots, the less they have to say to each other. Israeli Jews think that living in Israel, serving in the Israel Defense Forces, speaking Judeo-Hebrew, etc., are enough to guarantee that they and their children will remain Jewish. This is blatant nonsense. American Jews also live in a dreamworld, thinking that Jewishness is a given, and what must be done is to awaken in their children (or children's children) some affection for or sense of identity with that given. This is also nonsense. Both these delusions are based upon the unarticulated premise that the essentialist definition of what it means to be a Jew is correct. Were this definition indeed correct, then Jews could relax on their "laurels," secure in the knowledge that the "pintele Yid" would eventually express itself, that the "Jewish soul" would catch fire sooner or later, and that even if assimilation rages, eventually a "saving remnant" would be found. But working on that assumption has failed to stem the tides of rampant assimilation characteristic of Jewish society in Israel and the Diaspora. It is time to try something else!

That something else, I urge, is the Maimonidean understanding of Judaism as a challenge, not a gift. This approach demands action and negates complacency. No one, not even the most ostentatiously Orthodox Jews in deepest Brooklyn or B'nai Brak can ever feel that they are secure in their Jewishness. If we could only convince Jews in the Diaspora and in Israel to understand Judaism in this fashion, we would then have a basis for shared discussion of an important matter: what precisely are the challenges that we can agree upon that Judaism places on us. For Maimonides, the answer is clear, simple, and straightforward: the challenge of Judaism is understanding the Torah and obeying it. For us the answer cannot be so simple, since the very nature of our quest demands that we relate to all Jews, the observant and nonobservant, in ways that both can accept, but the very fact that we will look for it together will provide us with a crucially important project on which we can, indeed must, collaborate.

Viewing Judaism in this fashion would enable Diaspora Jewry to say to Israeli Jewry: "It is not enough for you to live as Israelis to guarantee your Jewishness—you must actually do something about being Jewish; you must learn what it meant to be Jewish in the past and decide what it means to be Jewish in the present, so that there will be a Jewish future." Similarly, Israeli Jewry would be forced to turn to the Diaspora and insist that sentimental attachment to the past is not enough, that reducing Judaism to Emil Fackenheim's "eleventh commandment" ("do not hand Hitler a posthumous victory") may be enough for the second or even third post-Holocaust generation, but is increasingly irrelevant to the lives of most Diaspora Jews. Israeli Jewry can then say to the Diaspora: "It is not enough that your parents or grandparents were Jewish; if you wish to be Jews, to share with us in the creation of the Jewish future, you must build that future and build your Jewishness with it."

CONCLUSIONS

The essentialist definition of Jewishness in effect relies upon the Jewish past to define what being Jewish is all about. I am calling upon Israeli and Diaspora Jewry to build a future together instead of relying upon a past that for many Jews is sadly growing ever less relevant and interesting. This is, of course, easy to write and hard to do. From my perspective the shared Jewish future must be built out of elements of the shared Jewish past. What must be done is to bring Jews from Israel and the Diaspora together to begin the process in a self-conscious, clearly articulated manner.

What is being proposed here is, in a certain sense, paradoxical. It might be thought that the easiest way of convincing Jews to build a future together is to tell them that Jews are by nature distinct from (and even superior to) other peoples. But for a number of reasons this is not so. First, while at some level many, if not most Jews, even the least observant, believe in this (to my mind false and pernicious) doctrine, very few of them admit to holding it when it is presented explicitly. If we are seeking some way to bridge the gap between observant and nonobservant, this will certainly not do. Holding the essentialist view in a self-conscious, clearly articulated manner demands either accepting a particular view of human nature rooted in Halevi, Kabbalah, Maharal, and hasidism or accepting dubious "scientific" claims based upon lists of Jewish Nobel-prize winners. Neither approach is likely to motivate secular Israelis or nonobservant

Diaspora Jews to commit themselves to a shared vision of Jewish continuity. Second, convincing Jews that they are special is a recipe for inaction and silence on Jewish matters, not the reverse. After all, if we are God's chosen people and inherently special, no special effort is needed to remain Jewish. No sincere and well-educated essentialist holds this view, but we are not addressing the already-committed in seeking some way to guarantee Jewish continuity.

Being Jewish, on the model here suggested, is like treading water: if you stop, you sink. The essentialist model maintains that your Jewishness cannot "sink." What has to be done is convince Israeli and Diaspora Jewry to swim, not sink.

What I am proposing here is in effect paraphrasing John Kennedy: "Ask not what the Torah can do for you; ask rather what you can do for the Torah." This is not, prima facie, the sort of challenge that will speak to generations raised to think that Judaism exists to solve their problems, to make them feel better about themselves and their place in the world. But other approaches have failed; it cannot hurt to try this one!

NOTES

1. This is the essence of the critique of Israeli secular education about Judaism found in a recent Israel Ministry of Education report authored by a committee chaired by Professor Aliza Shenhar, formerly Rector of the University of Haifa and now (1996) Israeli ambassador to Russia.

2. The seriousness of the matter may be gauged by the success of the immigrant party "Yisrael be-Aliyah" in the last elections; this party ran on a platform calling for civil marriage in Israel to solve the problem of non-Arab Israelis who are not halakhically Jewish.

3. "The Two Religions of American Jews," *Conservative Judaism 48* (1996), pp. 3–22.

4. See Jacob Katz, *Tradition and Crisis: Jewish Society at the End of the Middle Ages* (New York: Schocken Books, 1971), pp. 26–27.

5. The impact of Kabbalah on hasidut is obvious; its impact on mitnagdut comes through the influence of the Gaon of Vilna and his disciples.

6. For details on all this, see my *Maimonides on Judaism and the Jewish People* (Albany: SUNY Press, 1991), pp. 1–8.

7. See Ephraim E. Urbach, *Hazal* (Jerusalem: Magnes, 1969), pp. 208–220.

8. Niddah 30b.

9. Sa'adia Gaon, *Book of Beliefs and Opinions VI.3,* translated by Samuel Rosenblatt (New Haven, CT: Yale University Press, 1948), p. 241.

10. For an argument to the effect that Sa'adia's position is close to Plato's, see Herbert A. Davidson, "Sa'adia's List of Theories of the Soul" in A. Altmann (Ed.), *Jewish Medieval and Renaissance Studies* (Cambridge, MA: Harvard University Press, 1967), pp. 75–94. See Davidson's notes for further studies on Sa'adia's theory of the soul.

11. *Kuzari* I.1 and V.12.

12. Representative texts from the *Kuzari* on this issue include the following: "But the Law was given to us because He led us out of Egypt, and remained attached to us, because we are the pick of mankind" (I.27, p. 47); "Therefore you [the Jews] rank above all the other inhabitants of the earth" (I.96, p. 67); "The sons of Jacob were, however, distinguished from other people by godly qualities, which made them, so to speak, an angelic caste" (I.103, p.

73); "Israel amidst the nations is like the heart among the organs of the body . . ." (II.36, p. 109); "Thou knowest that the elements gradually evolved metals, plants, animals, man, finally the pure of essence of man [i.e., the Jewish people]. The whole evolution took place for the sake of this essence, in order that the *inyan elohi* should inhabit it" (II.44, p. 110); see further, II.50 (p. 114); III.1 (p. 136); III.17 (p. 152); and IV.3 (p. 207).

13. Gershom Scholem, *Major Trends in Jewish Mysticism* (New York: Schocken Books, 1941), pp. 241–251.

14. I use this term for the sake of convenience; I do not mean to assert (or deny) that philosophic views influenced the Rabbis or that Sa'adia, Halevi, or the *Zohar* derived their views from Plato and not from rabbinic sources.

15. The *Zohar* teaches that Jewish souls originate in holiness, while those of Gentiles originate in the *sitra ahra* (satanic forces). See, for example, *Zohar,* Pt. III, p. 25b. For a very useful analysis of these issues and for a nuanced exposition of Kabbalistic views on the nature of Gentiles, see Moshe Hallamish, "Some Aspects of the Attitudes of the Kabbalists Towards Gentiles" in Asa Kasher and Moshe Hallamish (Eds.), *Philosophiah Yisraelit* (Tel Aviv: Papyrus [University of Tel Aviv], 1983), pp. 49–71 (in Hebrew). On the issue of the holy origin of Jewish souls versus the impure origin of Gentile souls, see Hallamish, p. 53.

16. See *Kuzari* I.27 (p. 47: ". . . any Gentile who joins us unconditionally shares our good fortune, without, however, being quite equal to us") and I.115 (p. 79: "Those, however, who become Jews do not take equal rank with born Israelites, who are specially privileged to attain prophecy, whilst the former can only achieve something by learning from them, and can only become pious and learned, but never prophets").

17. Lasker's metaphor may be found in "Proselyte Judaism, Christianity, and Islam in the Thought of Judah Halevi," *JQR 81* (1990), pp. 75–92. My use of the expression "native Jew" is based on Lasker's locution, "native-born Jew."

18. For a summary and analysis of Zoharic statements to this effect, see Jochanan H. A. Wijnhoven, "The Zohar and the Proselyte" in Michael A. Fishbane and Paul R. Flohr (Eds.), *Texts and Responses: Studies Presented to Nahum N. Glatzer* (Leiden: Brill, 1975), pp. 120–140.

19. See *Zohar* Part III, p. 168a, and Part II, pp. 95b and 98b, translated into Hebrew with commentary in I. Tishbi, *Mishnat ha-Zohar I* (3rd ed., pp. 50, 62–64) (Jerusalem: Mossad Bialik, 1971). For rabbinic sources of this idea, see *Numbers Rabbah* XIII.15–16 and Shevuot 39a.

20. For other but related Kabbalistic positions on these questions, see Hallamish, "Some Aspects . . . " pp. 56–57.

21. *Maimonides on Judaism and the Jewish People* (Albany, NY: SUNY Press, 1991), cited above.

22. I should emphasize that Maimonides's universalism did not reduce his pride in being a Jew or his certitude that Jews had a tremendous advantage over Gentiles in the pursuit of perfection. The Torah is the source of this headstart.

23. Readers familiar with the writings of Yeshayahu Leibowitz will see his influence here. This is one of the few places where my understanding of Maimonides coincides with that of Leibowitz.

24. For details, see my *Maimonides on Judaism . . .,* pp. 23–32. (Cited above.)

25. For details, see my *Maimonides on Human Perfection* (Atlanta, GA: Scholars Press, 1990), and the appendix to my forthcoming, *Must a Jew Believe Anything?*

26. For a good example of this, see Julius Lester, *Lovesong* (New York: Henry Holt, 1988).

27. The view in question is expressed with brutal clarity towards the end of the first book of the *Tanya*.

28. Arthur Hertzberg hints at this in *The Jews in America* (New York: Simon & Schuster, 1989), p. 387. He argues that Jewish self-definition as loyalty to the Jewish people, without reference to theology, ". . . did not belong together with their usual rhetoric about ethnic pluralism. *An ethnic group cannot assert "chosenness" without falling into chauvinism or worse"* (emphasis added).

29. To my mind it is also a morally (and hence in my view Jewishly) superior position, but this, I admit, is a controversial point and I do not want to insist upon it here.

30. This is not an halakhic position, but a theological one. Maimonides does not deny that in halakhic terms, being born to a Jewish mother makes one a Jew. But for him this appears to be a necessary condition for being a Jew, not a sufficient condition. See *Maimonides on Judaism . . .,* pp. 59–64. (Cited above.)

31. For references to recent claims that Jews are inherently distinct from non-Jews, see David Ruderman, *Jewish Thought and Scientific Discovery in Early Modern Europe* (New Haven, CT: Yale University Press, 1995), pp. 1–4; see also pp. 285–289.

10

Jewish Involvement in the American Public-Affairs Agenda

JEROME A. CHANES

In a forum published in the *Journal of Jewish Communal Service* in 1991, Albert D. Chernin, an official of the National Jewish Community Relations Advisory Council (NJCRAC), asked, "The Liberal Agenda: Is it Good or Bad for the Jews?"[1]

The question might be framed along the lines of "the *political* agenda—right or left: good for the Jews?" All too often, the public-affairs and intergroup-relations agenda of the organized Jewish community have been identified with stances on either side—liberal or conservative—of the political aisle. In essence, the "political" agenda is one piece of the larger intergroup-relations agenda: the ways in which Jews in America act and react vis-à-vis the external world, to groups and individuals around them. This chapter will headnote the areas of activity in the intergroup-relations and public-affairs arena, and will track a longitudinal timeline of the Jewish communal activity in these areas.

The central theme is the paradox of democratic pluralism—that *sui generis,* singularly American, phenomenon—and how it works itself through Jewish communal-organizational structure. The varied and multilayered public-affairs agenda of the organized Jewish community in the United States will be surveyed. The following questions are addressed:

- What is the singular nature of American society that informs the workings of American Jewish groups on public affairs?

- How and why do issues become priorities on the agenda? Who decides? What dynamics inform the nature of the interaction of the Jewish polity with American society?

- How has the Jewish communal agenda changed over the decades of the twentieth century in response to the agendas of the larger society?

• What are the central issues of concern for the Jewish community as we approach the new century? How does the Jewish public-policy and intergroup-relations agenda of the mid-1990s differ from that of earlier decades?

Jewish involvement in the public-affairs arena—activity in law and social action—is an innovation, indeed a revolution, in the history of how Jews relate to the external world. In earlier times, when it was not within the power of the Jewish community to alter its condition, the norm was "quietism." The shift from quietism to activism marked Jewish activity from the last years of the nineteenth century, and characterizes Jewish communal activity to the present day.[2]

There are conflicting visions of Jewish community in America. On the one hand, the classic model of *kehilla*—the traditional model of the Jewish community—with its concomitant obligation, *tzedakah*—the model of charitable justice—have long informed the workings of Jewish society. But the Jewish community in America is no longer the *organic* community of the Eastern Europe of earlier centuries, but a *pluralistic* community in a pluralistic society. In the organic community *kehilla* and *tzedakah,* religious obligations both, were accepted as normative. In the pluralistic community anything that smacks of mandate from above, by fiat, is rejected. How does the Jewish community, therefore, make the connection in a pluralistic society between *kehilla* and *tzedakah* and the public-affairs agenda as crucial to Jewish security?

In recent years the salient items on the Jewish communal agenda have come under five rubrics: anti-Semitism; Israel; Jewish communities in distress, primarily the plight of Soviet Jewry; constitutional protections, primarily the separation of church and state; and social and economic justice.[3]

ANTI-SEMITISM

Is the glass half empty or half full? Nowhere is this question more apparent and pointed than in Jewish communal discussions of anti-Semitism. There is a profound paradox—"the riddle of the defensive Jew," in the words of Jewish communal leader Earl Raab—that plays itself out within the American Jewish community when it comes to the question of anti-Semitism. On the one hand, Jews, when questioned in surveys, consistently aver that they feel "comfortable" in America. Yet some eight out of ten American Jews believe that anti-Semitism is a "serious" problem in the United States. In 1985, in the San Francisco Bay Area, approximately one-third of those questioned[4] said that Jewish candidates could not be elected to Congress from San Francisco, citing anti-Jewish bias or prejudice. Yet three out of the four congressional representatives from that area—as well as the two U.S. senators and the mayor of San Francisco—were in fact well-identified Jews at the time the poll was conducted. (The population of San Francisco was approximately 97 percent non-Jewish, mirroring the national average.)

There are a number of explanations for these contradictions—the "perception gap" among American Jews—that are rooted largely in the historical experience of the Jews, especially the recent experience of the Holocaust. But the underlying reality of the Jewish condition in the United States in the post-World War II era is that of a steady and dramatic decline of anti-Semitism, and more to the point, an enhancement of Jewish security. Indeed, the hard data clearly indicate that levels of both *behavioral* anti-Semitism—what people do—and *attitudinal* anti-Semitism—what people think—have clearly declined from peak levels during the prewar years and during World War II. While Jewish security and anti-Semitism are concentric circles and clearly related, there is, in the America of the late 1990s, a clear distinction to be made between anti-Semitism and Jewish security. There is still anti-Semitism in the United States—witness the activities of extremist groups, the rantings of Louis Farrakhan and others who use anti-Semitism for the cynical reasons of enhancing their political power, and incidents of anti-Semitic vandalism—that needs to be monitored and counteracted.

Nonetheless, the condition of Jewish security in America is strong, largely because of the history and tradition of democratic and pluralistic institutions in this country. Anti-Semitism "where it counts" is simply no longer a factor in American life. Such anti-Semitism includes large-scale discrimination against Jews; the widespread cynical use of anti-Semitism in political rhetoric in order to achieve political gains; and most important, the inability or reluctance of the Jewish community (or of the individual Jew) to express itself on issues of concern because of anti-Jewish animus. This kind of anti-Semitism—the kind that makes a difference in terms of the security and status of American Jews—has declined to the point of virtual disappearance.[5]

What are troubling and different about the existing anti-Semitism in America as the Jewish community approaches the twenty-first century are that the efforts to introduce as legitimate what until now was considered "fringe" or extremist manifestations of bigotry into the mainstream institutions of society have increased. Nonetheless, there remains a qualitative difference between a pluralistic America of the 1990s and the Europe of the 1930s, in which anti-Semitism was embedded in the institutions of society and power.

The organized Jewish community, traditionally viewing anti-Semitism as a key item on the intergroup-relations agenda, has counteracted anti-Semitism in a number of ways. Popular among Jewish "defense" agencies has been the use of a variety of prejudice-reduction programs, although there are limited data that such programs result in the diminution of attitudinal anti-Semitism among members of the broad population. Legislative and judicial remedies—"hate-crimes" laws, for example—are important to the extent that the message that the government will not tolerate bigoted behavior is sent. The most efficacious counteraction of anti-Semitism, in my view, is the enhancement of social and economic conditions. The data, without fail, assert that in any population, in any geographic area, at any time, in which the conditions of society are improved, bigotry and racism decreases. This verity holds true across racial lines as well.

Finally, as anti-Semitism as an issue for American Jewish groups diminishes, the rubric of Jewish security expands to include *internal* or *endogenous* threats to security, such as assimilation and Jewish illiteracy. How this issue will play itself out on the Jewish communal agenda is an open question for the next decade.

ISRAEL

As we approach the twenty-first century, Israel remains the prime reality for American Jews. But few American Jews can recall or indeed conceive of a time when non-Zionism, or even anti-Zionism, were legitimate positions in American Jewish life. In point of fact, in the years preceding and immediately following the creation of the State of Israel in 1948, most groups[6] had expressed, at best, positions of neutrality with respect to the Zionist agenda, and were moved to support the fledgling State of Israel during the early years of its existence.

Nonetheless, Israel was not on the formal agenda of the organized Jewish community as a priority issue until 1967 when, with the Six-Day War, Israel was threatened with annihilation.[7] American Jews perceived that the threat to Israel was by extension a threat to the continued security and indeed survival of Jews in the United States and elsewhere. Hence for the first time Israel jumped to the top of the Jewish communal agenda, and has remained a top priority for American Jews for the thirty years since then.

The "Israel agenda" has for the most part played out in concrete terms for Jewish communal groups primarily in four areas: United States–Israel relations, the peace process, Israel and the international community, and the Middle East arms race (including arms sales to Arab countries). But in recent years—particularly since the Oslo peace process and the Arafat–Rabin "handshake" in September, 1993—other Israel-related issues have come to the fore for action by American Jews. While U.S.–Israel relations and the Middle East peace process during the administration of Israeli Prime Minister Benjamin Netanyahu remain salient, there is a growing recognition on the part of American Jews that Israel–Diaspora relations—particularly American Jewish–Israeli relations—require more attention. One flashpoint for the relationship in the closing years of this century is the question of religious pluralism in Israel, a concern nurtured by the deep sensitivity of most American Jews to civil rights and what are perceived as civil-rights abuses. Legislative efforts in 1997 in Israel to challenge the religious status quo have raised questions about the sense of solidarity that binds the Jewish people.

Beyond the relatively narrow albeit important issue of religious pluralism (an issue, by the way, that has more resonance for American Jews than it does for Israelis), the larger issue of Israel–Diaspora relations is evolving, and discussion on issues such as the Jewish character of the State of Israel, religious diversity, civil rights, and Jewish–Arab coexistence are crucial to the relationship and to the role Jewish groups (especially groups concerned with fundraising on behalf of Israel) will play with respect to Israel in coming years.

SOVIET JEWRY/JEWISH COMMUNITIES IN DISTRESS

The American Jewish community, with its profound sense of *Klal Yisrael*—the "community of Israel" and the concomitant commitment to the entire Jewish "family"—has always been deeply concerned with the fate of fellow Jews around the world: Ethiopian Jewry (the so-called Falashas), Syrian and Yemenite Jews, and other Jewish communities held captive by unfriendly regimes. The most notable effort over the past three decades has been that on behalf of Soviet Jewry. From the mid-1960s until the early 1990s the fate of Jews in the former Soviet Union was a high priority on the Jewish communal agenda, with advocacy on behalf of Soviet Jewry informing much of the political and community-relations activity of Jewish groups. The Soviet-Jewry issue galvanized the community, nationally and locally, with networks established that crossed Jewish religious and political lines. Major, successful efforts were undertaken to involve successive Administrations and the Congress. Noteworthy in this regard was the passage of the so-called Jackson–Vanik Amendment, which linked the granting to the Soviet Union of "Most Favored Nation" status to freeing up emigration of Soviet Jews.

In 1989, in an unprecedented shift in Soviet-government policy concomitant with other deep changes in the country, virtually all Jews seeking to emigrate were granted visas. With the collapse of the Soviet Union in December, 1991 there were opportunities and hope for the future of Jews and Jewish life; at the same time, the enormous dislocation in economic, political, and social conditions spawned by 74 years of Soviet rule posed fundamental dangers to Jews and Jewish life in the former Soviet Union (FSU). These developments signaled the beginnings of a new stage in the Soviet-Jewry movement, less concerned with political advocacy, and more with questions of Jewish continuity in the states of the FSU, and with the tremendous dilemmas of resettling hundreds of thousands of Soviet Jews in Israel and the United States. The Soviet-Jewry movement today is therefore not a *political* movement, but a social-service and Jewish-continuity issue.

SEPARATION OF CHURCH AND STATE

A long-held principle of Jewish activity in the public-affairs sphere is that the security of Jews depends less on the nature and extent of overt anti-Semitism, but more on the strength of the American-democratic process and of those traditions and institutions that foster and protect individual freedom and an open and pluralistic society. Chief among these institutions is the separation of church and state. The Jewish community has long been profoundly aware that maintaining a firm wall between church and state is essential, not only to religious freedom, but to the creative and distinctive survival of diverse religious groups, such as the Jewish community. The organized Jewish community has been aware that, given the historic ebb and flow of attempts to challenge the principle of strict separation between church and state in America, it is the consensus position of Jewish groups that rigorous efforts to protect that cherished constitutional right must continue.[8]

Questions involving the separation of church and state are those that come under the broad rubric of constitutional issues that most directly affect the Jewish community. The problem with church–state separation is that over the years, it has become more difficult to identify clear "villains." Most cases that reach the courts in the 1990s are those that test situations on the margin—"moment of silence," as against the composed prayer or Bible reading of forty years ago, for example, or public support of religious education. There are cases that test situations in which there is a conflict between two constitutionally protected guarantees: is distribution of religious literature in public schools protected behavior as freedom of expression?

Article VI of the Constitution prescribes "no religious test." But this mandate applies to officeholders only; ordinary citizens are not protected by Article VI nor by any other provision in the Constitution. The sixteen words of the First Amendment "religion clauses"—"Congress shall make no law respecting an establishment of religion or prohibiting the free exercise thereof"—apply to *all* citizens, by means, as is generally agreed, of the "due-process" clause of the Fourteenth Amendment. It is important to understand that the two clauses—"establishment" and "free exercise"—are not inherently in conflict; indeed, they enhance one another and together, religious liberty. Nonetheless, as is demonstrated from case situations, they do not always *reinforce* one another.

A series of cases from the late 1940s through the early 1960s, all addressing situations involving religion in the public schools, gradually expanded the rubric of establishment-clause violations and strengthened the "wall of separation." The Jewish community was heavily involved, indeed invested, in these cases. In recent decades a broader range of situations have been tested in the courts, the Congress, and in the state legislatures: religious symbols—crèches and menorahs—on public property, religion in the U.S. Census, creation of townships and other political entities on religious lines, and religious expression in public places. More recently, as demands from the Jewish-continuity agenda inform an increased emphasis on Jewish education, with a resultant call for government support of Jewish day schools and *yeshivot,* there may be a breakdown of the broad consensus on church–state separation. There is yet general agreement that the separation of church and state is essential to Jewish security, but the issue no longer has the salience for many Jewish organizations—and certainly for many in the Jewish grass roots—that it had in the 1950s and 1960s. Many Jewish groups are moving toward the view that in an era when the majority of American Jews are functionally illiterate in Judaism, the concerns of Jewish education have primacy over church–state concerns. The issue has therefore been joined, and needs to be resolved, by Jewish federations around the country, who are the agencies responsible for fundraising and allocations in local communities.

SOCIAL AND ECONOMIC JUSTICE

The fundamental premise of Jewish community relations and activity in the public-affairs sphere is that conditions that are conducive to Jewish security and creative Jewish life in a free society require a society committed to equal rights, justice, and opportunity. The denial of these rights breeds social tensions, conflicts, and dislocations, and has led to threats to the democratic process. When this happens, the security of the Jewish community—indeed all minorities and groups—is threatened.

Jewish communal groups have therefore traditionally been at the forefront of major movements and programs in the social-justice arena, notably the struggle for civil rights, the support of public education, and liberalization of immigration requirements. While the Jewish community has viewed activity in these important arenas as crucial to Jewish self-interest as well as being informed by the imperatives of justice, their implications in terms of intergroup relations are most salient.

Black–Jewish relations, and relationships with other minority and ethnic groups, have had an intense and profound history for all. With respect to relationships with the African-American community, the reality for Jews is that the issues that are salient in the relationship are not (contrary to conventional wisdom) those that involve anti-Semitism emerging from the black community; rather, the significant issues informing the relationship are those on the public-policy agenda such as affirmative action and redistricting under the provisions of the Voting Rights Act of 1965, issues that have nothing to do with anti-Semitism. Whither the relationship nationally is a serious question for American Jews as the decade draws to a close.

AN HISTORICAL GLANCE

In order to understand the agenda of the Jewish community of the 1990s, it is instructive to have a glimpse at what the agenda was during previous decades—a timeline of the priorities on the Jewish communal agenda.

During the 1920s, 1930s, 1940s—up to the early 1950s—the agenda of the Jewish community was defeating anti-Semitism, at home and abroad, and the corollary of anti-Semitism—discrimination, which was pervasive.

From the early 1950s to the mid-1960s the Jewish communal agenda was the civil-rights movement, to the exclusion of virtually everything else. Civil rights *was* the Jewish agenda.[9]

Two events occurred in the mid-1960s that radically altered that agenda: the emergence of the Soviet-Jewry movement in the United States in 1963, and the Six-Day War in 1967, with its profound implications for the community. The most crucial results of these two developments (aside from their importance as issues unto themselves) were that they led the Jewish community to become legitimately preoccupied with Israel and Soviet Jewry and to move away from the total agenda, the broad range of issues on the domestic plate that encompassed social- and economic-justice concerns. Overnight, the Jewish agenda became a particularistic, parochial, *Jewish* agenda.[10]

Not that the organized Jewish community had abandoned the total agenda. Jews have always deeply believed that the Jewish community—indeed any minority—exists and flourishes best in a society that is informed by social and economic justice, and especially by the principles and protections that inhere in the Bill of Rights, particularly the First Amendment and most centrally the separation of church and state. But if issues on the domestic agenda were still on the Jewish agenda—and they were—they were no longer the *priority* issues of the Jewish community. This had serious implications with respect to work with other communities, especially the Protestant world and the black community. The implications of this shift were profound, and remain so almost thirty years later.

Beginning around 1980, the Jewish community started moving back to the total agenda. It was with the rise of an aggressive "religious right" in 1979—the "Christianization of America"—that the Jewish community began to feel most acutely that there was a potential crisis with respect to constitutional protections that were under serious attack. With the advent of the Reagan Administration in 1981 there was a fearful consensus in the Jewish community that economic justice could be undermined by that Administration's restrictive policies and that social justice could be compromised. The Jewish community began once again to engage in a reordering of its priorities in the broad agenda.

THE CONTEMPORARY SITUATION

We are once again in a transitional period. In the international arena, with the receding of and changes in the Soviet-Jewry issue and in other captive-Jewish communities, the contours of the agenda are very different from what they were a very few years ago. The issue of Jews in the former Soviet Union, as we have noted, is less a *political* matter and more one of the delivery of social services.

With respect to Israel, the peace process—whatever its pitfalls and the divisions within the Jewish community regarding its implications—the Declaration of Principles led to a new way of thinking about Israel and a different advocacy agenda.

In the domestic arena the Clinton Administration—an Administration that defined its priorities as being those of the domestic agenda—placed before the Jewish community a range of issues on which the Jewish communal voice needs to be heard. The Republican-controlled Congresses in 1994 and 1996 placed its set of challenges before the Jewish community. The evangelical political movement—the "religious right," this time clothed as the Christian Coalition—would once again wish to make life very uncomfortable for those who believe in fundamental civil rights and civil liberties, including church–state separation and protection against discrimination. In the arena of constitutional protections, particularly in the church–state area, there is a new generation of church–state situations that are being tested by the courts—situations involving tough choices for the Jewish community—and new challenges in the Congress and in state legislatures around the country. Beyond this, although clearly related, there is the growing debate over the role of religion in American society, a debate that was kicked off by Richard John Neuhaus's trenchant slogan "the naked public square" of a decade ago, but a debate that has become much broader and deeper over the past two years. Americans of whatever political and social persuasion acknowledge the reality of a "values crisis" in this country. The Jewish community has been called upon to explore serious approaches to this crisis that go beyond the quick-fix of school prayer.

In the world of interreligious relationships there is a recognition that new priorities mean new opportunities for coalitional activities, and there have been new initiatives begun with the national Catholic and Protestant bodies on a number of issues. The contours of the interreligious agenda—Catholic–Jewish and Protestant–Jewish relationships—have been reshaped as Jews in America approach the twenty-first century.

There is anti-Semitism, in some ways the most devilish issue on our agenda. While Jewish security in this country remains strong, most American Jews view anti-Semitism as a serious problem. Yet the reality is that most threats to Jewish security in the United States have little or nothing to do with anti-Semitism; conversely, most manifestations of anti-Semitism today do not compromise the security of American Jews, either individually or as a polity. In sum, there are new contours to the entire Jewish agenda.

Curiously enough, all of this renewed activity on the domestic agenda—looking outward—comes precisely at a time when Jews as a community are once again looking *inward,* to their own values and indeed to their very continuity. Whatever the "Jewish-continuity" agenda means—Jewish education, family-life programming, renewed Zionist activism, social and economic justice—the challenge for American Jews is to develop a complementarity of the "continuity" agenda and of our broad public-affairs agenda during a time of scarce resources.

JEWISH SECURITY

The Jewish community is clearly in a transitional period. One principle, however, remains the central organizing principle for issues on the public-affairs agenda: the issues that the community addresses—that are "selected" for action—are those in which *there is a consensus of the community that they affect Jewish security.*

There is a growing debate within the community with respect to the parameters of the "Jewish security" rubric. I suggest that there is a set of concentric circles that describe the prioritization of issues on the Jewish agenda.

At the center, some issues immediately and directly relate to Jewish security: anti-Semitism, Israel, and the security of Jewish communities abroad. The area that is tautologically "security"—is the core area for Jewish communal activity.

We then move one concentric circle out. With some issues, in the penumbra of Jewish concerns, the relationship to Jewish security is less immediately apparent, but is nonetheless absolutely central. The separation of church and state—the central guarantor of Jewish security in this country—is the most obvious in this category. This circle includes First Amendment and other political-freedom questions such as what government *cannot* do to a person, and what one person cannot do to another. The disparate issues of gay-rights ballot initiatives, capital punishment, and reproductive choice fall into this category.

We then move to the next level of concentric circles. Some issues lie further out, at the periphery of "Jewish" concerns, but are clearly important to the health of the society and are therefore important to Jews as well as helping to ensure the health of American Jewish society. The questions are not of restraint, as are those of political freedom, but of positive beneficence: what government *can* and *should* do for a person, such as in economic justice and the environment.

As the agenda expands, even during a period of organizational shrinkage, there is the inevitable question, "Why is this issue a priority for the Jews?" Issues are priorities for Jews when they directly implicate Jewish security. The Jewish community became involved in civil rights not only out of liberal philosophies but out of *Jewish self-interest*. In the early 1940s, to cite one dramatic example, there was a consensus in the community that Jewish security (that was defined in the early 1940s as employment discrimination) was at stake. The struggle against employment discrimination, which was the first goal of what became known as the civil-rights movement, became in 1941 the point of entry for the organized Jewish community in that movement. But it was not without vigorous debate within the Jewish community over the question as to whether "relations with Negroes" was central to Jewish security.[11]

The Jewish agenda, therefore, ought not be viewed through the prism of the "liberal agenda"—and it never was in any case. The conventional wisdom that it is the "old-time religion" of 1950s and 1960s liberalism that has driven the Jewish agenda is only partly right—and therefore mostly wrong. It was not thus the case then (as we have seen), and it is not the case today. Jewish social and political tradition is neither liberal nor conservative: *it is Jewish*. American Jews have long understood that the domestic agenda is thus the enabler of all of our other agendas, and is the vehicle by which a contemporary realization of *kehilla* and *tzedakah* is expressed.

A UNIFIED COMMUNITY IN A PLURALISTIC SOCIETY

There are three further questions that derive from these discussions. First, is there a single "voice" for the American Jewish community, or are there multiple voices?

Second, how was coordination achieved in the past—if indeed it was achieved—and how is coordination now achieved among American Jewish organizations?

Third, regarding the nature of American society. American Jews live in a world that is informed by the principle articulated in the classic Yiddish saying: *"Yeden mentsch macht Shabbos far zich aleyn"*—"Every person 'makes Shabbos' (that is, does what he or she does) in his or her own way." How do we achieve, in a context of American pluralism, a unified Jewish community? Is it enough in 1997 to recite, like a mantra, the trilogy of "pluralism, voluntarism, federalism"? What is the nature of consensus in the Jewish community? Is consensus at risk? Whither, indeed, consensus? How is dissensus in the Jewish community addressed, and how much dissensus is tolerated?

The oft-asked question of the "voices" of the community is one that we need to nail down at the outset: Is there a "voice" of or for the American Jewish community? Ought there to be a single voice? In fact, there are many voices, some overlapping, sometimes cacophonous, that reflect views and that act along a broad continuum of ideologies, views, and needs, but that cohere on fundamental issues of Jewish security and survival.

In this country there has been a history and tradition of vibrant American voluntarism, a tradition that has been most productive in the Jewish community. Voluntarism has emerged as a forceful advocate for individuals and their groups, and for the policies put forth by these groups as realizing their visions of what society should be. *Kehilla* (community) and *tzedakah* (charitable justice) have in fact found fertile soil in the American experience. *Kehilla* and *tzedakah* have been transmuted in democratic pluralism to produce a highly effective, voluntary institutional framework, historically supported by Jews. The associational base of the American Jewish community, and the federated structure of that community, have both permitted and depended upon affiliation—with a synagogue, a federation, a "defense" agency, a Zionist organization—to a degree far greater than at any other time or place in Jewish history. Any and all connections in Jewish organizational life in the United States depend on a major degree of voluntary association. The sum total of these associations determines, defines, and informs American Jewry's organizational structure.

In this respect the American Jewish community has been absolutely unique. While the organizational structure varies among Jewish communities around the globe, the model elsewhere is that of the "single voice"—a board of deputies or delegates or rabbis, often subsidized by the government, that speaks officially on behalf of the community. There is no such official voice, except in limited circumstances, for American Jews. Nonetheless, the multiplicity of agencies remains an effective forum for discussion of issues of concern to the community, a vehicle for acting on those issues, and a voice for the community on the issues. What is evident is that this mechanism acts more effectively than those centralized, communal-organizational structures in other Jewish communities.

The day-to-day workings of the American Jewish communal system involving the local community, the national Jewish polity, and world-wide Jewry, suggest approaches to the questions of representativeness and consensus.

The boundaries of the American-Jewish body politic are not preset; the Jewish community is not a classical Greek polity, in which every citizen automatically has a vote. In the Jewish community everyone is born into eligibility, but affiliation requires some kind of voluntary action, even if the act is nominal, that represents a conscious decision on the part of the individual to be part of the community.

The fact is that no self-identifying group in the United States offers as many institutional forms that provide opportunities for expression as does the American Jewish community. The question of whether the organized Jewish community is representative is addressed, not on the basis of "direct elections," but on another criterion: If people feel that there is a vehicle for expression, and if by means of their choice through affiliation of that vehicle they can cast a vote on policy issues, then the community is representative. If an individual is not satisfied that the organization with which he or she has affiliated is serving his needs, he tries to change it from within. If this does not work, he goes "across the street" to another organization. And if the competing agency doesn't do the job, then the individual joins together with like-minded people to start a new organization. This is American voluntarism and associationalism at work. Thus the multiplicity of Jewish organizations is the strength, not the burden, of the Jewish community.

Moreover, the basic institutional format of the community, with its abundance of organizations, is one that provides for active debate on a range of issues. A good indicator of the representativeness of the agencies is that over the years the resolutions passed by the umbrella organizations of the Jewish community and the policies adopted by a range of national Jewish organizations across the political spectrum almost perfectly parallel the views that are observed in the periodic polling of the grass roots of the American Jewish community and that are consistently expressed in the voting patterns of the Jewish polity. The grass roots certainly does let the leadership know if its expressed positions are out of step with what American Jews are thinking and saying.

Nonetheless, there is a degree of asymmetry between where the grass roots and the organizations are, and that suggests questions about the fundamental consensus in the community. There have been a number of events and issues in recent years—public-sector aid to religious education, discussed earlier, is one that challenges the consensus in church–state separation—that have raised questions about some *components* of the consensus.

It is important to bear in mind that the Jewish community's consensus has been shaped over the years on the basis of pragmatic considerations, and not as a direct result of conceptual frameworks. There was of course a high degree of consensus on general conceptual formulations that did define the debate. Questions of values and priorities, while they always underlay the community's approaches, were rarely at the forefront of the debate. These questions have been sharpened in recent years. To cite but two dramatic examples over the years and most recently in 1996 and 1997, the "Who is a Jew?" question has forced Jews once again into defining and redefining themselves. The Soviet-Jewry issue over several decades moved the American Jewish community to ask if it ought to function on the basis of long-held, freedom-of-choice positions, or on the basis of the well-being of a Jewish national movement. These posed questions of values rather than responding to the pure pragmatics of an issue. This defining of the debate on the basis of values rather than pragmatics has added an important dimension to the question of consensus.

There have been a number of approaches to the question of consensus and dissensus. The core of the issue is not whether consensus is unraveling. The judgment of many observers is that it is a sign of increasing maturity that the American Jewish community can handle the degree of dissensus that exists on some issues without becoming defensive, as was the case in the past.

Further, an important distinction must be made between those issues in which there is some gap of perception or judgment between the grass roots and the organizational leadership—the extent of anti-Semitism in the United States, for example—and real dissensus on core issues. The former does exist on a number of issues; the latter is rare.

The Jewish community is not in danger of being "balkanized." Most Jews in America do not concede to any one organization the right to express their views; they may look to a number of different organizations, and this dynamic is very important in shaping the voices of the community. Thus American Jews are willing to accept a fair amount of elasticity on views and positions, as long as basic, elemental positions of consensus (such as the security of the State of Israel) are at their core. These basic positions remain strong and secure.

CONCLUSIONS

The strength of the Jewish community lies in its pluralistic communal structure. The Jewish community does not seek unity merely for the sake of unity, but in order to enable the community to achieve collectively its shared goals. The coordinated national and local organizations can and do reach the American Jewish community, and provide a collective voice for the community.

One commonly held perception has it that the American Jewish community, with its multiplicity of organizations, is chaotic. The reality is that the community possesses the instrumentalities that are capable of getting these disparate organizations to work together. The resultant voice is an effective one in terms of its impact on public policy and its fostering of a dynamic and creative Jewish life in America. It is not hyperbole to suggest that it was the collective voice of the American Jewish community, by virtue of its activity in shaping the civil-rights movement, in immigration reform (the repeal of the National Origins Quota System in the 1950s and 1960s), in the separation of church and state, and in providing the models for social-service federations, that was a major force in changing the face of American society. The vitality demonstrated in this coordinated activity and voice of the Jewish communal structure is strong and presages well for the best interests of Jews—and the Jewish community's coalition partners—everywhere.

NOTES

1. *Journal of Jewish Communal Service, 67,* no. 3 (Spring, 1991), pp. 166–173.

2. The "activism" of the late-nineteenth century was manifest in the wide-scale immigration from Eastern Europe during those years. Immigration, a favorite form of activity during that period, has been denied the glamor of an abstract noun (an "ism").

3. A sixth area, interreligious relationships, deserves a full discussion. But while relationships with American Catholics, Protestants, and Muslims do deal with issues of substance, activities in the interreligious arena are either those of coalition, or of dialogue on matters such as anti-Semitism, or address issues that are most often subsumed under the standard rubrics—for example, the stances of Protestant denominations on the policies of the government of Israel—and are addressed in those arenas.

4. Jews affiliated in some manner with the Jewish community were surveyed.

5. For a full discussion and detailed analysis of anti-Semitism and Jewish security in the United States, see Jerome A. Chanes, *Anti-Semitism in America Today: Outspoken Experts Explode the Myths* (New York: Carol Publishing/Birch Lane Press, 1995).

6. Except, of course, Zionist organizations.

7. This is not to say that Israel-related issues were not addressed by the organized Jewish community. To be sure, the first arms sales to Arab states in the early 1950s, the 1956 Suez Campaign, and other situations were addressed as they arose by Jewish communal organizations. But at no time before 1967 does "Israel and the Middle East" appear as a priority agenda item on the agendas of Jewish communal organizations.

8. For a full discussion of the history of church–state separation in the United States, see Naomi W. Cohen, *Jews in Christian America: The Pursuit of Religious Equality* (New York: Oxford University Press, 1992).

9. The separation of church and state played a significant role, to be sure, during these years as well. The great landmark cases, beginning with *Everson vs. Board of Education* (1947), were decided during this period, with essential participation of the Jewish community. But the *first* priority was civil rights.

10. It is important to note that the radicalization of key voices in the civil-rights movement was significant in this regard as well.

11. Indeed, at a Plenary Session of the National Community Relations Advisory Council (later NJCRAC, the National Jewish Community Relations Advisory Council) in the mid-1940s, a vigorous debate took place on the wisdom of coalition-building with blacks, and it was Rabbi Stephen S. Wise, an American Jewish Congress and NAACP leader, who made the case for continued involvement, and involvement based on Jewish self-interest. Wise's rationale was a re-articulation of the original reasons for Jewish involvement in the civil-rights struggle.

11

Cultural Adaptation in Soviet-Jewish Resettlement: A Reciprocal Adjustment Process

MARK HANDELMAN

A HISTORY OF SOVIET-JEWISH RESETTLEMENT

The rescue of Jews from the Soviet Union was initiated in the early seventies through the joint efforts of the Soviet-Jewry advocacy movement in the United States, the Israeli government, and the government of the United States. At that time, the Soviet Union did not have an emigration policy, since it was unthinkable that any rational citizen would want to leave the utopian Soviet society. However, in order to relieve pressure from the West and obtain certain concessions, the Communist government adopted a policy of Jewish "reunification." Under this policy, Soviet Jews were allowed to accept formal, written invitations from relatives in Israel to leave the Soviet Union for purposes of reunification with family and the Jewish homeland.

Thousands of invitations were delivered from both Israel and the United States to Soviet Jews. Invitations from "relatives" in Israel were the only ones deemed eligible for consideration by the Soviet authorities, despite the fact that the origins of these documents were somewhat questionable. An elaborate system of movement of the Jews who were granted exit visas for reunification was developed with the cooperation of the Dutch, Austrian, and Italian governments.

Jews issued exit visas by the "OVIR," the Soviet Exit Authorities, were transported by air or rail to Vienna, Austria, under the auspices of the government of the Netherlands. In Vienna, the refugees were greeted by the Jewish Agency, who arranged for care and maintenance, as well as transport to Israel. Those who chose to come to the United States were transported by the Hebrew Immigrant Aid Society (HIAS) to Italy, where they waited to be processed by the U.S. Immigration and Naturalization Service. The American Jewish Joint Distribution Committee (AJDC) provided care and maintenance to thousands of Soviet Jews in Rome, Ladispoli, Santa Marinella, Ostia, and other communities, while HIAS helped the refugees to prepare applications for admission to the United States with refugee status.[1]

Despite their cooperation in winning freedom for Soviet Jews, a major controversy raged between the American Jewish community on one side, and the Israeli government and American advocates for the Jewish Agency on the other: freedom of choice for Soviet-Jewish refugees—a right to immigrate to any part of the free world—versus an obligation to make "Aliyah" to Israel.

This controversy was further fueled by the erratic flow of Jewish refugees from the Soviet Union. In the seventies only a trickle of immigration was permitted by the Communist government. In 1979, however, a huge number of Jews was allowed to emigrate, with almost 25,000 refugees—presumably the largest group of Jewish refugees the American Jewish community would ever have to resettle—entering the United States. Then suddenly in the early eighties the doors of the Soviet Union slammed shut, with less than two thousand people a year getting out. In 1986 emigration out of the Soviet Union again began to escalate. The late eighties and early nineties saw almost 40,000 Jews from the former Soviet Union (FSU) immigrate to the United States, with almost 20,000 per year coming to New York.[2]

SOVIET-JEWISH IMMIGRATION TO NEW YORK CITY

Jewish immigration into New York in the eighties and nineties has dramatically altered the face of the city's Jewish community. Over 200,000 Jewish refugees from the former Soviet Union have settled in New York City (NYANA Arrival Statistics).

Arrival rates of Jews from the FSU into New York are projected to continue at levels of approximately 12,000 per year, although this could change due to possible cuts in the overall number of refugees admitted by the United States government and/or the loss of refugee status for Jews from the former Soviet republics. Even if the inflow of Jews from Russia, Ukraine, the Baltic, and Central Asian states decreases, by the year 2000 this population will constitute close to 25 percent of all Jews living in New York City.

The movement of over 200,000 Jews from the FSU into the New York Jewish community during the past 25 years has presented an enormous challenge for both the émigrés and the host community. Millions of dollars and unquantifiable hours of work have been devoted to the task of resettling this population in New York and assisting the newcomers in their efforts to achieve self-sufficiency and social adaptation.

THE MYTH OF ACCULTURATION

The organized Jewish community in New York has viewed the process of cultural adaptation, or "acculturation," as an unidirectional rather than a reciprocal process. While the established community understands that it has had varied degrees of success in its attempt to integrate and indoctrinate the émigrés, it has little insight into the impact of Jews from the FSU on Jewish New York. Cultural adaptation in resettlement is in fact a two-way process, and massive reciprocal adaptation has been underway in New York since the mid-seventies as this large group of newcomers from the FSU has steadily engaged with the host Jewish community.

RESTORING JUDAISM TO JEWS FROM THE FSU

One of the most significant thrusts of the American Jewish community's early resettlement programs for Jews from the FSU was in the area of promoting Jewish acculturation. During the first wave of migration from the Soviet Union in the eighties, the organized Jewish community in New York and throughout the country invested heavily in "Judaising the Russians."[3]

Under the Communist regime in the Soviet Union, Jews could not study and practice Judaism for over 60 years. With the exception of the Georgian and Bukharian Jews, most of the immigrants from the FSU came to the United States with little knowledge of Jewish ritual and history. And while many may have intuitively held a positive sense of Jewish identity as individuals, most did not identify with any organized or communal expression of being Jewish.

American-born Jews were surprised and somewhat upset when the émigrés did not immediately exhibit a strong impulse to connect with Judaism and/or to seek affiliation with Jewish institutions. The concern over this population's Jewish identity was exacerbated by recent studies on intermarriage and assimilation by American Jews. Fearful that the rescue of Soviet Jewry from the threat of assimilation in the Soviet Union would simply translate into assimilation in the United States, the host community in New York committed itself to ensuring that Soviet Jews would be resettled "Jewishly."

During the eighties, new arrivals into New York were offered free synagogue and Jewish community center (JCC) memberships, as well as day-school and camp scholarships. The UJA-Federation agencies in New York received priority funding to provide Jewish-acculturation programming. A great effort and large sums of philanthropic dollars were expended in order to bring these unaffiliated Jewish immigrants "into the fold."

Concern began to grow as many newcomers terminated relationships with Jewish centers, camps, and synagogues after the subsidies expired. The onset of activities by missionaries and cults in the large émigré communities in Brooklyn and Queens prompted the Jewish community to establish antimissionary educational programs, outreach campaigns, and a "cult-clinic." However, it soon became clear that a more sophisticated and less paternalistic approach would be necessary if these new Jewish Americans were to make positive connections to Jewish life in New York.

In the past seven years, both host and newcomer communities have made efforts to adjust their norms and move toward each other. The host community began to understand that the émigrés tended to identify Jewishly in terms of individual rather than communal or organizational relationships. A series of dinner dialogues, sponsored by the New York Chapter of the American Jewish Committee, for leaders of the émigré and host communities did a great deal to promote mutual understanding and insight. Implementation of programs staffed by Jewish volunteers that clearly demonstrated the extension of a "communal helping hand"—such as Passover food-package distributions, English-language-acquisition discussion groups, and orientations to New York—were well received by many of the newcomers and helped connect them to the Jewish community.

New York Association for New Americans (NYANA), the agencies of the UJA-Federation network, synagogues and other Jewish organizations, and institutions in New York offered the émigré population hundreds of specially designed Jewish cultural programs. The Wexner Heritage Foundation developed a seminar for Jewish émigrés from the former Soviet Union who held promise as future Jewish communal leaders in New York. Classes, workshops, and dialogues on Jewish history and literature were held, bilingual publications with Jewish cultural and issue-oriented themes were printed and distributed, newcomer families were "adopted" by Jewish families from the host community. The perceptions and behaviors of the host community were reoriented to the cultural context from which the newcomers came, while the émigrés moved toward the host community.

PERCEPTIONS OF THE RESETTLEMENT SYSTEM

At the outset, Jewish immigrants from the FSU coming into New York tended to see the agencies of the New York Jewish community as extensions of the United States government. Jews from the FSU had no experience with voluntary human-service organizations funded by philanthropic contributions. The staffs of NYANA and the UJA-Federation communal agencies were viewed as government bureaucrats, who were to be dealt with as one dealt with Soviet authorities—always placating but never really trusting. The service providers at the agencies, on the other hand, viewed the émigrés as manipulative and unappreciative of their assistance.

Over time, both providers and consumers have gotten in touch with each other's realities and have developed better understanding and respect for their respective values and frames of reference. Agency staff have had to modify their resettlement practice to accommodate the cultural context from which their clients come. Resettlement workers have discarded the notion of the "melting pot" and have embraced the concept of cultural pluralism. Cultural adaptation rather than assimilation to the host culture has become the goal of resettlement. The émigrés, for their part, have begun to realize that the help they receive is extended through the philanthropy of the organized Jewish community and its concern for the welfare of fellow Jews.

"Professional social workers are significant in facilitating the acculturation process and are usually the most-available societal role models for immigrants during the initial stage of resettlement" (Handelman, 1983). In an innovative approach to the promotion of cross-cultural understanding and adjustment, NYANA, the Jewish Board of Family and Children's Services, and the Wurzweiler School of Social Work of Yeshiva University have jointly developed subsidized programs of graduate education in social work for Jewish immigrants from the FSU.

Bicultural social workers who can encourage bilingualism, model culturally appropriate behaviors, provide corrective feedback, and help newcomers develop analytic problem-solving skills can be of great value in helping immigrants move into the mainstream (Longres, 1991). The development of a cadre of professionally trained, bilingual social workers also created another bridge between the émigré and established communities. These bilingual, bicultural service providers have been valuable communicators and interpreters of the expectations and normative patterns of the newcomers to both professionals and lay members of the organized Jewish community, while helping newcomers adjust to the mainstream culture.

Another valuable mediating force has been a networking project developed by NYANA and UJA-Federation known as "ACE," Advisory Committee for Émigrés. Members of the émigré community and New York-born Jews who have achieved success in such fields as science and engineering help recent arrivals from the former Soviet Union prepare for the American job market and find employment. ACE volunteers mentor newly arrived engineers, mathematicians, and scientists; help them prepare resumes and conduct job searches; and offer networking through referrals. The ACE program has provided established émigrés with an opportunity to experience an important Jewish value of the host community—to engage in one of the highest forms of *Tzedakah* by helping others earn their own living. It has also helped to better acquaint native-born volunteers with émigrés in the context of a joint endeavor to resettle newcomers, thus helping both communities to view each other as equal and essential partners.

ÉMIGRÉ COMMUNAL ORGANIZATIONS

During the past few years yet another normative pattern on the part of the émigré community in New York appears to have been significantly modified. Émigrés from the FSU have until recently displayed a distrust of formal organizations—and thus the organized Jewish community—due to the negative experiences they were subjected to under the Soviet Communist regime. A dozen formal organizations have now emerged in the émigré community based on either professional, geographic, or cultural themes. These groups have almost simultaneously reached out to the agencies of the New York and national Jewish communities for both technical assistance and funding. In New York, the ACE program has been expanded to provide these groups with technical assistance in organizational development. NYANA has also extended its resource-development staff and physical facilities to these newly emerging organizations.

These fledgling organizations have had somewhat unrealistic expectations of the host community. Their frame of reference may be based to a certain degree on a sense of entitlement, emanating from the experience of having lived in a welfare state, which was both totalitarian and paternalistic. In any case, the leaders of these groups have periodically criticized the host community for being less than forthcoming, particularly in providing funds. There is an evolving understanding on the part of these groups, however, of how fundraising and distribution of philanthropic funds are carried out in the New York Jewish communal system. The UJA-Federation network, at the same time, has been responding to pressure from the émigré organizations and has directed more staff resources toward these groups.

Many Jewish communal agencies have made a special effort to recruit leaders of the émigré community to their boards of directors. While this effort is in its infancy, those émigrés who have accepted board positions have seriously committed themselves to this responsibility. Émigré board members, however, have showed little patience for the process-oriented discussions and deliberations of many Jewish organizations. They tend to prefer concise and "to-the-point" decision-making. Organizations desiring émigré leadership participation have had to take this fact into consideration in terms of the existing Jewish "corporate culture." Where this has not happened, many émigré members have excused themselves from board membership.

EMERGING SELF-RELIANCE

In the nineties, NYANA for the first time instituted a Relative Assistance program in order to help underwrite the resettlement of Jews emigrating from Russia, Ukraine, and the other former Soviet republics. Stateside relatives in the émigré community were asked to contribute cash on a per capita basis or to assume some of the costs for services provided to their arriving families through an interest-free loan made available by the Hebrew Free Loan Society of New York.

Stateside relatives in the émigré community were extremely forthcoming and responsive to this program. The repayment rate on loans has been over 85 percent, indicating a shift in the norms of a population that entered the United States only a few years ago with an entitlement perspective regarding what the host community "owed" immigrants.

As a result of the success of the loan program under Relative Assistance, the perception of the émigré community by the host community has been altered. The Hebrew Free Loan Society, for example, considers émigrés from the FSU as good credit risks and has enthusiastically developed other interest-free loan programs—for example, small business loans—for this population.

Stateside relatives have also been asked to provide interim housing for arriving relatives. The total value of this in-kind contribution is equal to approximately $10 million per year. Between housing and Relative Assistance funding, the émigré community is thus contributing close to $15 million per year to refugee resettlement in New York. This is an indication that the émigré community has begun to assume responsibility for a major Jewish communal effort.

AN UNEXPECTED PHILANTHROPIC ASSET

After years of supposition that a philanthropic campaign in the émigré community would yield little, the host community created the Russian Division of UJA-Federation of New York. This division has not only raised significant funds to help pay for Jewish communal services in New York and Israel, but has encouraged both the newcomer and the host communities to generalize their identities and to move toward a new Jewish communal collective conscience. The establishment of a formal institution of philanthropic giving in the émigré community clearly indicates a change in the values of a population that had no previous experience with volunteerism or Jewish communal responsibility. The belief held by American-born Jews that this population of immigrants had no inclination to affiliate with the organized Jewish community has also been altered as a result of the involvement of the émigré community in the UJA-Federation campaign.

The new fundraising structure began its activities by emulating the programs of other established fundraising divisions, but with a decidedly "home-country" frame of reference. Its first fundraising dinner was held at a Russian restaurant in Brighton Beach, with typical Russian and Ukrainian fare and speakers from the émigré community. Recent fundraising events, however, display clear evidence of cultural adaptation: They have become gala affairs, held at major hotels in Manhattan, requiring black-tie attire, and featuring keynotes from major politicians in state and federal offices.

THE CHANGED FACE OF RESETTLEMENT

Many immigrants from the former Soviet Union experience adjustment difficulties that stem from cultural disorientation. "Culture shock" is often the result of a lack of validation of the newcomer by the host culture. The immigrant feels uprooted and adrift emotionally and "predictability and familiarity in life may be replaced by a sense of chaos and perceptual disorganization, resulting in extreme emotional stress . . ." (Westwood & Ishiyama, 1991).

Although new arrivals experience the same challenges of cultural adaptation as their predecessors, the host environment has changed dramatically. Émigrés from earlier waves have had a positive impact on the New York Jewish community, which now has more realistic perceptions and greater understanding of their "cousins" from the FSU.

The émigré community has also changed since the early years of migration to New York. Many of those who arrived in the eighties have achieved a great deal and have become successful in their professions or in business. Those who arrived in their teens have been especially successful in developing careers, in fields as diverse as law, computer science, publishing, and financial markets. In addition to financial success, many of the 200,000 Russian-speaking Jews living in New York have taken on leadership roles in both the émigré and larger Jewish communities. Their insight and guidance in helping to shape and improve the cultural adaptation process of the newcomers and the host community on a continuing basis makes "starting over" a smoother, less-daunting task for the present wave of immigrants from the former Soviet Union.

CONCLUSIONS

Cultural adaptation is a reciprocal process. Newcomers adapt to the mainstream host society and, at the same time, affect the established culture. A new, generalized collective conscience results. However, it is often surprising to find that Jewish immigrants who have been in the United States for some time still are unclear about the structure and dynamics of the established Jewish community, and that many American-born Jews in New York still stereotype newcomers from the FSU. The cultural-adaptation process is developmental, and although significant movement along the cultural-adaptation continuum has occurred in New York, both the émigré and host communities must continue to struggle with this mutual task.

NOTES

1. In the nineties, after the fall of Communism, it became possible to process Jewish refugees coming to the United States from the former Soviet Union directly out of Moscow, thus eliminating the extraordinary expense of care and maintenance in Italy that had been incurred by both the Jewish community and the U.S. government.

2. HIAS referred 50 percent of the Soviet-Jewish refugees coming to the United States to Jewish communities throughout the country, while approximately 50 percent of the caseload was referred to the New York Association for New Americans (NYANA) for resettlement in New York City.

3. Ironically, this was the reverse of the strategy employed by the host New York's German-Jewish community in the resettlement of Eastern European immigrants during the 1800s, when the newcomers were thought to be "too Jewish" and were encouraged to assimilate into mainstream American culture.

REFERENCES

Handelman, M. (1983). Social workers as socializing agents, *Practice Digest, 4,* 3.

Longres, J. (1991). Toward a status model of ethnic sensitive practice, *Journal of Multicultural Social Work, 1*(1), 46–47.

New York Association for New Americans (NYANA), arrival statistics.

Westwood, M. J., & Ishiyama, F. (1991). Challenges in counseling immigrant clients: Understanding intercultural barriers to career adjustment, *Journal of Employment Counseling, 28,* 134–135.

12

Reengineering the Jewish Community

STEVEN M. COHEN

The idea of discussing "Reengineering the Jewish Community" is in accord with a long-standing tradition in North American Jewry. For many years, for better or worse, American Jewish institutions have looked to North American business for ideas on structure and management. So, at a time when Jewish professional and volunteer leaders sense that something is awry with North American Jewish organizational life, it is perfectly understandable that they turn to some of the latest thinking in the business world. Here, the hope is to identify ideas as to how to design a more efficient, more effective, and in a certain sense, a more Jewishly profitable voluntary community.

In theory, the reengineering approach can teach us something about how to reshape organized Jewry. To begin our exploration, we need at least a rudimentary understanding of the concept, for which we can turn to the writings of Michael Hammer of Boston, a leading management expert and, as it so happens, an active and involved Jew who addressed the 1995 Council of Jewish Federations (CJF) General Assembly (Hammer, 1996; Hammer & Stanton, 1995).

Reengineering begins with the view that many current corporate structures are obsolete. Throughout most of the earlier part of this century, North American corporations succeeded grandly by perfecting a style of management and corporate design well-suited for the Industrial Age. They constructed highly bureaucratized and tightly controlled multilayered hierarchies. They broke-up work processes into tiny pieces, allowing them to assign their workers very simple, discrete tasks to perform. They engaged highly trained professional managers, who adhered to well-articulated, detailed, and comprehensive established procedures.

This business organization flourished at a time when producers, not consumers, held the upper hand, a time when a Henry Ford could say with both arrogance and impunity, "Americans can have any color car they want as long as it's black." These corporations ably produced large numbers of similar products for mass markets; that is, markets where millions shared similar tastes and consumers sought to conform rather than to stick out.

Yet now, toward the end of the twentieth century, consumer markets are increasingly differentiated and segmented. Consumers have more choice and more power. They've learned to demand more specialized, highly tailored goods and services, along with more personalized attention to their delivery. But, more broadly, rapid change is now endemic, universal, and a constant.

To contend with this highly fluid and dynamic environment, today's companies need to become more highly efficient and more consumer-oriented. They need to redesign their business processes to dramatically reduce the time and cost of accomplishing their objectives. This redesign is essential for companies whose losses are up or profits way down; but it is even useful (if not eventually essential as well) for successful corporations seeking to stay ahead of the ever-innovating competition. Although Jewish Communal Service Association (JCSA) had called for a discussion of reengineering the Jewish community as a cry of exaggerated distress, reflecting an unwarranted and overly pessimistic view of the community, the desirability for reengineering can also apply to basically healthy situations as well.

FEATURES OF REENGINEERING

Hammer defines reengineering as "the fundamental rethinking and radical redesign of business processes to achieve dramatic improvements" (Hammer & Stanton, 1995). It is characterized by certain key features, given below.

Reengineering identifies and discards old assumptions. It focuses on business processes, a series of several connected steps that may well take place across several departments within a corporation. Examples include product development, order fulfillment, or handling claims.

It breaks down and reconfigures established organizational structures. Often the prime reason for doing so is to eliminate or sharply reduce the number of transfers of responsibility between organizational divisions. After reengineering takes effect, fewer workers operating out of fewer organizational units are responsible for the same process. Downsizing is not the immediate goal of reengineering, although it often is the sought-after by-product of a successful redesign, one that brings about vastly increased efficiency.

Another key feature of reengineering is that companies become more directly oriented to the customer, rather than requiring the customer to adapt to the structure of the business organization. One common reengineering product is the formation of teams of professionals drawn from different divisions who, as a self-contained group, handle an entire business process from start to finish or provide for all the needs of the customer in one place. Some reengineered companies go further and create the position of "case manager," a single staffer who manages customers' relationships with the various parts of the complex corporation.

Reengineering frequently means giving workers more authority and responsibility. In doing so, it demands that workers become more widely competent to handle more diverse tasks. Reengineering often utilizes breakthroughs in information technology.

Lastly, reengineering efforts succeed only if correctly advocated and executed by top leadership—those whose high positions allow them the breadth of vision to discern the system-wide difficulties and who wield the degree of influence to overcome the inevitable objections of those with vested interests in the current organizational design, of whom veteran middle-managers may be the most outstanding type. The reengineering effort requires and engenders an ongoing process of intensive analysis, deliberation, planning, and advocacy on the part of committed, talented, and respected corporate leaders.

CHALLENGES OF CONTEMPORARY JEWISH LIFE

Certainly, the North American Jewish community differs in critical respects from the major corporations that originally fashioned reengineering. The end result of a successful North American Jewry cannot be determined by a year-end profit-and-loss statement. Its objectives are measured in historical, cultural, religious, and transcendental terms. To make matters more difficult, our alternate Jewish ideologies assign different values to different objectives, making the measurement of success even more ambiguous. The managerial inefficiencies that are the target of reengineering may, for the voluntary community, constitute desirable objectives. Consensual decision-making and maximal consultation, even at the expense of efficiency, are generally contrary to the interests of most businesses, but consistent with the mission and culture of most good communities.

Nevertheless, notwithstanding the differences between corporations and communities, many useful concepts can be derived from the reengineering approach, and these will now be addressed.

The term "Jewish community" will signify the typical constellation of agencies found at the local level: synagogues, schools, Jewish community centers (JCCs), human-service agencies, the federation, as well as defense agencies, Zionist organizations, fraternal groups, museums, and numerous smaller, innovative endeavors. Reengineering suggests that we subject these institutions, with all their value, strength, and history, to fundamental scrutiny. We need to look at the processes these organizational units perform and see whether we indeed have the best structures to perform those processes.

Just as reengineering begins with an analysis of the changing economic environment, so too must we begin by examining recent changes in the United States and Canada. In fact, the emerging challenges of contemporary Jewish life in many ways resemble the portrait of North American markets, consumers, and corporations offered by the reengineering advocates.

For example, reengineering speaks of an explosion in consumer choice. In like manner, in recent years we have been witnessing the acceleration of the impact of modernity. The key feature of modernity entails the expansion of choice—the freedom to choose, and the sometimes disconcerting necessity to choose, once all the givens of the past have been swept away (Berger, 1979). The absence of rules and social conventions, seen at first blush as a sign of freedom, puts heavy burdens and stress on the individual who needs to make choices that were unavailable to the previous generation (Fromm, 1971).

More than ever before, Jews in contemporary North America are free to choose whether to be Jewish, and if so, how, when, where, and how much to be Jewish. Indeed, one major Jewish denomination—the Reform movement—makes choice the centerpiece of its theology. The Jewish movement from fate to choice usually has been portrayed by social historians as tied to the transition from traditional to modern society, or the experience of the Enlightenment and the encounter with Emancipation (Katz, 1971). But the expansion of choice neither starts nor stops with these truly momentous developments in Jewish history. Choice continues to broaden in our own lifetimes. As recently as the mid-sixties we could presume that Jews had to be Jewish and that there were certain things a Jew had to do and ought to know. The last 10 to 20 years have underscored the freedom of the individual Jew to opt out of both the formal and informal Jewish community. Jews no longer have to marry, make friends, have neighbors, or maintain organized affiliations with other Jews. The Jewish individual has gained ascendancy over the Jewish tradition and the Jewish community. Educators now speak of learner-centered, rather than text-centered, Jewish education. Donor-directed giving is yet another response to the expansion of choice and the modern rise of autonomy.

Reengineering analysts point to consumers' increasing sophistication and their greater demands. In like fashion, several recent studies of Americans' religious affiliation have described them as treating their churches and other religious institutions as consumer products. So long as their religious communities provide them with the services they seek, the adherents remain committed. When the communities fail them, when the institutions fail to produce the benefits their members seek, they move elsewhere, either to other local churches of the same denomination or to other religious movements altogether (Bellah et al., 1985).

North American Jews have become sophisticated and demanding consumers of community services, whereby becoming less automatically connected to the Jewish community. Their allegiance (or what we may call their religious "brand" loyalty) can no longer be taken for granted. One of the more curious findings of the National Jewish Population Survey (Kosmin et al., 1991) is that in reinterviews three years later, a good number of respondents and their spouses had switched their religion in the interim period, a finding with parallels in research on other American religious and ethnic identities.

The reengineering theorists point to market segmentation and the consequent necessity for more differentiated products, serving narrower slices of the market in a more highly tailored fashion. Here too we find a parallel with the contemporary Jewish condition. Modernity (and what we may call the last few decades of supermodernity) has meant increasing individuation and differentiation. With the rapid geographic mobility experienced over the lifecourse and the diversity in denominations if not in other features as well, we can no longer presume as having as many similarities in life experiences. Jews, particularly outside of Orthodoxy, find themselves thrown together in synagogues, centers, schools, federations, and human-service agencies with Jews who, in some ways, are very much unlike them. We encounter more highly idiosyncratic Jewish biographies, generating a more culturally diverse population with respect to Jewish interests, tastes, and commitments.

Modernity delegitimizes the past, and that process has also proceeded apace in recent years. Traditional Judaism, and the premodern world in general, presumed the wisdom of ancient thinkers and the authority of the words they spoke and texts they wrote. With today's rapidly changing environment, the "new-and-improved" takes precedence over the "tried-and-true." No longer do we automatically presume the authority of the past or its usefulness for the present.

The multiplication of choices witnessed in the general marketplace has a special parallel among American Jews (and with some modification, among Canadian Jews as well). For the Jews, America—and especially post-sixties America—has meant new opportunities for advancement and acceptance. With this development comes less of a need to turn as clients to Jewish agencies for services, or as members to community, or as leaders for status. Jews are the most highly educated Americans (Goldstein, 1992), with all the implications of liberal education for traditional beliefs. They have the most opportunities to express themselves outside their religious and ethnic communities. Scholars of religion have noted that, in general, it is the more subordinated— the blacks, the women, the poor, and the least educated—those with fewer alternative social outlets, who are the most religiously active and most philanthropically generous in relative terms (Iannacone, 1994). The extraordinary success of individual Jews makes them less needy of the Jewish community and its institutions. In a way, Judaism and the Jewish community would be better off if Jews were less successful and as a result, had fewer attractive options outside the Jewish community. Moreover, they are the most highly entrepreneurial, by far, of any religioethnic group in the United States (Goldstein, 1992). Their highly professionalized, entrepreneurial backgrounds clash with the governance cultures of most Jewish organizations that seem more structured towards building consensus rather than drawing upon this highly independent entrepreneurial talent.

Recent research among mainstream American Jews finds experiences and attitudes toward organized Jewry that mirror those found among some consumers with respect to some corporations or industries. Individual Jews—even many who are active in Jewish life at home or the community—find formal Jewish organizations out of touch, remote, and even distasteful (Cohen & Eisen, in press). Many, perhaps most, have no satisfying personal relationship with an official representative of organized Jewry.

The last key change of which we need to be aware is that during the middle and latter part of this century, the organized Jewish community has managed to achieve many of its key objectives: it has adapted large immigrant populations to Canadian and American societies; it helped end nearly all forms of anti-Semitic discrimination; it advanced recognition of the Holocaust; and it secured broad political support for endangered Jewry, be it in Israel, the former Soviet Union, Ethiopia, or Syria (Chanes, 1995; Goldberg, 1996). The old challenges of relief and rescue, of opening the United States and Canada to Jewish immigration, and of combating anti-Semitism and other threats to Jewish life and livelihood are, thankfully, largely behind us—but so too are some of the most compelling reasons to be active in organized Jewish life.

The result of all these and other crucial developments is a variety of unhealthy outcomes: stagnant centralized-philanthropic campaigns; the aging and numerical decline of most long-established membership organizations; widespread resistance to affiliation; alienation; under-utilized buildings; disheartened professionals and lay leaders; petty lay-professional conflict; and interinstitutional rivalry of the unproductive sort. Perhaps worst of all, we find the devaluation of Judaism occasioned by the lowering of standards in a vain attempt to entice more Jews into our institutions for lower cultural costs and obligations.

The troubles in what we may call the "public sphere" of North American Judaism are all the more significant when seen in contrast with the relative health of the Jewish private sphere. The public sphere consists of federations, major organizations, attachment to Israel, political involvements, and other related phenomena. The private sphere refers to spiritual concerns, education, culture, ritual practice, and such matters. Against the difficulties in the public sphere, we have relatively good news in the private sphere: synagogue attendance and ritual performance have held steady; day-school enrollments are way up, and climbing, as are the proportions who have enrolled in university-level Jewish-studies courses; book-publishing, including religious texts, scholarly tracts, and popular works on Judaism seems to have reached new heights both in number of titles and quantity of sales. What's more, we seem to be in the midst of a particularly productive period for Jewish spirituality and Jewish learning. In broad terms, American Judaism may be becoming more religious and less ethnic, more individualist and less collectivist, more spiritual and less tribal.

REENGINEERING THE NORTH AMERICAN JEWISH COMMUNITY

The emerging weaknesses in the public sphere demand attention. The reengineering perspective offers a way of thinking, a critical stance, and a license for imagination that may prove useful in generating new ways of organizing the Jewish community. The early stages of redesigning the corporation, Hammer (1996) writes, demand "imagination, inductive thinking, and a touch of craziness. In redesigning processes, the reengineering team abandons the familiar and seeks the outrageous." In this spirit I offer a few half-baked ideas that have benefited from conversations with a small number of friends, colleagues, and close family members.

Let us begin with ideas applicable to individual agencies—synagogues, schools, centers, etc.—and then move on to the local Jewish community as a system worthy of reengineering.

1. The Primary Liaison. An agency staff member or a volunteer, veteran lay-person would be designated as the principal, ongoing contact for newly arrived families or individuals with the given agency. Thus, upon joining a synagogue or center or enrolling one's child in a day school, one would be assigned a liaison or what some companies would call an "account executive." His or her responsibilities would be to orient and introduce the newcomer to the agency and other member-families, to provide an ongoing source of information, and at times to mediate the disputes and misunderstandings that inevitably crop up in agency–member relations.

But more than these narrow, institutionally related responsibilities, the liaison—who figures to be fairly knowledgeable and well-connected, certainly in comparison with the newcomer—would tend to the newcomers' wide spectrum of Jewish needs. Liaisons would advise families on the availability of alternative services in the entire community; they would serve as advocates of Jewish growth and learning; they would handle such delicate interactions as day-school or summer-camp scholarship applications; and—in the context of the ongoing relationship—attend to fundraising.

Not only would such a system give newcomers and relative outsiders a friendly connection with the Jewish community, it would also elevate the seriousness, knowledge, and commitment of the liaisons. In a sense, this idea builds upon Rabbi Harold Schulweis' innovation of the para-rabbi, as well as the Shalom committees found in many smaller communities. But unlike the para-rabbi, this role is meant for synagogues and other agencies alike; and unlike the Shalom committees, this idea is meant as an enduring relationship.

2. Team Case Management. One of the more amusing recurring scenes in the television series *LA Law* was the firm's staff meeting where attorneys were brought up-to-date on each other's cases. Looking past the entertainment value, we may find a lesson here for synagogues, centers, and perhaps other agencies as well. Such agencies can adopt what is standard practice in geriatric and many health-care facilities, and regularly review entire families at meetings of several agency professionals. The rabbi could sit with the educational director, the office manager, and the cantor, or the physical education director could sit with the preschool director and the adult education director and discuss a sampling of the agency's members in a weekly session. The implications for a better-informed staff and more personalized and thoughtful service are obvious.

3. Broad-Banding Professional Responsibilities and Skills. If professionals are to deal with the whole person and not just the part that relates to their particular program, if they are to effect more personalized relationships with their clientele or members, if they are to work closely with professionals from other departments and other professional backgrounds, and if they are to adapt to the rapid pace of change, they will need to acquire and utilize a wide range of professional skills. It is no accident that social workers in Jewish agencies are now increasing their Judaica background, while rabbis are learning more about community organization and case-work skills. Some of the cross-disciplinary training will occur organically, through cross-disciplinary case management, and some will be sponsored by organizations such as the JCSA. However undertaken, programs of in-service training can (and do) address gaps in professional skills outside one's original area of training.

Beyond reengineering the individual agency, we could also imagine advances inspired by the reengineering perspective on the community level. Here we are talking about processes that cut across synagogues, schools, centers, federations, and human-service agencies. On one level, these are all departments of the larger entity known as the local Jewish community. On another level, these are competing corporations in the same industry. One would hardly expect Taco Bell to reengineer with McDonald's to make sure that more North Americans "affiliate" with fast food. Yet even in the competitive world of the local Jewish agencies one can imagine eventually instituting innovations that make operations cheaper and more efficient, and the community more personalized and more responsive to the needs and interests of its individual members. It is in this spirit that I offer the following ideas.

4. Centralized Billing and the Integrated Community Database. Consistent with reengineering's emphasis on simplification and use of new technology, the community would maintain a single database, bringing together all basic information and accounting under one roof. Families will pay one billing office for all Jewish community services and donations. The centralization of billing should allow for the reduction of the labor costs resulting from individual institutions presently implementing their own book-keeping and billing procedures. The system also allows for innovative billing practices and financial management: the use of credit cards; standing orders to place payments on a monthly basis; the management of sizable community assets by taking advantage of cash-flow opportunities; the ability to market lists to direct-mail companies, and to market Jewish products to the list's enrollees.

But the information technology ought not to stop with financial management. We ought to be able to make use of new technological capabilities to collect, store, and make accessible a wide variety of appropriate information on Jewish families in the community. A community database on each Jewish family, complete with all appropriate information on its relationships with the Jewish community, can facilitate its ongoing attachment to the community. It would also allow professionals an opportunity to scan the entire family and its numerous relationships with local Jewish agencies.

Ideally, a call that came to a preschool director from a certain home or business telephone number would cause the family's summary data to appear on his or her PC monitor as she spoke. The director would immediately have access to all family-members' names, their ties to the center, synagogue, day school, camps, and other agencies, as well as other pieces of relevant information.

5. Interagency Cooperation and Communication. Parallel to the team approach emergent from several reengineering efforts, front-line service agencies (synagogues, schools, centers, and, at times, human services) need to become more seamless, share more information, effect smoother hand-offs. Somehow we need to increase the likelihood that the center's preschool teacher will advocate the Jewish day school, or that the supplementary-school principal will advertise the center's camp, and that all agency professionals, including synagogue rabbis, will have a direct interest in a successful federation campaign.

6. Joint Facilities. Reengineers (and management experts generally) look at stored inventory as a sign of something amiss and as a place to economize through greater efficiency. Ideally, at any point in time, only small fractions of goods or capital facilities should be idle. Over the course of the week or the calendar year, an audit of most Jewish communities' buildings would find many of them empty at different times. The opportunities for more efficient utilization of the entire capital infrastructure are apparent when we realize that "down-times" are often complementary. Centers are empty on holidays, but that's when synagogues are heavily utilized. Day-school classrooms are vacant when supplementary schools are in session. These kinds of patterns allow for joint utilization of capital facilities and, obviously, joint planning as well.

7. Federation as a Headquarters Institution. For almost twenty years federations have experienced a kind of organizational gridlock, a development so disturbing and obvious that federation leaders have increasingly been discussing such steps as shedding some current responsibilities, acquiring new ones, and redesigning still others. Their freedom to maneuver is in decline along with their resources as money, leadership, and ideas flow elsewhere.

The long-held notion of a single federation campaign supplanting fundraising by individual agencies is an ideal that has long since passed. For years, agencies in some communities have been running their own fundraising drives, and for years, federations in many communities have been unable to provide meaningful funding for some major agencies. It may be time to sanction agency fundraising in some organized and orderly fashion.

I propose that federations increasingly emphasize their "headquarters functions." These are the responsibilities that cut across functional agencies, such as the management of information, lay- and professional-personnel recruitment and training, the distribution of direct subsidies for Jewish community services, centralized purchasing, communal planning, etc. In other words, federations would assume prime responsibility for managing the infrastructure of Jewish communal life.

8. Harnessing Jewish Entrepreneurial Abilities. Earlier I discussed the clash between the entrepreneurial talents and inclinations of successful North American Jews and the consensual, committee-based style of governance of most of our institutions. We need a fundamental revolution in the way we make decisions, one that will free lay leaders with a highly individualist bent to make significant, creative contributions, yet at the same time not destroy the community process. One possibility is that potential funders, provided that their aims are consonant with those of the Jewish community and contingent on their commitment to maintain a serious gift to the overall campaign, could have the opportunity to "purchase" staff assistance and professional expertise to help them design their own philanthropic contribution to the community. In short, the funders—with federation approval, encouragement, assistance, and influence—would run their own planning processes. In such a world, federations' products for sale would include their technical expertise and experience with the community and its needs.

The specific ideas offered are both flawed and unrefined. They are not meant to be seen as finished proposals ready to be accepted or rejected, but to illustrate the sorts of thinking that can emerge. The one clear implication of the reengineering literature is that in many communities, key stakeholders and influential leaders, both lay and professional, from diverse institutional backgrounds ought to sit together and accept the challenge of thinking about designing the Jewish community from scratch. They may well come up with exciting structural alternatives to make the Jewish community more efficient, more effective, and more accomplished.

CONCLUSIONS

Notwithstanding the value of treating Jewish life as a product to be marketed to the Jewish consumer, we also need to bear in mind that the excessive adoption of this approach ultimately undermines the very endeavor we seek to enrich. Specifically, by catering too closely to the Jewish consumer, a policy that is not all that far from abandoning traditional norms and historic demands to make Jewish participation easier, we run the risk of demeaning the Jewish communal enterprise in its entirety. According to much of the research literature, since the early 1970s the most successful communities, those with the highest rates of growth and the most committed adherents, have been the ones that have made relatively high demands of their members, although not so high as to devolve into closed and zealous sects rather than open and vibrant churches. Applying rational economic principles, one sociologist argues that lowering the price of participation in religious communities—be it a moral or a financial price—demoralizes and demobilizes the most committed. If such is the price of following the consumer, then the price is too high. Especially for a numerically small, minority religious community, it is the presence or absence of the most dedicated that in the long run will make or break the successful Jewish community and its agencies.

As we are seeking to make the community more attuned to the needs of the ever-changing Jewish-consumer marketplace, let us also recall the specific features of a religious community in general and of Judaism in particular that set it apart from other goods and services in modern North America. For ultimately, this is a "business" whose bottom line is measured by a "higher authority."

REFERENCES

Bellah, R. N., et al. (1985). *Habits of the heart: Individualism and commitment in American life*. Berkeley: University of California Press.

Berger, P. (1979). *The Heretical imperative: Contemporary possibilities of religious affirmation*. Garden City, NY: Anchor Books.

Chanes, J. A. (Ed.). (1995). *Anti-Semitism in America today: Outspoken experts explode the myths*. New York: Carol Publishing.

Cohen, S., & Eisen, A. (in press). *The Jew within*. London: Routledge.

Fromm, E. (1971). *Escape from freedom*. New York: Avon Books.

Goldberg, J. J. (1996). *Jewish power*. New York: Addison-Wesley.

Goldstein, S. (1992). Profile of American Jewry: Insights from the 1990 National Jewish Population Survey. In *American Jewish Year Book, 1992, Vol. 92*. (pp. 77–173). Philadelphia: The Jewish Publication Society of America.

Hammer, M. (1996). *Beyond reengineering*. New York: Harper Business.

Hammer, M., & Stanton, S. A. (1995). *The reengineering revolution: A handbook*. New York: Harper Business.

Iannacone, L. (1994, March). Why strict churches are strong. *American Journal of Sociology, 99*(5), 1180–1211.

Katz, J. (1971). *Tradition and crisis: Jewish society at the end of the Middle Ages*. New York: Schocken.

Kosmin, B., Goldstein, S., et al. (1991). *Highlights of the CJF 1990 National Jewish Population Survey*. New York: Council of Jewish Federations.

Index

About the Contributors

STEVEN BAYME, national director, Jewish Communal Affairs Department, American Jewish Committee, adjunct assistant professor, Wurzweiler School of Social Work, Yeshiva University

JOEL A. BLOCK, executive director, Suffolk Y Jewish Community Center, Commack, New York

JEROME A. CHANES, program director, National Foundation of Jewish Culture, adjunct assistant professor, Wurzweiler School of Social Work, Yeshiva University

STEVEN M. COHEN, professor, The Melton Centre for Jewish Education, The Hebrew University, Jerusalem, Israel

DONALD FELDSTEIN, associate executive vice-president (retired), Council of Jewish Federations

SYLVIA BARACK FISHMAN, assistant professor of contemporary Jewish life, Near Eastern and Judaic Studies Department, Brandeis University

SHELDON R. GELMAN, Dorothy and David I. Schachne Dean, Wurzweiler School of Social Work, Yeshiva University

DRU GREENWOOD, director, Commission on Reform Jewish Outreach, Union of American Hebrew Congregations and the Central Conference of American Rabbis

LAWRENCE GROSSMAN, director of publications, American Jewish Committee

JEFFREY GUROCK, Libby M. Klaperman Professor of Jewish History, Yeshiva University

MARK HANDELMAN, executive vice president, New York Association for New Americans

MENACHEM KELLNER, Wolfson Professor of Jewish Thought, Haifa University, Israel

NORMAN LINZER, Samuel J. and Jean Sable Professor of Jewish Family Social Work, Wurzweiler School of Social Work, Yeshiva University

JEFFREY SCHECKNER, research consultant, Council of Jewish Federations

DAVID J. SCHNALL, Herbert H. Schiff Professor of Management and Administration, Wurzweiler School of Social Work, Yeshiva University

ISBN 0-275-96022-6

EAN

9 780275 960223

HARDCOVER BAR CODE

90000>